WHAT'S MOTHER GOT TO DO WITH
PROTECTING CHILDREN FROM SEXU

In this book, Julia Krane offers a first-hand look at everyday child welfare protection practices from the perspective of mothers of sexually abused children and their female social workers, charting their complex, contradictory, and often costly relations with the child welfare arm of the Canadian state. Drawing on interviews with social workers and mothers of sexually abused children, examinations of client files and court documents, and reviews of training and procedural manuals, Krane argues that child welfare procedures designed to protect children and help parents often end up as methods to scrutinize and punish mothers for their inadequacies, transforming them into a protective labour force expected to safeguard their children. Protection practices, she contends, essentially reproduce legacies of mother blame and responsibility for child sexual abuse, relieving the abuser and the state of liability.

This study lays bare the role of gender in relation to child sexual abuse and child protection, and locates child welfare practice in feminist scholarly debates about women and the welfare state. Krane uses her analysis to identify problem areas and make recommendations for change, such as creating services and resources that take into account the gendered nature of protection, offering support to women in their protective efforts, and allowing opportunities for women to explore and reflect on the context of maternal care and protection.

JULIA KRANE is an associate professor in the School of Social Work at McGill University.

What's Mother Got to Do with It?

Protecting Children from Sexual Abuse

JULIA KRANE

UNIVERSITY OF TORONTO PRESS
Toronto Buffalo London

© University of Toronto Press Incorporated 2003
Toronto Buffalo London
Printed in Canada

ISBN 0-8020-0958-1 (cloth)
ISBN 0-8020-7921-0 (paper)

∞
Printed on acid-free paper

National Library of Canada Cataloguing in Publication

Krane, Julia
  What's mother got to do with it? : protecting children from sexual abuse / Julia Krane.

  Includes bibliographical references and index.
  ISBN 0-8020-0958-1 (bound).   ISBN 0-8020-7921-0 (pbk.)

  1. Mothers of sexually abused children. 2. Child sexual abuse.
  3. Sexually abused children – Family relationships. 4. Child
  welfare.   5. Child welfare workers.   I. Title.

  HV6570.K72 2003   362.76'3   C2003-901044-9

This book has been published with the help of a grant from the Humanities and Social Sciences Federation of Canada, using funds provided by the Social Sciences and Humanities Research Council of Canada.

University of Toronto Press acknowledges the financial assistance to its publishing program of the Canada Council for the Arts and the Ontario Arts Council.

University of Toronto Press acknowledges the financial support for its publishing activities of the Government of Canada through the Book Publishing Industry Development Program (BPIDP).

Contents

ACKNOWLEDGMENTS vii

1 Introduction 3

2 Women and the Welfare State 17

3 Family Ties: Child Welfare and the Protection of Children from Sexual Abuse 38

4 Understanding Child Sexual Abuse: Highlighting the Inadequacies of Women 58

5 Shifting the Focus in Practice: Women's Deficiencies as Wives and Mothers 83

6 Transforming Women into Mother Protectors: The Investigation and Its Aftermath 105

7 Enforcing, Reinforcing, and Maintaining Mother Protector 129

8 Critical Reflections: Workers' and Mothers' Thoughts on Mother Protector 155

9 Protection as Gendered and En/Gendering: Implications
  for Theory, Practice, and Research   176

NOTES   197

REFERENCES   201

INDEX   213

Acknowledgments

In its completed format, this book bears my name. However, this piece of work, like so many other activities, has been inspired and influenced by my family, friends, and colleagues. Their contributions to my development have been enormous in ways that cannot be easily expressed in print. Speaking from the heart, I hope that my appreciation for all that they have done for me will come through in the following passages.

It is befitting to start with thanks to my mother, Evelyn Krane. She is an incredible woman, intelligent, intense, wise, strong, and outspoken. I love her for her belief in me throughout my life and for her sound advice that seems all the more meaningful as I journey down the path of motherhood with my own young son, Jacob. I also wish to thank my husband, Daniel Paul, for encouraging me in my professional development, for sharing my struggles and celebrating my accomplishments, for expressing faith in my abilities not only as a scholar but as a mother, and for providing unconditional love.

I am deeply appreciative of the scholarly contributions from two exceptional women, Dr Sheila Neysmith at the University of Toronto and Dr Linda Davies at McGill University. I thank them for their outstanding guidance in matters of theory and research and for the generous support, tremendous encouragement, and thoughtful critiques they have given to me over the years.

My original research was made possible through doctoral fellowships from the University of Toronto (Open Fellowship Program) and the Department of National Health and Welfare. I am grateful for the publishing subvention from the Aid to Scholarly Publications Programme with the Humanities and Social Sciences Federation of Canada. I thank the anonymous reviewers for their insightful suggestions that compelled me to rethink and rewrite the manuscript, and the editorial staff at the University of Toronto Press for bringing clarity to my prose. I am especially appreciative of the guidance and support I received from Virgil Duff, Executive Editor with the University of Toronto Press.

   This book is based on women's accounts of protecting children from sexual abuse. With eloquence and courage, frontline workers and clients of a child welfare agency shared their experiences with me. I thank each woman for allowing me into this aspect of her life. I hope that this work reflects an understanding of and respect for their accounts.

WHAT'S MOTHER GOT TO DO WITH IT?
PROTECTING CHILDREN FROM SEXUAL ABUSE

1

Introduction

This book is concerned with the social relations that lie hidden beneath child welfare practices pertaining to the protection of children from sexual abuse. In this book, I examine social work practice in cases of child sexual abuse from the perspectives of mothers of child victims and their female workers in order to investigate how and why the legacies of mother blame and responsibility are reproduced through these practices, and thereby to uncover the workings of the child welfare arm of the state.

Family Ties

Fifteen-year-old Tonya Kline kept getting into trouble with the law. Charged with truancy, shoplifting, and breaking into a home, Tonya was placed in a juvenile detention centre, where she resided for two months. When it looked like Tonya would be remanded to juvenile detention until the date of sentencing, her mother 'offered to do whatever it takes' to maintain Tonya at home until the next court appearance. On 7 December 1995 in Summerville, South Carolina, a family court judge ordered Deborah Harter to keep her teenaged daughter Tonya tethered to her side with a belt and chain normally used for shackling prisoners. Deborah Harter was required to hold onto the chain attached to the belt, sleep next to her daughter at night, and sit beside or behind her at school. If Tonya were to escape, her mother would face thirty days in jail. According to a newspaper article entitled 'Family ties: Judge orders teen-age daughter chained to her mother for a month,' the teen was nonchalant about the sentence. In contrast, her mother's sentiments could hardly be regarded as indifferent. Now responsible for regulating her daughter's every move, Deborah Harter found that she and her husband were less able to spend time together, in and out of the home, with or without friends. Though she hoped that the measure would aid her daughter, she felt as though she were being punished. 'I feel like I've got a sentence here as well,' stated Harter. Less than a month after this case of 'unusual punishment' attracted international press coverage, the following headline appeared: 'Tethered teen's mom hospitalized: Woman treated for anxiety drug overdose.'[1]

On the surface, this is the story of a seemingly outlandish state intervention – shackling a troubled teen to her mother in order to restrain the girl's activities for a specified period of time. Beyond the surface view, arguably, this story is not atypical. It is both an account of the willingness of a woman to monitor her child and a reflection of dominant Western expectations of mothers as available, capable, and responsible for the care, nurturing, and supervision of children. It is the story of the ease with which the welfare state – in this case the judicial arm – shifts responsibility for the well-being of children to mothers in families, and thus participates in the reproduction of gender relations. Although not readily apparent, it is also a tale of the dearth of support and absence of regard for the effects on women of the shift in monitoring duties from the state to mothers. As seen in this case, Deborah Harter's offer to do 'whatever it takes' necessitated profound adjustments to her relationships with her husband and daughter and led to a drug overdose. In its totality, the story of Deborah Harter is a narrative of the complex, contradictory, and often costly relationship between women as mothers and the welfare state. Broadly speaking, it is this relationship that I address in this book. The springboard from which I launch into this analysis is that of the protection of children from sexual abuse.

Within the last two decades, the intricate relationship between women and the state has been a major area of study for feminists in Canada, the United States, and Britain. In their analysis of the relations between the welfare state, families, and women, feminists have examined such matters as how women's issues have been taken up by the state as well as the 'changing boundaries of public and private, the interrelationship between state, family and labour markets, the complexity of women's role in the home and in society, [and] the need to investigate the contradictions of women's lives' (Sassoon, 1987a, p. 22). In an era of critical feminist appraisal of women–state relations, curiously absent has been the topic of child welfare. According to Elizabeth Hutchison (1992, p. 67), it is possible that an analysis of child welfare as a women's issue both reveals diminished concern for the vulnerability of children and raises the painful question, 'must the welfare of children come at the expense of the welfare of women?'

These issues are indeed important, yet they have received scant consideration by scholars, policymakers, and practitioners in the field of child welfare. Instead, the traditional focus has stressed studying, planning for, and serving children and their families without giving special attention to the needs of female caregivers (Hutchison, 1992). In fact, child welfare analysts have tended to assume that mothers' and children's needs are synonymous and thus met by the same programs. As such, the effects on female caregivers for the well-being of children have largely remained invisible (Hutchison, 1992). One wonders if the consequences for Deborah Harter might have been different had the effects of the court order to monitor her child been acknowledged or forecast. Given that the care of children is delegated almost exclusively to women, that women are held accountable for the welfare of their children, and that the rights and needs of women and children can and do compete, feminist attention to child welfare seems most compelling.

This book is concerned with those features of child welfare that have to do with the protection of children from sexual abuse. By protection, I am referring to those actions that are required to defend a child from harm or maltreatment in cases of child sexual abuse, including investigation of complaints, provision of therapeutic and other services to the child and family that are negotiated with or without court involvement, or the removal of a child from her or his parent(s) or guardians for varying lengths of time.

My interest in the protection of children from maltreatment arose from my years of experience as a frontline social work practitioner in a child welfare agency. In that capacity, I investigated, assessed, and intervened in cases of child abuse, including sexual abuse. These activities could not be described by any stretch of the imagination as a dispassionate charge. I was deeply committed to the protection of children from sexual (and other) abuses, and firmly believed in the goal of securing the safety and well-being of children in their families, accompanied by the necessary support and service programs. I was perplexed and distressed by actions that threatened to continue placing children at risk. My job, as I saw it, was to engender family support, compliance, and adherence to a given plan of action to protect the child. After all, the dominant belief was, and continues to be, that family care is certainly preferable to state apprehension and state care of the child. Family care met the best interests of children and offered workers, such as myself, a way to think about the protection of children. At the time, it did not occur to me to critically examine what might lie beneath a protection mandate, or the assumptions inherent in the dominant understanding of child sexual abuse and interventions in these cases. Looking back now, I might say that protection appeared so abstract as to render neutral and gender-free the activities involved in securing protection.

Once removed from the frontlines of practice, and granted opportunities to read the vast literature on the topic of child sexual abuse, I became aware of a number of recurring themes in the discourse (Krane, 1989). For one, in the context of adult sexual abuse of children in its many forms, preoccupation with incestuous families prevailed. This focus on incest families concealed individual members' experiences as victim, abuser, nonoffending parent, and sibling. It also provided fertile soil for the continued implication of women in establishing and maintaining the problem of (male-perpetrated) sexual abuse of children. Second, in contrast to marked attention to offender behaviour and treatment, studies of mothers were negligible (Krane, 1989). Though little knowledge was being produced about mothers of sexually abused children based on their experiences and accounts, it was apparent that scholars and clinicians alike had much to say about these women. While these studies have been important and useful, they provide only a fragmented knowledge. As Carter (1999) notes, only a smattering of efforts continue to be made to understand, firsthand, women's experiences of the sexual abuse of their children. Even fewer have been the attempts to examine those experiences in the context of child protection practice. In response, this book explores the protection process from workers' and mothers' perspectives and theorizes about women's complex and contradictory relations with the welfare state.

For this book, I have drawn on passages from over 100 hours of interviews with a purposive, albeit select, sample of mothers of sexually abused children and the female social workers involved in their cases (Krane, 1994). I asked the women about their thoughts on the problem of child sexual abuse, their experiences as workers and clients in dealing with the problem, and their insights into the strengths and weaknesses of everyday interventions. I juxtaposed the against official documents such as theoretical, practice, an discourse; recordings in case files and court documents; and training, policy, and procedural manuals for protection workers. In doing so, I sought to explore how and why the state seemingly protects children from sexual abuse through the transformation of their mothers into mother protectors. Such an exploration emanates from the perspectives of women in child welfare.

Protection, I will suggest, comes about through a complex process of taken-for-granted, gendered, and 'en/gendering' activities and relations that reverberate with varying costs and consequences throughout the lives of women in families. It is a process that seems to translate the problem of child sexual abuse into one of failure to protect. This conversion comes about through casework practices that accentuate women's inadequacies in the problem of child sexual abuse. Coupled with obsessions about a mother's awareness of the abuse – if not assumptions that she 'should have known'[2] – the problem is rewritten in such a way as to shift the focus from offences committed predominantly by men to transgressions or acts of omission by women as wives and mothers. Rewritten in this way, it is not surprising to find that protection seems to materialize through casework practices that largely scrutinize and transform multidimensional women into one-dimensional 'mother protectors.' As I will detail throughout the text, such practices include efforts: to persuade the mother to accept her responsibility as central to both problem and resolution; to establish the protection priority for mothers; to elicit expressions of belief and support for the child from the mother; and to encourage the mother to denounce the offender's actions and, if need be, separate from him.

Throughout the pursuit of protection, the mother's multiple dimensions as a woman are understandably often overlooked as are any meaningful explorations of her reactions and needs. Although mothers' protective labour is obligatory, it is often disregarded if not rendered invisible. This inattention is not without significant repercussions for workers, women clients, and their children. Most ironic, even counterproductive, is alienation from the state of the very women needed to protect children from further acts of harm and maltreatment.

As will be seen, and in keeping with the observations of feminists in this field (Carter, 1999; Hooper, 1992; Johnson, 1992; Swift, 1995), mother blame appears to be a pervasive feature of child protection work. It permeates not only professional and expert discourses but everyday practice, wherein mothers' inadequacies and responsibilities are central to the construction of the problem and the social work response to it. Coupled with taken-for-granted assumptions about mothers and mothering that inform everyday practice in child sexual abuse and a shift in the protection mandate from the public to the private sphere and to women in families, the analyses presented here speak volumes about the relations between women and the welfare state. Thus, this book locates protection practice in cases of child sexual abuse in the context of feminist debates about women's intricate relations with the welfare state. This analysis seeks to awaken an appreciation for how and why the legacies of mother blame and responsibility are reproduced in child welfare practice. These understandings are quite different from the image of protection as it emerges in official discourse.

Describing the experiences of protection from the perspectives of women – heretofore 'missing persons'[3] – in child welfare, and explicating the process of protection in the context of women–state relations, this book intends to inform and instruct. As Marilyn Callahan (1993b, p. 174) put it, 'why not make what are viewed as the exceptions (the way women think and do) the rule (the way the system operates)?' When we listen to the voices of women in child welfare, we learn not only about the experiences of our clients but about ourselves. How is it that professional social workers with the best of intentions and up-to-date practices reproduce gender, class, and race relations? The final goal of this book is to glean instruction from women, caseworkers, and mothers on the sites and means to challenge and rethink child welfare. In its totality, it is this woman-centred analysis that I hope will contribute, in the feminist critical tradition, to effecting change for women in child welfare.

By way of an overview, this chapter introduces the women who so generously shared with me their experiences in addressing child sexual abuse within the context of child welfare practice. Chapter 2 situates my emerging analysis of their accounts in a broader theoretical discussion of the state, families, and women as pursued by modern-day feminist scholars. Details of the 'official' child protection discourse – that is, Ontario's child protection legislation, practice, protocols, and procedures related to the identification of and intervention into child sexual abuse – are found in Chapter 3. A review of dominant theoretical and empirical literature on the conceptualization of the problem of child sexual abuse is undertaken in Chapter 4, with particular emphasis on the shifting but consistent legacy of mother blame in this discourse. It is against this 'official' backdrop that I articulate concealed, albeit crucial, workings of state interventions into families via the transformation and maintenance of women as mother protectors. Whereas the first four chapters summarize scholarly discussions of three intersecting substantive areas, chapters 5 through 8 present interview and documentary data. Chapter 5 elaborates on the conceptualization of the problem of child sexual abuse as it emerges in everyday practice. This conceptual framework spotlights women's inadequacies as wives and mothers, thereby shifting the focus from the atrocities committed by sexual offenders to the failings of women as the rightful and expected protectors of children. Such a shift in emphasis logically necessitates interventions that would address and redress women's inadequacies as wives and mothers. This reworking of the problem of child sexual abuse parallels dominant themes in the scholarly literature. Chapters 6 and 7 examine investigative and administrative practices and legal and therapeutic procedures. I suggest that these specific interventions and procedures are based on expectations of women as mothers, speak to failed mothers, and seek to instruct, enlighten, and transform them into better mothers, specifically, into mother protectors. As such, they reveal how our everyday child welfare interventions into families for the protection of children are likely interventions into the lives of women, and offer insights into how everyday practices and procedures legitimate and reproduce gender relations in general and reinforce and maintain the concept of mother as protector in particular.

Though I will suggest that 'mother protector' is a central feature of contemporary intervention strategies, I also conclude that mothers do not receive sufficient support to fulfil this mandate and that the effects on all involved in the protection of children are significant. Chapter 8 explores the costs and consequences for women of these interventions, which are implicated in the broader reproduction of gender relations. As well, I report on workers' and mothers' disappointments and frustrations. In Chapter 9, I revisit the topic of the relations of women and the welfare state from the perspective of my foray into practice in cases of child sexual abuse.

Voices from the Frontline

This book draws on a case study of a particular child welfare agency in Ontario. The agency offered a vast array of treatment services to the client population of interest to me and prided itself on forging progressive practice in sexual abuse investigation, assessment, and treatment. Such services could be considered 'best practice' in that every effort was made to ensure the security and well-being of child victims while offering intervention to support victims, their mothers, and offending fathers (for details, see Krane 1994).

This study was undertaken to allow me to gather a large amount of information on a select number of sexual abuse cases within the context of everyday child protection practice. The emphasis was on capturing the fullness and richness of the protection processes under investigation. As other researchers have put it, case studies are suitable for explaining processes, modifying or challenging generalizations, exploring uncharted issues by starting with a limited case, or proposing provocative questions (Reinharz, 1992; Yin, 1984). Case studies allow the collection of evidence from a variety of sources (Yin, 1984), which include interviews, observations, and written discourse.

In this book, I refer to interviews with seven female social workers and eight nonoffending mothers on the topic of child sexual abuse. Four other nonoffending mothers are discussed with varying degrees of detail; however, they were not interviewed.

Of the seven worker participants, four held positions at 'Intake,' a site of child protection practice that often investigates and assesses reports of allegations of abuse. The other three workers all functioned as 'family service' workers, who, for the most part, offered ongoing services throughout the life of the opened case. The participating workers are identified with a last name that begins with 'W' (for 'Worker'): Anne Wade (AW), Barb Wayne (BW), Carol West (CW), Dina Ward (DW), Emma Webber (EW), Fay Winters (FW), and Gail Wydell (GW). Of these women, two had been employed by the agency for over fourteen years. The others had held their positions for approximately four years. All workers had completed one or more university degrees: Bachelor of Arts, Bachelor of Education, Bachelor of Social Work, and Master of Social Work. Despite formal social work education, continued training, and years of child protection experience, some of the workers expressed inadequacies with their knowledge base. One described herself as a 'novice.' Another noted that she doesn't 'know very much. I'm new at this.' As will be seen, this work is tough. At times, even seasoned professionals feel unprepared to tackle the complex issues they face daily.

The workers ranged in age from twenty-eight to fifty-three years. Four were involved in long-term marital relations, one worker was divorced, and two women had not been married. Both single women described themselves as 'wrapped up in the job.' One worker noted that 'marriage and social life are on hold.' She expressed 'hope to have the package deal some day – marriage, children, a family.' The other spoke of pursuing an MSW and securing a supervisory position. Her 'family and friends,' however, 'hassle and pressure' her to 'settle down, be happily married, as if happy and married go together, and have children.' After all, she disclosed, 'everyone thinks I'd be a great mom.'

The mothers who took part in interviews with me or whose situations were discussed by the workers are identified with a last name that begins with 'M' (for 'Mother'): Abby Main (AM), Bella Mews (BM), Chris Mack (CM), Donna Munt (DM), Eve McKay (EM), Fiona Maye (FM), Gina Merton (GM), Harriet Miller (HM), Irma Morgan (IM), Jane McNab (JM), Kayla Miles (KM), and Lucy Mann (LM).

The women were related to the alleged offenders in different capacities. These men were their current or former husbands, the woman's common-law partner, the common-law partner's brother, and the common-law partner's nephew. They also included a woman's son, adoptive grandson, a son's friend, and a daughter-in-law's husband. In relation to the victims, the men were their biological fathers, stepfathers, and grandfathers; others were related as a step-brother, brother, or uncle. Two offenders were unrelated to the victim in the case. The victims comprised sixteen females and one male child. With the exception of the one son, the victims were the daughters, stepdaughters, or granddaughters of the women whose accounts are heard in this book.

Most of the mothers had a close (as in familial) relationship with the offender. Irma Morgan, Eve McKay, Bella Mews, and Chris Mack were all married to, and living with, the offender/husband when the allegations of sexual abuse became known and investigated by the child protection agency. For these women, length of marriage ranged from fifteen to twenty years. They all separated from their husbands following the disclosure of child sexual abuse in accordance with the intervention plan. Over the course of the interviews, two of the four women were in the process of reuniting with their husbands.

In the other cases, Harriet Miller had been married for over fifteen years to her first husband and over ten years to her current husband, the accused in the case; they did not separate following the allegations and investigation. Similarly, when allegations were made against Jane

McNab's common-law partner of two years, no long-term separation occurred. Fiona Maye, whose ex-husband had also been accused, had been married to him for sixteen years. Abby Main's first marriage had lasted seven years; she had been married to her current husband for ten years. He was not the offender in the case, and no act of separation took place as a result. Gina Merton's first marriage had been for two years; her current marriage had lasted nearly twenty years. In this case, her granddaughter was sexually abused by the child's father and brother. Donna Munt had been engaged in a common-law relationship for four years; it was her partner's brother who allegedly assaulted her son and daughter.

The mothers ranged in age from twenty to fifty-four years. Some of the women reared their own children as well as their grandchildren, step-children, or common-law partner's children, totalling forty-six children. Aside from one mother who had raised fourteen children, including her biological son and her husband's children and grandchildren, the average number of children raised was 3.5, with seven women rearing between three and five children. The mothers were engaged in a range of activities from paid labourers in the public workforce to private labourers in their own or others' homes. One woman was a longtime employee of the postal system. Six of the women were employed in a local factory; one also worked as a waitress at the same time. Five of the women described themselves as homemakers, with other activities including babysitting, volunteering at the church, and assisting on the farm. Following disclosure of child sexual abuse, two women quit their paid employment positions. The range of education achieved among the women was between grades eight and twelve.

The women whose accounts are distilled through my exploration of child protection practices in cases of child sexual abuse were by no means selected at random. All female workers at the agency spoke to me about their experiences in this field of practice. It is widely known, though relatively poorly documented, that women comprise the majority of the workforce in the social welfare industry (Land, 1991) as well as the frontline child welfare workforce (Callahan, 1993b; Voight, 1986).

Similarly, women account for the greatest number of social welfare clients. However, accessing mothers for their insights into protection proved to be somewhat challenging. Identifying and engaging current or former clients of child welfare in the hopes of securing their thoughts on dealing with child sexual abuse are common problems (see Carter, 1999 and Johnson, 1992). Though I had the agency's approval to meet clients, provided their consent had been secured beforehand, I encountered some barriers. For one, the number of sexual abuse cases addressed by the agency fluctuated regularly from as few as four to as many as twelve investigations per month. Furthermore, not all cases investigated were 'founded' – meaning there was insufficient evidence that the child might be in need of protection to warrant ongoing contact – and as a result some cases closed at the level of Intake. This information meant that it was not possible to include cases that had a known probability. I then turned to the workers for their assistance. I asked each worker to select, from among her sexual abuse caseload, two cases for discussion and interview that differed on the basis of length of involvement. The decision to explore two cases was made in order to minimize the likelihood that selection and discussion of one case would somehow be case-specific or idiosyncratic and maximize the likelihood that case discussion would touch upon different facets of the protection and intervention process.

I was guided by the techniques of theoretical sampling in that I sought to generate a group of mothers for participation who might differ according to the nature and extent of relationship with the particular worker. My aim was to include mothers who represented recent cases, ones that had been active with the agency for about six months, and those near termination. I imagined that this procedure would enable me to examine and explore how conceptualizations of the causes and consequences of child sexual abuse, and the construction of mother as child protector, had or had not changed over the passage of time. The workers advised me that categorizing cases according to length of involvement was rather meaningless. For example, they told me that while a disclosure of child sexual abuse might in fact be the most recent one on a worker's caseload, this very same case could easily have been involved for an extensive period of time with the worker or agency. One case in point was raised by Fay Winters. Just as she was about to close the Miller long-term case, a disclosure of sexual abuse was made. This rendered the case to be her 'most recent' one in terms of disclosure, even though it was by no means a 'recent' case.

Ultimately I met with the workers to identify all potential mothers for participation in interviews. I found that regardless of how cases were clustered, choice was often not available. To illustrate, Anne Wade was not actively investigating any cases of child sexual abuse at the time of the interviews. She did, however, identify three cases recently transferred to the Family Services Unit: Eve McKay, who agreed to participate; Risa McKoll, who moved out of the county and was thus unavailable for consideration; and Chris Mack, who permitted Anne to discuss her case but refused an interview with me.[4]

Having spoken to each worker about her caseload, I found nineteen mothers who were potentially available for interviews. Eight women were eliminated,[5] eight agreed, and three refused to participate. While it is difficult to evaluate the refusals, these women did comment to their workers that the thought of having to stir up the past was unappealing. As one woman later told me, 'the agency wasn't very helpful and I don't want to have to go through discussing it (the abuse and her experiences) again.' Another woman said 'it's too hard on my nerves.' Chris Mack, one of the three women who refused to participate, said 'I can't express myself properly.' Though I explained my interest in hearing about her experiences in her own words, she maintained her position. Having spoken with other mothers who had spoken with me, she later agreed to an interview.

The interviews with workers took place at the agency. Formal interviews were held in individual offices and informal discussions took place in the agency kitchen, over coffee and lunch. Many of the mothers shunned the idea that we meet at the agency; some outwardly rejected that suggestion. Based upon their preference and availability of transportation, all interviews with mothers took place either in their homes or at an agreed-upon location other than the agency itself.

Our discussions were facilitated by the use of an interview guide that was enhanced by my years of experience as a former child welfare practitioner. Particular ideas were garnered from interview schedules used by Belenky, Clinchy, Goldberger, and Tarule (1986) and Russell (1986). The interviews focused on two areas of interest. The first centred on the child sexual abuse case. It addressed three major subject areas: (1) the conceptualization of the causes of child sexual abuse; (2) the effects of the disclosure; and (3) the perception of services needed and rendered. The second interview explored each woman's background, perception of self, mothering, family, marriage, and relationships.

A total of thirty-nine interviews were held. All women were interviewed at least twice, giving rise to over 100 hours of material. All interviews were tape-recorded and transcribed verbatim, creating over 700 pages of single-spaced, typewritten text. Once in typed format, each interview was examined and supplemented by notes (a summary of the interview, questions for further exploration, and thoughts about emerging themes). This procedure is of course in keeping with qualitative methods of data collection and analysis in that these routes to understanding protection practice took place simultaneously. As has been noted by methodologists (Bogdan & Biklen, 1982; Dooley, 1984; Glaser & Strauss, 1967; Lofland & Lofland, 1984), this process increased an understanding of the interview and documentary data and generated theoretical ideas.

Talking for many hours with each woman in light of my appreciation of the bureaucratic, legislative, and scholarly contexts within which protection practice takes place made it possible to emerge with a more detailed, complex, and meaningful understanding of the experiences for workers and mothers alike. Hearing these voices from the frontline alongside the official written discourse allowed me to articulate the women's discrepant and often invisible experiences as they come together to protect children from sexual abuse, trace the process of protection (that is, show how protection seems to come about), and reveal some of the costs and consequences of securing protection in the way it is achieved.

Critics might well question the veracity of this analysis and its conclusions on the grounds of the small and nonrepresentative sample of women interviewees who were involved with one particular child welfare agency. By no stretch of the imagination would I suggest that the women who shared aspects of their experiences of child protection are 'representative' of all women embroiled in the protection of children from sexual or other forms of maltreatment. To generalize in this way requires, first and foremost, an established understanding of women's experiences of the protection of children from sexual offences. From that knowledge base, I might well have asked a different research question warranting a methodology that enabled generalization from sample to broader population. Bearing in mind that few researchers have ever heard from mothers about the sexual abuses of their children, let alone attempted to understand their experiences in the context of child protection, I posed a question for inquiry that sought to unearth a (heretofore unidentified) process of protection. I asked 'how does protection seem to come about?' In hearing a selection of voices from the frontlines alongside scholarly, legislative, and bureaucratic discourses, I was able to look critically at what is commonly known and what is commonly done in terms of the protection of children from sexual abuse. I used these voices to contribute to an understanding of the workings of the child welfare arm of the state as they relate to the actual experiences of women. My exploration begins with feminist insights into women's intricate relationships with the welfare state.

2

Women and the Welfare State

To ask 'How does the state protect children from sexual abuse?' raises questions about the very conceptualization of the state. As noted by Ng, Walker, and Muller (1990), definitions of the concept and nature of the state, and the way in which they are employed, have yielded little consensus among analysts. Though often equated with government, the state is a term frequently used to refer to decision-making bodies and bureaucracies normally associated with governments, to the judiciary, and to government-funded institutions such as schools, hospitals, daycare centres, and children's aid societies (Armstrong & Armstrong, 1990).

According to Adamson, Briskin, and McPhail (1988), it is limiting to restrict a definition of the state to the realm of government. Government is the site of legislative and electoral processes and is delegated the authority to define areas of public good and enact legislation; government and its representatives are seen to be 'responsive to citizens, and responsible for the shape and success of Canadian society' (Adamson et al., 1988, p. 112). However the state, and women's relation to it, is different from government. Adamson et al. (1988, p. 113) elaborate:

> The state is a powerful and complex force that intervenes daily in all citizens' lives; yet, unlike the government, it is largely invisible and unnamed ... It includes agencies such as child welfare, immigration, and housing and coercive forces such as the police. The state is more amorphous – less a question of people and personalities than a process of regulation, administration, and bureaucracy.

In her review of literature on the subject, Ng suggests that the prevailing conception of the state is that of 'a machine or a set of apparatuses that performs different functions for the ruling or dominant classes' (Ng, 1988, cited in Ng et al., 1990, p. 17). This view presents the state as a monolithic force 'over and above people' which controls our lives through governance, bureaucracy, and coercion. This view makes it difficult to relate the state to real people and our lived experiences (Heald, 1990; Ng et al., 1990). Heald (1990, p. 149) further argues that conceptualizing the state as a 'kind of animate being' is problematic for it leaves us to decide who is and is not a part of the state, and it sees people – 'particularly women – as products of other forces, of others' actions and desires,' thereby depriving women of action, power, motivation, and resistance.

In discussing the relation between women and the state, Gillian Walker (1990, p. 4) also argues that 'it is increasingly evident that one-dimensional views of a monolithic state apparatus are not adequate to the task.' She offers a conception of the state as a set of social relations and practices. This view enables us to identify how we participate, more or less, in state operations, and how we are organized in ways which seem 'natural' and 'insignificant' (Heald, 1990). Walker (1990, p. 5) elaborates:

> We have to look at what we do as professionals, activists, and women in general, and see how our activities are part of the way in which social relations are brought into being and reproduced. We must also come to see how the state is articulated to these activities, as a part of how ruling is accomplished.

This conception of the state is instructive for gaining an appreciation of how everyday child protection practices in cases of child sexual abuse might give rise to the reproduction of certain social relations, for example, gender stereotypes of woman as, above all, 'Mother.' Conceiving of the state as a monolithic entity obfuscates boundaries of the state and denies enormous differences and subdivisions within the state, especially women's relations to it. These are the issues taken up in this chapter.

Child Protection – An Arm of the State

The specific segment of the state under consideration here is child welfare. In Canada, the United States, and the UK, child welfare has tended to the more narrow and juridical construction of child protection. Whereas a detailed presentation of Ontario's child protection legislation, practice, protocols, and procedures appears in Chapter 3, here I discuss the supposed boundaries of the state through the example of child protection.

The child welfare system is that arm of the state concerned with 'the division of rights and responsibilities for children between parents and the state and between parents themselves' (Callahan, 1993b, p. 189). The major features of the child welfare system as derived from child protection legislation are: definition of a child in need of protection; receipt of complaints; investigation; action to ensure the protection of the child; court supervision and decision making; and guardianship and discharge of guardianship. Briefly, child welfare legislation defines the circumstances in which the state can intervene in the family – for example, in response to child abuse, neglect, and the like. Following receipt of a complaint, social workers intervene according to child welfare law in order to assess risk to the child and any protection concerns. The worker is required to act to ensure the protection of the child, whether such protection is pursued with or without court involvement and within or external to the child's family.

Child welfare has been described as the arena of social service practice in which the state, operating according to specific statutory laws, takes over or replaces certain functions normally carried out by parents for children (McCall, 1990, cited in Macintyre, 1993). In this context it is generally assumed that parents (families) are responsible for rearing and caring for their children and that the child welfare arm of the state has an obligation to intervene, protect, and provide care only when or after parental care has fallen below a certain standard or when parents disagree over custody and care issues (Callahan, 1993b; David, 1991). This conception of responsibility for the development and care of children is residual in nature in that the child protection agency only becomes involved when the 'normal structures of supply, the family and the market, break down' (Wilensky & Lebeaux, 1965, p. 138, cited in Armitage, 1993, p. 42).

As such, much child protection discourse is concerned with ascertaining, clarifying, and substantiating the extent of and limit to state intervention in the autonomous life of families, and energies are expended on defining the conditions that justify state intervention or intrusion in intrafamily relations, the procedures for those interventions, and their effects.

Although the residual formulation has been remarkably consistent over time and across Canada (Herringer, noted in Wharf, 1995), a number of concerns have been raised regarding the increasingly narrow focus on investigation, assessment, and protection of children from maltreatment that characterizes the approach described above. On a general level, an emphasis on clarifying state/family responsibilities and delineating state interventions in response to failures in parenting means a de-emphasis on providing for social welfare or concerning ourselves with social relations or attending to structural and material factors that shape the well-being, care, and protection of children. Furthermore, it is assumed that state authorities – for example, child protection workers – can define normal or expected standards of parental care and can identify when those standards of care have been breached (Armitage, 1993; David, 1991). It has been proposed that the residual approach, anchored in the principle of least intrusiveness, is paradoxical. By refraining from intervening until maltreatment of children has occurred, residual legislation 'virtually ensures that intervention will be intrusive' (Wharf, 1995, p. 5).

More specifically, through the concept of 'parental responsibility,' child welfare policies and practices 'reinvigorate notions of the privacy of the family' (David, 1991, p. 115). Not only is 'the family' reified as an autonomous unit but such reification is blind to variations according to gender, ethnicity, socioeconomic status, and composition.

Finally, through the rhetoric of ascertaining the boundaries of state intrusion and the nature of that intrusion into 'the family,' state interventions, goods, and services appear to reside in the public realm, which is reinforced as distinct from the private sphere of family. This is not uncommon. References to the welfare state in general reflect the notion of 'public' provision of assistance, and social welfare is often presented as the 'distribution of society's benefits,' in cash or in kind, to its members in the face of inequalities (Djao, 1983, p. 6). State child welfare services in particular are presented as aiming to support or assist parents in their responsibilities to care for their children or provide alternative or substitute care when the need arises. Actual services are delivered by provincial social welfare departments or private organizations such as a children's aid society (Djao, 1983).

The image of child welfare services that prevails is one of provision of aid and/or service delivered by the state through the children's aid society to the family. An important part of this conception is the bifurcation of public and private spheres, a subject of much critical analysis by feminists.

Public and Private: An Examination

The relationship between the public and private spheres is an important theme in the development of feminist theory. These spheres have been conceptualized as 'state' and 'family,' as the domain of men and the domain of women, respectively.[1]

The private sphere of family, including care of the home and children, reproduction, and sexuality, is associated with women. Even when women are employed in the public sphere, they are expected to care for children and oversee the everyday affairs of the household (Andersen, 1988). Within the family it is assumed that the woman, meaning biological mother, is best able to care for the children. She does so with relative ease given that tending and caring are believed to come naturally to her. Men on the other hand are associated with the public sphere of 'paid work, institutionalized religion, and political authority' (Andersen, 1988, p. 338).

This image of the ideal nuclear family has dominated middle-class consciousness despite the fact that this family composition has only fleetingly comprised the majority pattern throughout history. In the contemporary North American context, this particular family form is far from the norm. The 'vast majority of American families' are two-earner families; female-headed or single-parent households; postchildbearing couples or those without children; not to mention households made up of singles, gay and lesbian couples, and cooperative living (Andersen, 1988, pp. 147–8). Thus the idealized nuclear family only accounts for about 13 per cent of American families.

In Canada, the nuclear family consisting of breadwinner/father and homemaker/mother, legally married and living with their children, is equally mythical. From the 1960s to the 1990s, lone-parent families increased from 11 to 20 per cent of all families with children. According to Statistics Canada (1996), lone-parent families headed by women outnumber those headed by men by a ratio of more than four to one. 'In addition to one-parent families created by separation and divorce, more babies are now born outside marriage ... In Canada, 24 per cent of live births in 1990 were to women who were not married, compared to 4 per cent in 1960' (Baker, 1996, p. 27).

Regardless of marital status, women's labour force participation has undergone dramatic change since the Second World War:

> Before the Second World War, Canadian women usually left their paid jobs when they announced their engagement to be married ... In 1941, only 4.5 percent of married women were in the paid labour force ... By the 1960s, women's labour-force participation was influenced by marriage, the employment status and income of husbands, and the presence of children. If a woman was married, she was less likely to be working outside the home ... Now, however, younger women are more likely than older women to be in the labour force regardless of marriage or the presence of children. (Baker, 1996, pp. 21–4)

Baker reports that approximately 75 per cent of mothers with children under twelve are now working for pay outside the home. 'Married women are as likely, or more likely, to be working for pay as separated, divorced, or widowed women' (Baker, 1996, p. 24). In fact, Statistics Canada reports that two-income families are now in the majority. In 1996, for example, of all husband–wife census families, dual-income-earner families accounted for 63 per cent. Of the lone-parent families surveyed, 83 per cent were female headed. These women comprised 80 per cent of the total lone-parent labour force (Statistics Canada, 1996). This snapshot confirms the myth of the nuclear family as delineated previously.

Despite the demise of the idealized nuclear family, women continue to bear the brunt of caregiving and housework duties (Baker, 1996). Equally significant is the following observation by Baker (1996, p. 274):

> Although family life has changed considerably throughout the last fifty years, many of our social programs and policies were created from the 1940s to the 1970s when society differed substantially. Although some programs have been amended since then, many still over-emphasize the homogeneity or uniform nature of families, implying that most people live in nuclear family units consisting of breadwinner/father and homemaker/mother, legally married and living with their two or three children.

In the traditional dichotomy between public and private worlds, the family of the late twentieth century is associated with privacy and autonomy from state interference. 'Home and family usually conjure up images of free emotional expression, privacy, and protection from the impersonal world of politics and bureaucratic rule' (Pupo, 1988, pp. 207–8). The private world of the family is 'one where conflicts are supposed to be self-contained, without the intervention of the state' (Pupo, 1988, p. 149).

Much public debate has been based on this dichotomy with respect to the provision of services, as the following statement attests: '*Either* the state provides services *or* the family/woman or the market does' (Sassoon, 1987b, p. 174; italics in original). Discussions centre on when the state should intervene and on the intents and effects of such interventions for families and, of concern to feminist scholars, for women; state intervention is said to relieve or support the family or take over family functions, as if the family and state are distinct, as if private is separate and separable from public, and as if the family is the smallest unit of analysis.

A critical analysis of 'the family' as the smallest unit of analysis has been undertaken by Margrit Eichler (1988) in her operationalization of the multifaceted concept of sexism. She describes familism as one form of sexism wherein the family is regarded as a solitary unit rather than a collection of individuals who engage in particular actions. Considering the family as if this unit 'experienced or did things in the same manner, or as if any differences in the impact on, or activities of, individual family members are irrelevant' likely 'has a pervasive impact on policy formation' (Eichler, 1988, p. 118). In her discussion of the development and effects of social policy, Eichler argues that one cannot assume that a particular policy is good for the entire family unit until the effects of such a policy are demonstrated to be beneficial – or at least not harmful – to each family member. In this book, I am concerned with exploring the nature and effects of state interventions in response to allegations of child sexual abuse. While such interventions purportedly support autonomous families in the least intrusive ways, one cannot conclude that they are actually good for families when the experiences of women in families are brought to the surface.

Public and Private Spheres from the Perspective of Women: An Examination of Complex Relations

When examined from the perspective of women, the notion of state intervention as being good for families or supporting family functions takes on new meaning. State support for the family sounds innocent enough until one explores the relationship among women, the domestic sphere of the family, and state interventions to support family functions.

Women relate to the state in several interconnected and often invisible ways. They are unpaid caregivers, consumers, paid human service workers, and intermediaries who link state goods and services to household needs. Though women's relations with the state vary historically and according to class, race, ethnicity, marital status, age, and sexual orientation, for the most part women as a social group are the principal subjects of the welfare state. They comprise the overwhelming majority of program recipients and paid social service workers. They are also

> the wives, mothers, and daughters whose unpaid activities and obligations are redefined as the welfare state increasingly oversees forms of caregiving. Since this beneficiary–social worker–caregiver nexus of roles is constitutive of the social welfare arena, one might even call this arena a feminized terrain. (Fraser, 1989, p. 147)

Women as Unpaid Caregivers and Motherworkers

The state relies on women to provide a range of unpaid caring services to children, the elderly, and the infirm 'through families, partly as a result of an ideology that sees nurturing as part of women's natural role, and partly as a result of the complex division of labour ... which structures women as secondary workers' (Adamson et al., 1988, p. 114). One such service is that of 'motherwork.'

Motherwork is gendered. As Pascall (1986) says, motherwork is the province of women, it belongs to the domestic arena, and it is unpaid. Women, the biological bearers of children, are 'socially, legally and ideologically responsible' for rearing their children and as such are 'contained in the home and constrained in the world of work' (Mandell, 1988, p. 49). Though the relationship between women and children has varied through time and across social classes and ethnoracial groups, since the 1800s bourgeois notions of childhood as a distinct developmental stage and of a 'cult of domesticity' for women have prevailed[2] (Mandell, 1988). Alongside these themes are the beliefs that children are malleable and require full-time care by mothers, particularly in the early years, and that mothers are 'uniquely equipped' to care for them (Contratto, 1986, p. 71). It takes no mental leap to then relate failures in children to bad mothers. Similarly in child protection, 'when children's needs are not being met, mothers are scrutinized and held accountable' (Hutchison, 1992, p. 72).

Motherwork is teeming with deeply ingrained contradictions. On the one hand, motherwork can be isolating, tedious, tiresome, lacking in social recognition and social support (Rosenberg, 1988). On the other hand, women are expected to make a trouble-free transition into motherhood and are 'not supposed to need or have the right to need social services or social funds' (Rosenberg, 1988, p. 387). A second contradiction centres on the status of motherwork. Through the concepts of 'mother,' 'motherhood,' and 'mothering,' motherwork is romanticized and glorified as an instinctive labour of love, private, located in the individual called mother, and seemingly high in status (Rosenberg, 1988). Glorification, however, suggests normative and public expectations of women as mothers, expectations that are open to public scrutiny and evaluation by individuals other than mother. Alongside the idealization of motherhood is a 'misogynist tendency to blame mother for whatever problems arose with a child' (Contratto, 1986, p. 71). Heather Jon Maroney (1985) spoke of a third paradox: whereas mothering is relegated to women, they have lost control and authority over its activities. The expectation of women to provide unpaid caring and motherwork, with all of its contradictions, can be seen when workers and mothers of sexually abused children describe their experiences of protection.

The idealized model of motherhood has largely derived from the experiences of 'the white, American, middle class,' though it has been projected as 'natural, universal and unchanging' (Glenn, 1994, p. 3). Historical and anthropological evidence suggests that the concept of mothering is culturally constructed and that social and economic circumstances significantly influence expectations of mothers and motherhood. Ethnographic investigations reveal a variety of childcare arrangements and ideologies that justify them (Braverman, 1991). This means that the contemporary emphasis on the primacy of mother care in this society is not widely shared. In a study of 186 different societies across the globe, mothers are the primary or exclusive caregivers in only 46 per cent; 'after infancy, mothers provide the primary care in less than 20 per cent of these societies. In another 40 per cent, siblings provide the primary care' (Braverman, 1991, p. 230).

The universalistic construction of mothers as idealized nurturers has also been challenged for its ethnocentrism. Historically, poor women, immigrant women, and women of colour (African, Latina, and Asian) have been excluded from the cult of domesticity (Glenn, 1994). Rather than being valued for their family roles, these women have been looked on as sources of cheap labour, especially as domestic workers in white households or as low-level service workers (Glenn, 1994). For many social work agencies, cultural variation in client population is a fact. Yet assessment and intervention in child sexual abuse is, I will show, premised on the assumption of mother as primary caregiver and protector. This may contradict, if not violate, cultural norms.

Women as Recipients or Consumers

Women also rely on the state to provide an array of services to the sick, elderly, and the young. In North America women and children comprise the overwhelming majority of clients of means-tested and age-tested programs. 'Because women as a group are significantly poorer than men ... and because women tend to live longer than men, women depend more on the social-welfare system as clients and beneficiaries' (Fraser, 1989, pp. 147–8). However, social welfare services are often inadequate not only with respect to availability but because of the way in which the services are provided, and because of the ways in which needs are defined, interpreted, and satisfied by the state, as will be elaborated later in this chapter. Suffice it to say here that services 'make women overly responsible, often control their behaviour, and limit their choices and options' (Adamson et al., 1988, p. 114).

Women as Patchworkers

Women also function as intermediaries or patchworkers (Balbo, 1987). In order to make use of state services that are available, someone must 'supply the links which enable services provided elsewhere to be used' (Sassoon, 1987b, pp. 171–2). That 'someone' is a woman. She deals with these agencies, adapts to their 'complex, time-consuming, rigid and bureaucratic procedures' and negotiates, organizes, and transforms public services and resources for personal need; women meet with teachers, bring children to clinics, and visit social service agencies (Balbo, 1987, p. 49). In other words, women's patchwork is central to the processes through which resources are produced, delivered, and distributed (Balbo, 1987). Women's servicing and patching are, in Balbo's words, 'required, interchangeable (provided within families, through state agencies, by the market according to changing requirements), flexible, cheap' (1987, p. 65). Women provide huge amounts of work at little or no pay, and women's work represents 'ingenuity in the innumerable concrete ways of piecing and patching resources, their understanding and response to personal needs, and their ambivalence in dealing with the prevailing rules' (Balbo, 1987, pp. 65–6). As I will suggest, protection – a seemingly gender-neutral and state-based activity – is very much a feature of women's work, unpaid caring, servicing, and patching.

Women as Employed Providers

Finally, women relate to the state as the majority of frontline providers of service: teachers, childcare and social workers, welfare administrators, and so forth. In the Australian child welfare system, Smith and Smith (1990, p. 66) reflect that 'women do everything except manage it'; their work tends to be badly paid, low in status, frequently unrecognized, and yet essential. According to Swift (1995), Canada's child welfare workers are mostly young, white, middle-class women. 'More of them than in the past are well educated, with special training in social work and often specific training in child welfare, although a significant minority continue to work with little training or education' (Swift, 1995, p. 65). Callahan (1993b, p. 172) estimates that 'at least 70 percent' of frontline child welfare workers in Canada are women. Since the Second World War, Callahan explains, men increasingly entered into and moved up the promotional ranks of child welfare agencies. Simultaneously, women activists developed alternative/separatist services. Thus, although women are substantial in number, feminist influences in child welfare have been slight.

Contradictory Effects

Such intricate relations between women and the state, and the effects of state interventions for women, have given rise to much feminist debate. For one, while the state often appears amorphous and invisible, its activities reach into the lives of many Canadian women who engage in a constant process of negotiation with the state about the provision of services, particularly with the caring services, as discussed above. Second, women in Canada continue to face 'escalating violence, inadequate wages, discrimination in the workplace, continuing responsibility for child care and housework ... sexual harassment, racism, heterosexism, sexual objectification [and] the double day of labour' (Adamson et al., 1988, pp. 5–6). This reality for Canadian women persists despite legislative changes that have resulted from organized pressure by women, increased funding to services required by women, growth of women's organizations, and increased public awareness of women's inequality and rights. As a result, the extent to which the state functions as an oppressive or liberating force in the lives of women has been, and continues to be, critically examined by feminists.

Feminist positions on this issue differ. Whereas some feminists stress the state's role in reproducing male dominance or unequal social relations, others view the state as a site for protection, service, regulation, and redress (Armstrong & Armstrong, 1990). Despite these differences, few feminists argue that the state acts as a neutral arbitrator of competing demands. Feminists increasingly recognize that 'the state is not simply an instrument of class or male rule; [rather] it can ... work for the benefit of at least some women' (Armstrong & Armstrong, 1990, p. 114).

The debate on the liberating and oppressive functions of the state is summarized well by Pascall (1986). According to her, a number of feminists emphasize the social control function of the state. Through the professions of medicine, teaching, and social work, for example, public control is exerted on the private sphere associated with women. Social control analysts emphasize that social policy, 'based on a breadwinner/dependent form of family with the woman at home,' has 'played a part in controlling women by keeping them in the private sphere and out of public life' (25). This underlying paradigm ensures that women are available for caring labour and simultaneously 'exempts men and state services from these tasks' (25). This discussion is taken up in greater detail later in this chapter when women's relationship with the state as caregivers and intermediaries is revisited.

Linda Gordon (1990) has critically examined the social control position. She suggests that social control analysts tend to assume that 'social-control practices in question served (were functional for) the material interests of a dominant group and hindered (were dysfunctional to) the interests of the subordinate' (p. 180). She notes that such analyses are based on dichotomous relationships of 'them' and 'us' or 'oppressed and oppressor' (p. 180). A perusal of child protection case records from the progressive era enabled Gordon (1988, 1990) to challenge key premises of social control theory. She found evidence to contradict the notions that agency intervention into family life is 'automatically evil,' that families are autonomous and immune from social regulation, and that initiatives move from 'top to bottom' or professional to client (Gordon, 1990, pp. 191, 192). Gordon discovered that while there is some validity to this directionality, clients were not passive but 'active negotiators in a complex bargaining' (p. 192). She hypothesized that denial of the active role of agency clients by social control theorists was likely, given the conception of the family as a homogeneous unit. To refer to the family as a unit is to mask differences and conflicts of interests among family members. Gordon's analysis also found that social worker involvement actually changed 'existing family power relations, usually in the interest of the weaker family members' (p. 192). Gordon (1990) did not discard the 'experience' of social control; she found considerable discrimination and victim blaming by 'helping' professionals, as well as the experience of 'loss of control' as articulated in the case records (p. 195). 'Often the main beneficiaries of professionals' intervention hated them the most, because in wrestling with them one rarely gets what one really wants but rather another interpretation of one's needs' (p. 195).

In addition to debates about a social control function, the welfare state has also been seen as operating for the social good by redistributing income, goods, and services to the poor and the aged, the majority of whom are women (Pascall, 1986; Sapiro, 1990). Whether the state provides cash or service-based programs, Piven (1990, p. 254) finds that women are rendered 'a little less insecure' and 'a little less powerless,' for such programs reduce dependence of women with young children on men and of older women on their adult children, meaning daughters.

As far as Scandinavia is concerned, Borchorst and Siim (1987) argue that women's relation to the welfare state is neither wholly oppressive nor liberating but contradictory. There, the welfare state has vastly improved women's social and economic position through increased labour force participation and state benefits and services. At the same time the labour market is markedly sex-segregated, and women's influence on the development of the welfare state and participation in decision-making processes pale in comparison with men's authority in such domains.

Given that women in Canada, the United States, and the UK have campaigned for state recognition of and support for issues of concern to them,[3] it is difficult to hold firm to a view of the welfare state as being only an instrument of oppression. Resistance to women's demands, however, provides evidence to challenge the liberating role of the state. Current feminist scholars recognize that the welfare state has both progressive and repressive strands; its effects for women are contradictory in that state policies are not simply instruments of oppression or liberation.

Revisiting Relations between State, Families, and Women

In discussions about women's positions as consumers, unpaid caregivers, service workers, and employees, certain aspects of the role of women vis-à-vis the state rise to the surface.

For one, the traditional notion of separate spheres is rendered inaccurate for women. 'In reality, the private home stands in a complex, entangled, and historical relationship to the public sphere' (Pupo, 1988, p. 208). These spheres are 'reflected in one another' in that for women 'private life is not private from social policy, and public life reflects the division of labour in the home' (Pascall, 1986, p. 24). Whereas analytic distinctions might be made between production and reproduction or between paid and servicing work, and whereas the separation of public and private does reflect everyday experience, the 'concrete reality of women's lives' suggests that the domestic sphere is 'enmeshed with institutions and relations outside the home' for women and by women (Sassoon, 1987b, p. 179).

That women function as service workers and intermediaries indicates an assumption, even expectation, that women's roles are flexible, their participation in the labour force marginal, and their location in the home a fact (Sassoon, 1987b). This is not the case. Most women are employed out of economic necessity and few women are confined to the home (Andersen, 1988). Apparently women are expected, able, and willing with little or no hesitation or consequence to alter, jeopardize, or forgo remunerated labour force participation. Anette Borchorst and Birte Siim (1987) raise this very point. With women's increased participation in the paid workforce in Denmark and Sweden has come a more vivid perception of women's double roles as caregivers and wage earners. State policies, they note, continue to rely upon women's responsibilities for the 'psychic and physical well-being of the family members' (Borchorst & Siim, 1987, p. 128).

Social care policies assume that women are able to relinquish paid work and make themselves available as unpaid caregivers because it is further assumed that women are economically dependent on a husband's (or any male partner's) wage (Dale & Foster, 1986). Assumptions of marital stability and the adequacy of a male wage as a family wage fly in the face of the reality that more and more women and children experience lone parenthood at some stage in their lives and that a single income is woefully inadequate to cover household needs.

Though state policies and practices are based on the notion that women 'should' remain at home to care for their children (and others), the state is not prepared to pay for such labour in order to make this option a 'realistic' one for families (Dale & Foster, 1986).

It is also assumed that if a woman leaves the labour force to care for her child, aged parent, infirm or disabled relative, the costs to her and her household are insignificant at worst and 'invisible and unspoken' at best (Sassoon, 1987b, p. 172). On a general note, the very invisibility of women's caring labour must be costly regardless of the experience of caring, which may well range from burdensome to fulfilling. On the one hand, women's expected caring and servicing are so invisible that 'it is not even considered to be work' but rather 'love and self-denial and care for the needs of others' (Balbo, 1987, p. 52). On the other hand, Balbo adds, 'its worth is known to all' (p. 52), particularly men, whose 'familial patterns of caring ... have changed only marginally' (Sapiro, 1990, p. 49), and the welfare state, whose financial crisis would surely skyrocket if it were required to pay for women's invisible and essential service work.

Balbo (1987) reminds us that the costs and consequences of servicing work for women become all the more apparent when placed in the context of labour force participation. That is, women's increased involvement in the public/paid labour force has simply been added on to women's work in the family and 'nearly exclusive responsibility for the everyday care of their children' (Andersen, 1988, p. 182). Protection of children from sexual abuse, a feature of women's work, is both invisible and costly to women, as will be detailed in this book.

In light of women's relation with the state, the notion of supporting the family shifts in meaning. Pascall (1986) argues that 'the real meaning of supporting the family is *supporting family responsibility*, as distinct from state responsibility, for dependants young and old' (p. 38; emphasis added). Support for family responsibility, while appearing neutral with respect to family members, is very much gendered. As has been suggested, family responsibility for the care of children, the aged, infirm, disabled, and even one's (supposedly able-bodied and self-reliant) male age-mate/partner is a misnomer given the gendered division of caring labour. As Pascall points out, 'the existence of a relative, particularly a female relative, is enough to justify the absence of state support' (1986, p. 38). When 'services in kind' are available to support children, the aged, or disabled, such services are intended to supplement women's caring, servicing, and patching activities and 'fill gaps only in the absence of female relatives (Dale & Foster, 1986, pp. 109–10). Thus women often are – and often feel – responsible for the well-being of those who depend on them. This responsibility, and the accompanying ideology that women inherently provide servicing, are daily reinforced by concrete experience (Balbo, 1987). Anne Showstack Sassoon is rather blunt in her analysis of state–family relations: 'The welfare state will only provide what cannot be provided elsewhere. The less the welfare state does, the more is done by women and vice versa' (Sassoon, 1987b, p. 171).

Thus women in families have not lost the responsibility for caring, servicing, and linking. However, as will be seen in upcoming chapters, having the charge, obligation, or burden for service and patchwork is not equated with having the control over defining the problems, articulating the needs, and thus realizing the service and patchwork. As Gillian Pascall has indicated, 'one rather unattractive light in which to see the Welfare State, then, is as an erosion of women's power' (1986, p. 32).

Not only is support for the family steeped in gender, but the actual notion of support or taking over is questionable. Kari Waerness (1984, p. 75) put it this way:

> Seen from the mother's perspective, the 'taking over' has meant that a greater share of her caregiving work consists of cooperation with different agencies outside the family and not a release either from the practical care-giving tasks, or from having the main responsibility for the well-being of her children.

Contemporary feminist critics have argued that the welfare state, through social policies, plays a large part in sustaining the dependent position of women in families. As Sassoon (1987b, p. 160) points out, 'the domestic sphere, the world of work, the welfare state are all organized as if women were continuing a traditional role,' that is, as if women were full-time mothers and housewives. With cutbacks in the public sector, women can expect to take on heavier burdens as caregivers, and state policies are foreseen to continue to promote the bourgeois family 'through framing social policies on the assumption that women perform unpaid labour in the home and are economically dependent on men' (Dale & Foster, 1986, p. 61).

As consumers, paid human service workers, unpaid caregivers, and intermediaries, women are the principal subjects of the contemporary welfare state. The state however 'does not deal with women on women's terms' (Fraser, 1989, p. 149). Rather, social welfare programs and services have their own characteristic ways of interpreting women's needs and positioning women as subjects, thereby reinforcing gender stereotypes for women as wives and mothers, homemakers, and caregivers (Fraser, 1989, 1990).

The Welfare State as Gendered: Positioning Women as 'Mothers' and Interpreting Their Needs Accordingly

The works of feminist philosopher Nancy Fraser (1989) offer insights into how gender norms and meanings are encoded in the structure of the social welfare state. Though 'officially' the state and its social programs are gender neutral, Fraser (1989) views the social welfare system in the United States as organized by a gender subtext.[4] One set of programs (for example, unemployment insurance or social security) is oriented to individuals and tied to participation in the paid workforce. The majority of 'rights-bearing' recipients are males. As 'consumers' they have a right to cash benefits given that they, in partnership with employers, have already paid for what they deservedly receive (p. 151). A second set of programs (such as public housing) is oriented to households or families. It 'is designed to compensate for ... family failures,' generally meaning those families that lack a male breadwinner (p. 149). Financed largely through tax dollars, these programs position recipients as 'dependent clients' (not consumers), whose claims to benefits are appraised as worthy or undeserving; recipients, primarily women, are regarded as human failures, that is, as 'welfare mothers.' Both categories of programs are sustained by the assumptions of separate spheres and their respective sexual division of labour wherein women's priorities are 'housewifely and maternal responsibilities' regardless of paid workforce involvement (p. 149).

This two-tiered system constructs women 'exclusively as mothers.' As such it interprets women's needs as 'maternal needs' and women's sphere of activities as that of 'the family'[5] (p. 153). By constructing women as mothers, the welfare state fortifies the idea that a woman's natural vocation is wife and mother (and, as will be seen, mother protector). Of course the persistent and idealized location of women in families clashes with the reality of contemporary households, and women's relations with the domestic sphere, the world of production, and civil society. In this book, I examine protection practices in cases of child sexual abuse in order to reveal how such practices seem to identify need, position women, and thus reinforce gender norms and meanings.

The State as a Juridical-Administrative-Therapeutic Apparatus

Fraser (1989) proposes the 'JAT' – 'juridical-administrative-therapeutic state apparatus' – as an analytic tool for scrutinizing how the welfare state operates particularly in regards to interpreting and transforming problems and needs into legal, administrative, and/or therapeutic matters that coincide with the social institutions established to address those needs (p. 154).

By juridical, Fraser refers to the rights of clients or recipients of social welfare and services. Rights are appraised, meaning claimants are required to 'translate their experienced situations and life problems into administrable needs, to present their predicaments as bona fide instances of specified generalized states of affairs that could in principle befall anyone' (p. 154). In a sense, then, one's needs are subject to a 'rewriting operation' (p. 155). As problems are translated into administrable needs – that is, into a social service – and as 'the latter are not necessarily isomorphic to the former, the possibility of a gap between them arises' (p. 155). This gap is particularly possible in the 'feminine' subsystem of the welfare state, wherein clients are constructed as deviant, defective, or failed as families. In response to failures are service provisions that often include some 'therapeutic' dimension wherein 'gender-political and political-economic problems' are constructed as 'individual, psychological problems' (p. 155).

The social welfare system as a JAT 'imposes monological, administrative definitions of situation and need' and thus appropriates 'dialogically achieved self-definition and self-determination' (p. 155). In other words the interpretation of needs is pregiven, considered unproblematic, and (re)defined to 'system-conforming satisfactions' (p. 156). The JAT positions its subjects as passive clients or recipients of such predefined services (Fraser, 1990) and not as 'active co-participants involved in shaping their life conditions' (Fraser, 1989, p. 155). Subjects are personalized as 'cases' and their collective identification is stifled; thus, they are not empowered by the state (p. 155). Discontentment with these arrangements is construed 'as material for adjustment-oriented, usually sexist therapy and not as material for empowering processes of consciousness-raising' (p. 155).

Needs as Interpretations

Fraser takes the position that 'the identities and needs that the social-welfare system fashions for its recipients are *interpreted* identities and needs' (Fraser, 1989, p. 153; italics in original). In late capitalist societies that are 'differentiated into social groups with unequal status, power, and access to resources, traversed by pervasive axes of inequality along lines of class, gender, race, ethnicity, and age,' Fraser maintains that 'socio-cultural means of interpretation and communication' are also organized in ways that are compatible with relations of dominance and subordination (1990, p. 203). She explains that

> dominant groups articulate need interpretations intended to exclude, defuse, and/or coopt counter-interpretations. Subordinate or oppositional groups, on the other hand, articulate need interpretations intended to challenge, displace, and/or modify dominant ones. In neither cases are the interpretations simply 'representations.' In both cases, rather, they are acts and interventions. (pp. 203–4)

Fraser suggests that needs are translated into objects of potential state intervention through 'expert needs discourses,' including those of social workers, therapists, policymakers, and welfare administrators. Expert needs discourses include: social science discourses generated in universities; legal discourses produced in judicial institutions and their satellite schools, journals, and professional associations; administrative discourses circulated in various state agencies; and therapeutic discourses disseminated in public and private health and social service agencies. Chapters 3 and 4 present overviews of statutory, administrative, and therapeutic child protection 'expert' discourses related to the identification of and intervention into child sexual abuse.

Expert needs discourses redefine needs to correlate with a predefined social service, as noted above. Expert redefinitions reposition the people whose needs are in question. They become individual cases. They are 'rendered passive, positioned as potential recipients of predefined services rather than as agents involved in interpreting their needs and shaping their life conditions' (Fraser, 1990, p. 212). Though the identities and needs that the social welfare system fashions for its recipients are 'political interpretations' and thus subject to dispute, they are rarely recognized as such (as in the construction of women as mothers with maternal needs) and 'too often ... are rendered immune from analysis and critique' (Fraser, 1989, pp. 153–4). However, because interpretations emanate from specific locations in society, they cannot be assumed to have equitable impact or consequences. For example, feminist scholars have demonstrated time and again that 'authoritative views purporting to be neutral and disinterested actually express the partial and interested perspectives of dominant social groups' (Fraser, 1990, p. 219). To evaluate needs interpretations, Fraser (1989, 1990) suggests that we ascertain who is dis/advantaged by the interpretation and whether or not societal patterns of dominance and subordination are challenged or accommodated.

Conceptualizing the state as a JAT reveals how a political issue can be translated into a manageable legal, administrative, therapeutic, and frequently individual matter. When the issue is translated, it becomes depoliticized. Swift's (1995) analysis of child welfare agency files reveals how, through the JAT, neglect is produced and reinforced. Though poverty is arguably the defining factor of neglect, Swift demonstrates through recordings in case files that maternal deficiency, inadequacy, neediness, immaturity, and dependency become the central focus. Even though the mothers' lives are rife with multiple problems such as long-term poverty, resource deprivation, and violent intimate relations, and even though some positive images of mothers appeared in case records, the 'gaps, lapses and problems' in maternal care are emphasized (Swift, 1995). Interestingly Swift observes a glaring contradiction. 'Mothers must appear incompetent in order to qualify for the resources they need. In appearing incompetent, they bring the supervision and scrutiny of the agency upon themselves' (p. 125).

Here, too, the gaps, lapses, and problems in maternal care are accentuated. Conceiving of state practices in the context of a JAT, I suggest that the problem of a child being *sexually abused* (an offence committed predominantly by men) is rewritten to that of a child needing and having a right to *protection* (which entails the many acts of omission by women as wives, mothers, and protectors). This transformation embroils women such that they appear not as self-determined co-participants but as predefined mother-clients whose protective skills and obligations have obviously failed and thus are in need of repair. The transformation of the problem, its definition, and responses to it expose an unmistakable yet often hidden gendered subtext in official and largely gender-neutral child protection policies and practices.

3

Family Ties: Child Welfare and the Protection of Children from Sexual Abuse

Across Canada, adult children are successfully suing their parents for the abuses they endured in their childhood years. Such lawsuits target not only the parent directly involved in the alleged offence but also the parent who is seen to have breached her or his 'fiduciary duty.' In a newspaper article entitled 'Woman sues mother for not preventing sex abuse by father,'[1] an Ottawa woman claimed that her mother 'knew' of the physical and sexual abuse she suffered as a child, that her mother 'did nothing to stop the assaults,' and thus failed in her 'obligation to protect.' 'Parents have a duty to protect their children,' stated the woman's lawyer. 'We take the position that the mother was definitely aware of it. If she wasn't, she should have been.' Though the mother could not be reached for comment, she reportedly denied the allegations.

It has only been in the recent past that the silence shrouding children's experiences of sexual abuse has been lifted. Whereas children's allegations of sexual abuse were once commonly dismissed as the product of a child's rich fantasy life or as acts of maliciousness, today's helping professionals are more prone to listen, believe, act, and prevent. Though secrecy and denial of the very existence and pervasiveness of the problem still prevail (Glaser & Frosh, 1993), the story of the Ottawa woman reveals the considerable strides made in accepting allegations of child sexual abuse and in protecting victims. But the story also offers insights into the direction protection has taken, and it reflects a reworking of the balance between state and family in terms of accountability and responsibility for protecting children from sexual abuse.

This chapter looks at the statutory discourse on the problem of child sexual abuse and protection from it. It focuses on the cardinal policies, principles, and practices that are currently in place in the child welfare arena to deal with the problem.[2] In this chapter and in Chapter 4's review of the dominant theoretical, empirical, and clinical literature on child sexual abuse, a picture of the protection of children from sexual abuse emerges and serves as a backdrop against which the accounts of workers and mothers can be understood and analysed.

Child Welfare

Child welfare has been a long-standing and significant aspect of social welfare in Canada (Levitt, 1985). Child welfare refers to a broad range of policies, programs, and services provided by both public and private organizations that respond to problems experienced by families in caring for their children (Wharf, 1985). Child welfare policy, suggests Melichercik (1987), strives to create and reinforce conditions that secure children's wholesome growth and sound development.

Recognizing the multifaceted nature of Canada's child welfare system, Marilyn Callahan (1985, p. 6) once described it as a system designed to guarantee children 'the resources required for their development and the rights essential for their fair treatment.' It does so 'by providing supportive, supplementary, and substitute services to children and their families and advocating changes in economic, health, education, and social policies which have a significant impact on their well-being' (p. 6). Callahan further conceptualizes the child welfare system as three concentric circles. At the centre are those policies designed to ensure economic equality and freedom from discrimination. The middle ring includes universal programs (such as public education, family allowances, etc.). The outermost circle consists of policies and services fashioned to meet the basic needs of some children and families. These include protection programs, emergency shelters, foster care, and the like. As noted in the last chapter, analysts suggest that the bulk of current-day child welfare practice is occupied with activities related to this outermost circle: assessing abuse and neglect, dangerousness, and risk; policing families; and providing involuntary/coercive services. It is this outermost circle – child protection policies in relation to child sexual abuse – that forms the basis for the discussion in this chapter.

Child Protection: An Examination of State–Family Responsibility

It has not always been accepted that the state has a duty to protect children. For a long time, children were considered parental property or, more to the point, the father's property. This attitude was ensconced in both Roman law and English common law, whose traditions shaped early approaches to children's welfare in Canada (Melichercik, 1987). Ancient Roman law recognized the concept of *patria potestas*, meaning power of the father. This concept gave the father complete authority over his children. It 'provided the foundation for the legal systems of most European countries and ... carried the notion of almost exclusive parental jurisdiction into the twentieth century' (Melichercik, 1978, p. 188). The role of the state was that of protector and enforcer of parental rights (Harris & Melichercik, 1986). In England, the concept of *parens patriae* was prominent. Literally meaning 'parent of the nation,' this doctrine 'viewed the king as the father of the country and gave him (later the state) the right and the obligation to intervene on behalf of children' (Melichercik, 1987, p. 196). Originally designed to protect the property rights of orphaned children of nobility, the doctrine was gradually extended to include other government interventions for children.

Both traditions found their way into Canada with the early settlers. Whereas parental rights were emphasized in Lower Canada (Quebec), some governmental provisions were favoured in an attempt to achieve balance between the rights of parents and the rights of children in Upper Canada (Ontario). Thus the notion of social responsibility for the well-being of children to be achieved by state intervention on behalf of children was introduced (Harris & Melichercik, 1986; Melichercik, 1987). Though the principle of societal responsibility seems somewhat obvious in modern-day Canada, its appearance is a relatively recent development in most countries, including Canada.

In Ontario, the notion of state responsibility for assuring a minimum standard of well-being for all children was not established in legislation until the late nineteenth and early twentieth centuries. At that time, private children's aid societies were organized and provincial child protection legislation was enacted throughout Canada. In Ontario, the Act for the Prevention of Cruelty to and Better Protection of Children was passed in 1893, thereby granting children's aid societies legal authority to remove neglected or abused children from their homes and become their guardians (Bala, 1991). This legislation 'empowered private organizations to administer a provincial statute and use public funds for that purpose' (Melichercik, 1978, p. 190) and authorized state intervention in families in the name of child protection.

Enormous developments in the field of child protection have occurred within the last forty years. Extended definitions of abuse and neglect, limitations on temporary care by the state, establishment of criteria for the provision of child protection services via standardized accountability mechanisms, mandatory reporting laws, and the development of child abuse registers to track abusers and victims were just some of the changes undertaken in the 1950s and 1960s.

By the 1970s, attention shifted to the questionable adequacy of the state's child protection efforts that removed children from their families. According to Trocmé (1991), the belief that the state was able to know and provide what was best for children came under close examination and heavy criticism during this decade. As a result, the child welfare system again underwent legal and administrative reforms. In Ontario, key changes were numerous. The balance between children's best interests and the least restrictive course of state action was reworked. The definition of a child in need of protection was specified, and the principle of due process was introduced (Trocmé, 1991). The impact of these revisions on child protection proceedings was significant. They signified legalization of the protection process, greater recognition of the rights of parents and children, and greater controls on the power of the state to intervene in families (Bala, 1991). These changes are evident in the legislation in place to regulate child protection.

Provincial Child Welfare Legislation

Nationwide, child welfare agencies have been established with a legal right and responsibility to investigate reports that a child may be in need of protection and take action to protect children from illtreatment. The activities of such agencies are guided by provincial legislation. In Ontario, the Child and Family Services Act establishes the roles of children's aid societies and offers direction in how they are to function. This legislation was significantly revised in 1984, and further amendments to the Act were passed by the Ontario legislature in May 1999. Of particular interest here are the principles upon which the Act rests and the delineation of conditions rendering children to be in need of protection.

PRINCIPLES

The 'paramount objective' stated at the outset of the Child and Family Services Act (1984) is to promote 'the best interests, protection and well-being of children.' Alongside this cardinal principle is the notion that 'while parents often need help in caring for their children, that help should give support to the autonomy and integrity of the family unit and, wherever possible, be provided on the basis of mutual consent.' The Act further declares that 'the least restrictive or disruptive course of action that is available and is appropriate in a particular case to help a child or family should be followed' and that children's services should be provided in a manner that 'respects children's needs for continuity of care and for stable family relationships' (Ontario, 1984, pp. 3–4).

These principles were intended to reveal the general policy underlying the specific sections of the Act and the provision of services to children and families and to 'serve as an interpretive guide to the courts and to protection agencies' (Barnhorst & Walter, 1991, p. 18). Such principles demonstrate a particular balance between the rights and needs of children, their families, and the state, a balance that underscores support for self-sufficient families, minimal interference in families, mutual consent, and continuous care for children. In the Child and Family Services Amendment Act (1999), the promotion of the best interests, protection, and well-being of children was featured as the paramount purpose of the Act. This revision attempts to position the objective of protection as primary in practice rather than balanced against any other purpose. Its translation into actual change in practice remains to be seen.

FUNCTIONS OF CHILD WELFARE AGENCIES

As well as establishing principles, the Child and Family Services Act (1984) clarified the functions of child welfare agencies and modified the terms and conditions justifying involuntary intervention in families. The Act states that children's aid societies are mandated to 'investigate allegations' that children 'may be in need of protection,' to 'protect where necessary,' and to 'provide guidance, counselling and other services to families for protecting children or for the prevention of circumstances requiring the protection of children' (Ontario, 1984, pp. 13–14).

Intervention by a local child protection agency can involve a diversity of provisions from voluntary to court-ordered services, the latter of which may result in removal of the child from her or his family. Contemporary child protection services are most often thought of as involuntary, given that clients are brought to their attention usually by a third-party report (versus self-report). From the report, clients are subjected to child protective intervention 'until it is determined that the child has not suffered any harm and is not endangered in his or her current situation' (Wells, 1994, p. 438). Involuntary intervention does not imply apprehension of children from their families. In fact, as 'evidence has grown of the risks involved in separating children from their families and communities,' the maintenance of children with their families has replaced 'rescue' as the intervention/philosophy of choice (Jackson, 1995, p. 324).

According to Rivers (1993), the maintenance of children in their own homes is the most striking change in child welfare. A topography of clients served by the Children's Aid Society (CAS) of Metropolitan Toronto, the largest board-operated child welfare agency in North America, reveals that the overwhelming majority are assisted in their own homes. Most of these children, well over 80 per cent, were living at or below the poverty line. For every child admitted to state care, seven more are maintained in their families (Rivers, 1993). This ratio is neither accidental nor confined to a particular child welfare agency, as confirmed by similar trends across Canada, the United States, and the UK (Jack, 1997). Aimed at reducing the number of children removed from their families, child welfare statutes direct this shift in practice largely through such notions as family autonomy, least intrusion, permanency for children, and family support (Barnhorst & Walter, 1991; Rivers, 1993). A feminist critical analysis of the translation of these principles to protection practices in cases of child sexual abuse forms the crux of this book.

DEFINITION OF A CHILD IN NEED OF PROTECTION

The Child and Family Services Act (1984) further specifies twelve conditions under which a child is deemed to be 'in need of protection.' These conditions refer to children who have suffered or are at substantial risk for suffering from different kinds of harm. According to Ontario's legislation, a child is in need of protection specifically related to child sexual abuse when 'the child has been sexually molested or sexually exploited, by the person having charge of the child or by another person where the person having charge of the child knows or should know of the possibility of sexual molestation or sexual exploitation and fails to protect the child' or when 'there is substantial risk that the child will be sexually molested or sexually exploited as described [above]' (Ontario, 1984, p. 33). This definition links harm or substantial risk of harm to the child to the behaviours – acts or omissions – of the person having charge of the child (parents, caregivers, etc.). Actual or

44   What's Mother Got to Do with It?

potential harm warrants intervention by the child welfare state and it does so according to the principles described earlier.

The Act to Amend the Child and Family Services Act (Ontario Ministry of Community and Social Services [MCSS], 1999) extended the conditions defining a child in need of protection and revised the conception of the threshold of risk. A 'pattern' of neglect in caring for, providing for, supervising, or protecting the child was added to the list of protection conditions. As well, the threshold for risk of harm was lowered by replacing the phrase 'substantial risk' with 'risk that the child is likely to be harmed.' This revised phraseology recognizes that the word 'substantial' created too high a test for action to be taken to protect a child.

The definition of a child in need of protection is a crucial provision in the legislation for it establishes the legal justification for involuntarily intervention into families. Most provincial child welfare statutes contain vague definitions of a child in need of protection. Such ambiguity permits a wide variety of interpretations and considerable discretion for social workers and judges. However, in Ontario the approach taken to define a child in need of protection contains more precise and 'objective' language (Barnhorst & Walter, 1991, p. 20). This approach aims to provide a more consistent interpretation of a child in need of protection, limit intervention to cases in which there is specific harm or risk of harm, and regulate the range of discretion afforded to judges and social workers. It is consistent with due process 'since it gives parents a clearer idea of the problems they have to address' (Barnhorst & Walter, 1991, p. 20).

The aforementioned revisions and trends suggest that in the face of conflict between the best interests of a child considered to be at risk and respect for parental autonomy, the child's interests are paramount and the state's right to intervene takes precedence. Throughout this discourse reference is made to the rights and autonomy of gender-neutral families. I will suggest that interventions into families are most likely interventions into the lives of women as mothers. For the most part, their privacy is invaded and not without consequences for the women.

Whether or not statements of principles actually influence child protection workers and other involved systems is debatable. In her study of child abuse practice in Britain, Davies (1990) found that it was not unusual for workers to be unaware of management-initiated structures and procedures and to be unfamiliar with child abuse manuals. Even when aware of formal processes, workers used their own judgments to interpret those rules and procedures. Although a certain degree of worker discretion is to be expected, it should be noted that statements of principles and descriptions of the functions of children's aid societies (CAS) do not exist in a vacuum. They are supplemented by detailed particulars regarding the procedures followed to promote the best interests and protection of children garnered from the Standards and Guidelines for Management of Child Abuse Cases (Ontario MCSS, 1986). Such procedures include responding to an allegation of child abuse by seeing the child immediately and ensuring her or his safety; informing the police prior to the investigation; and interviewing the referral source, victim, siblings, alleged abuser, parent(s), and the person who had charge of the child.

Statements of principles and the functions of children's aid societies are also supplemented by community-based protocols that aim to ensure consistent and thorough handling of complex matters such as child sexual abuse investigations. Protocols were adopted in all parts of Canada by the late 1980s. While their contents vary to correspond with the distinctive constitution of a given jurisdiction, protocols augment, clarify, and specify existing policies and legal codes, and translate them into concise practice guidelines (Horejsi, Bertsche, Francetich, Collins, & Francetich, 1987). Protocols aim to facilitate reporting, investigation, assessment, and/or treatment of child sexual abuse, and coordinate activities of the CAS, police, criminal justice and child welfare legal systems, hospitals, mental health professionals, schools, daycares, and so forth. The next section elaborates on the investigation, assessment, and intervention by CAS in cases of child sexual abuse. The discussion is supplemented by excerpts from the protocol adopted in Metropolitan Toronto.

The Role of the CAS in Protecting Children from Sexual Abuse

'Child protection agencies are charged with the legal and moral obligation of promoting the welfare of children, by ensuring that they are not subject to abuse or neglect' (Bala, 1991, p. 10). More than fifty child protection agencies serve Ontario's 2.2 million children. In the early 1990s, over 18,000 allegations of child abuse came to the attention of these agencies. Sexual abuse accounted for approximately 44 per cent of the allegations (OACAS, 1991, Fact Sheet #5).

In Ontario, as in other Canadian and American jurisdictions, members of the public are required by law to inform child protection authorities when there are reasonable grounds to suspect that a child is suffering from physical or sexual abuse or neglect. Mandatory reporting laws have resulted in a child welfare system that must accommodate spiralling reports of suspected child maltreatment. Whereas 10,000 child abuse reports were made in the United States in the early 1960s, child protection agencies responded to over 1.3 million reports on 2.7 million children in the early 1990s (Wells, 1994). A proportional increase in reports also occurred in Canada (Lindsey, 1994).

Upon receipt of a complaint of child sexual abuse, the child protection agency is required to investigate. The protocol calls for reciprocal reporting between CAS and the police (each must inform the other of complaints received) and sharing the responsibilities of investigating and assessing the report of sexual abuse. To investigate is to establish whether or not an offence has occurred according to the Criminal Code and/or child protection legislation. This aspect of investigation entails identifying and establishing abusive behaviour and assessing the degree of risk to a child in her or his home. It is during the investigation of a report that the worker is positioned in a quasi–law enforcement role as she or he is faced with the tasks of verifying the abuse and deciding upon immediate and future courses of action to be taken by the agency and court systems. This initial investigation is a crucial decision-making point in the life of a case. Though the judgments made at this time can have a significant impact on children and families, they are often based on incomplete information, cultural and personal biases, and personal values on childrearing, parenting, and the like (Alter, 1985). In making decisions to substantiate allegations of abuse or neglect in the absence of evidence of serious harm to children, Alter found that workers call upon abstract factors such as parental will to harm the child or poor parent–child relationships.

Provincial child protection standards require that an investigation be undertaken within one hour after the report. Pursuing an initial report includes reciprocal contact between the CAS and police and involves checking CAS records, the Child Abuse Register, the Canadian Police Information Centre (CPIC), and police records regarding the alleged offender (Metropolitan Toronto Special Committee on Child Abuse [MTSCCA], 1986). Investigations of reports are not limited to new cases. Over half (51.6 per cent) of sexual abuse reports made to child protection agencies involve currently opened protection files on worker caseloads (Badgley, 1984).

When the sexual abuse is committed by a friend, acquaintance, or stranger, CAS involvement may be limited. In ascertaining the nature and degree of involvement, the CAS considers: protection concerns within the victim's family (e.g., insufficient supervision, inappropriate reaction by parent); protection concerns within the circle of the alleged offender (e.g., other children at risk); potential caretaker relationship between the alleged offender and the victim (neighbour, babysitter, known to the victim); site of disclosure; status of the case with the CAS; and immediate availability of a designated CAS worker (e.g., after hours, weekends).

While the police are required to report such cases to the CAS, limited resources often prevent the agency from becoming actively involved in all extrafamilial investigations. However, such reports enable the agency to determine any protection concerns; support, assist, and reassure the sexually abused child and family; and refer victims and their families to appropriate treatment or support services (MTSCCA, 1986).

Intrafamilial child sexual abuse refers to those abuses perpetrated by anyone related to the child by blood, adoption, or marriage, or anyone who acts in the capacity of the parent. In response to allegations concerning intrafamilial child sexual abuse, the CAS is more likely to intervene immediately and over a longer period of time. In these cases, suspects are more likely to be removed from the victim's home, the 'child is more likely to be apprehended or placed elsewhere,' and 'the suspect's access to [the] child is more likely to be restricted' (MTSCCA, 1986, Appendix C, p. 12).

Once all available information has been gathered from police and CAS sources, the police/CAS team arranges to interview the child. This interview can take place at the school or home, CAS office, police station, hospital, and so on. It can proceed without prior knowledge and in the absence of the parents if it is deemed to be in the child's best interests. Commonly, when the perpetrator is a parent/parent figure, or when the investigation team believes that the nonperpetrating parent will jeopardize the investigation, parental consent is not sought to interview the child. In cases of intrafamilial child sexual abuse, for example, Cage (1988) suggests that specific details of the abuse should not be revealed to the mother until the team meets with her in person. The rationale is that she may experience excessive upset, contact her spouse, and discuss the charges with him. It is feared that this advanced notice to the alleged offender destroys the element of surprise and gives him the opportunity to collect and eliminate potentially damaging evidence. Thus, the degree to which the mother is or is not informed is intended to contribute to the protection of children. However, the extent to which the mother is informed is not limited to the initial investigation, and although the intent is to protect, it may in fact come across as a disregard for these women. As will be seen, such disregard bears consequences for mothers, workers, and, potentially, for children.

The protocol calls for interviews with the child to be tape-recorded. This enables the investigative team to establish rapport with the child, focus on the disclosure, and reduce the number of times the child will be required to repeat his or her disclosure. The tape may be used to encourage a guilty plea on the part of the offender and assist the non-offending parent to support the child (MTSCCA, 1986).

Because the disclosure point 'is a critical situation for the victim,' sensitive responses and maximum support from authorities are essential (MTSCCA, 1986, p. 5). Disclosure of sexual abuse often produces a crisis for all family members, especially the child. The child fears she or he will be blamed or disbelieved. Thus the interviewer expresses belief in the child's disclosure, firmly states that the abuse was not his or her fault, and conveys to the child an intention to protect and help (Dawson, 1984, pp. 30–2). The technique of coaching – preparing a verbal response (to the disclosure) – is often used with those persons who are in close contact with the child. As will be seen in this case study, the mother is often asked to express support and belief in her child during the investigation phase of intervention. Regardless of her experiences at the moment, the forces compelling her to protect her child are potent.

The team proceeds on the assumption that the child's report warrants a full investigation. A retraction by the child should not be taken as proof that the abuse did not occur (MTSCCA, 1986). The team determines whether an offence has occurred and seeks evidence required for criminal prosecution. It also assures the immediate protection of the child. Thus details of the abuse are sought: its duration, severity, and frequency; the dynamics of secrecy and coercion; and the like.[3] To verify child sexual abuse is no easy matter, particularly in cases of father-perpetrated sexual abuse. Commonly, denial is thematic and the child ends up withdrawing allegations; corroborating evidence (forensic evidence, witnesses) is also usually lacking (Dawson, 1982). As Pezdek (1994) put it, distinguishing false from real claims of child sexual abuse is truly an ambiguous task. It involves decisiveness in the face of uncertainty; it is a process that occurs in a highly emotional situation and that has dire consequences for error.

The investigation continues with the nonoffending parent and any siblings who may be at risk. The nonoffending parent (often the mother) is assessed for her capacity to protect the child. According to Faller (1988a, pp. 122–3) clinicians should attend to the mother's economic and emotional dependence on the offender; her relationship with the victim, particularly the extent to which she is 'warm,' 'appropriate,' and 'loving'; and her protective response, that is, her awareness and toleration of abuse and her cooperation with professional interventions. If she does not present as an ally to the child and demonstrate an ability to support and protect him or her, the child will likely be removed from the home (Cage, 1988; Everson, Hunter, Runyon, Edelson, & Coulter, 1989; Horejsi et al., 1987; Pellegrin & Wagner, 1990). While assessing the mother's capacity to protect is a central feature of intervention, I will suggest that this feature is by no means a neutral exploratory process. Rather, it is a process wherein protection is effected through the mother at almost all costs. Such themes are detailed in chapters 6, 7, and 8.

The police officer interviews the alleged offender. If the suspect confirms the abuse and indicates a desire to seek help, he may be referred to a crisis support group program and/or a treatment facility. In dealing with the offender, the team considers the immediate protection needs of the victim and any other children potentially at risk. This is accomplished by halting all unsupervised access to the child. In intrafamilial situations, the team makes every effort to remove the offender rather than the child from the home. Voluntary agreements or criminal charges with bail conditions around access are used to accomplish this goal (MTSCCA, 1986). Though this practice of removing the offender ensures the protection of children with the 'least intrusion,' it can stir a range of reactions from mothers. It is a practice that seems to defy the meaning of 'voluntary' and ignores the many dimensions of their lives given their positions as mothers of sexually abused children. These consequences are likely unintentional on the part of social workers. Workers, too, struggle with the increased emphasis on legalism and danger in the face of their efforts to help all those involved in a case of child sexual abuse. As Jack (1997) observed in the UK, social workers' fears of 'getting it wrong,' of making mistakes that might render a child at risk or danger, have led to an 'atmosphere of mutual suspicion and mistrust ... [and] a defensive orientation to practice' (664).

While investigating complaints and attempting to verify abuse, the CAS worker embarks upon an assessment of risk, needs, and case management issues. When assessing risk, the worker might consider substance abuse, violence, psychiatric status, history of sexual orientation and sexual abuse, and response to disclosure and treatment on the part of the father. She or he might also explore the ability to protect, the degree of dependence on or control by the husband, and the response to disclosure and treatment on the part of the mother. The child's age and developmental capacity, frequency and severity of abuse experienced, degree of fear, and refusal to return home are also likely factored into the assessment of risk. The degree of chaos, transience, geographic or social isolation, the attitudes of siblings to the abused child, and the presence of multiple problems or marital problems in the family might also come under scrutiny in the risk assessment (Dawson, 1982; Spencer & Nicholson, 1988).

The worker also begins a psychosocial assessment of the child and family and designs a specific management plan for the case. Ideally this plan incorporates the findings of the investigation, the needs of the child, objectives for the case, the manner and extent of child welfare intervention and court intervention, and services to be provided (MTSCCA, 1986). In consultation with colleagues who routinely meet to review sexual abuse or other high-risk cases (internal agency review teams), decisions are made regarding the provision of voluntary services only, the use of voluntary agreements, or the use of the child protection court for the purposes of obtaining a supervision or wardship order. It should be noted that the outcome of the criminal investigation should not be a factor affecting the decision to involve child protection court.[4]

Debate has raged as to whether child protection proceedings should be initiated in all intrafamilial sexual abuse cases. Certainly court involvement has its advantages. It confirms to the child that she or he is believed and steps toward protection will be made; it enables a judge to order an assessment of the child and family, to enforce counselling, and to specify target changes. It thus changes the balance of power from the offender to the CAS and has the potential to reduce dropout and to act as an incentive for change (MTSCCA, 1986). However there are disadvantages in pursuing court involvement. These include the risk of insufficient evidence for a finding, lengthy delays in contested cases, and the potentially traumatic and intrusive nature of court proceedings themselves. As a result, the CAS may embark upon a signed voluntary agreement to service with a stipulation that, in the event of noncompliance, the agency would appeal to the provincial court for a finding that the child is in need of protection. All examples discussed in this book included at least a voluntary agreement or supervision order.

The investigation results in a determination of the status of the case. The sexual abuse will be 'unfounded,' 'suspected' to have occurred, or 'verified.' When child sexual abuse is suspected but not substantiated, there are no legal grounds to impose involuntary services. The agency may remain involved contingent upon the clients' willingness to engage in service. 'Verified' cases of abuse are made known to the Child Abuse Register. When the child remains at home, she or he is to be seen regularly until risks diminish; contact with the family is required until conditions are considered to be safe; 'missed contacts' are considered to be 'danger signals' (Ontario, MCSS, 1986). The Child Abuse Register is currently being phased out of practice (Personal communication with the Ontario Association of Children's Aid Societies, 2001).

The case remains an open protection file until the child is no longer at risk or in need of protection or until his or her environment is considered to be safe. While there is no authoritative approach to attaining these goals, ongoing therapeutic intervention ideally involves multiple treatment modalities for up to two years. Following crisis intervention, treatment may entail individual and couple counselling; group treatment for victim, siblings, mother, and father; and/or family therapy (Dawson, 1982; Giarretto, 1982; Hoorwitz, 1983; Keller, Cicchinelli, & Gardner, 1989). Increasingly hefty caseloads, unanticipated crises, and responsibilities in competition for their time render social workers most unlikely to offer such a range of interventions and in such an organized fashion. Unlike its appearance in the written discourse, the provision of sequenced multiple modality treatment is unusual in a child welfare setting.

Much attention has been given to ascertaining the roles for nonoffending mothers throughout the phases of intervention. During the investigation/crisis-intervention phase, the nonoffending mother's ability to protect the child is of utmost concern. Investigation protocols and guidelines direct protective service workers to assess the nonoffending parent's reaction to the allegations, degree of support for the child, thoughts on the offender's behaviour, willingness and ability to protect the child, and the like (Faller, 1988b; Horejsi et al., 1987). In their inquiry into the most influential factors that predict placement decisions for sexually abused children, Hunter, Coulter, Runyan, and Everson (1990) found that maternal support of the child emerged as the only significant predictor of immediate and long-term placement decisions in cases of child sexual abuse. In fact, 'the attitude of the non-abusing parent (almost exclusively mothers) towards the alleged perpetrator is seen as a litmus test of children's likely safety' (Waterhouse & Carnie, 1992, p. 51). Along with an assessment of the mother's knowledge of the abuse prior to disclosure, her primary alliance with child or offender, and the extent of her collusion with the perpetrator after the disclosure, it is apparent that case management decisions depend crucially on the mother (Waterhouse & Carnie, 1992).

According to the first *Sexual Abuse Training Manual* used in Ontario, the mother should be helped early on to accept appropriate personal responsibility for the deficits of her marriage and for colluding or failing to be aware of the abuse (Dawson, 1982). The manual suggests that the mother apologize to the child in order to ensure that the child feels blameless for the abuse and its aftermath. In the two revised versions of the manual, detailed in the next chapter, concern with maternal collusion and awareness continues to prevail. However there is also recognition that she needs support and understanding, and that efforts should be made to refrain from implying that she was neglectful or somehow responsible for the abuse. Learning about her child's sexual abuse and accusations against her partner can be both shocking and devastating. Bearing her emotional trauma in mind, the manual recommends that she be evaluated for her immediate ability to protect the child. These themes are well established in the contemporary scholarly literature on mothers of sexually abused children. As will be seen, worker sensitivity to the mother's position does not relieve her of the expectations to protect her child.

While intervention proceeds differently according to the service setting and availability of or access to resources, the mother of the sexually abused child may engage in individual counselling and group treatment. Here she can explore and vent feelings of guilt, shame, and anger; confront denial; learn to protect her children and set reasonable expectations for husband and child; examine her childhood and marriage; and improve communication, social skills, and assertiveness (Bagley, 1985; Cammaert, 1988; Sgroi & Dana, 1985).

Since most mother–child relationships are strained as a result of the disclosure and investigation, one of the key goals for the social worker is to 'release the bonds of trust and love' (Spencer & Nicholson, 1988, p. 169). This goal is considered crucial in efforts to break the intergenerational abuse cycle (McDonough & Love, 1987) and to move toward family reconciliation (Spencer & Nicholson, 1988). Sessions with the mother and her victimized child(ren) are intended to help the mother nurture and protect her child and to foster an alliance between them. These goals are thought to be essential for effective family treatment.

Maternal support not only affects the child's immediate fate but has been found to enhance a child's long-term recovery from sexual abuse (see Esparza, 1993; Everson et al., 1989; Wyatt & Mickey, 1987). While a significant number of women believe, comfort, and reassure the child in the face of the disclosure and take immediate protective measures (Carter, 1990; Krane, 1994; Myer, 1985), it is not surprising that the discovery of the sexual abuse is rife with distress for the mother herself (Deblinger, Hathaway, Lippmann, & Steer, 1993). The mother's distress, I will suggest, is inadequately acknowledged, most probably unwittingly so. She is expected to forgo her own needs and ignore her own state of turmoil in order to support her child. She is expected to calmly and effectively cope with the situation, no matter how disruptive and distressing.

Finally, a plan of service might include marital therapy to address such issues as power between spouses, anger, intimacy, communication, and role boundaries (Hoorwitz, 1983). In cases of father-perpetrated sexual abuse wherein the offender has separated from his wife and children, 'courtship' between spouses is encouraged (Hoorwitz, 1983). In this sense, courtship is far from a private activity between partners; reestablishing their relationship is very much a public/state matter, as will be seen in Chapter 7.

Numerous clinicians advocate for family treatment at the end of intervention in order to improve family relations and problem-solving methods. Others recommend that family sessions be initiated as soon as possible for delays may lead 'mother [to] refuse to participate' (Hoorwitz, 1983, p. 522). Hoorwitz views these sessions as offering opportunities to enrich the mother–child relationship and direct mothers to set limits and provide guidance to the children.

Commonly the mother is seen as the key to treatment and the crucial player in the reconciliation process. After disclosure, she is expected to support her child and separate the child from the offender. Frequently she is asked to accept partial responsibility for not having known or for having failed to protect her children. Over the course of intervention,

54 What's Mother Got to Do with It?

she will learn to tune into her children and husband, and monitor family dynamics prior to family reunification.

Contemporary Child Welfare Practice: Strains and Struggles for Workers

The foregoing review of the context within which child welfare practice takes place gives rise to a number of themes, not the least powerful of which is an image of child welfare as an arena of social work practice that is under fairly strict legal and administrative control. We have seen not only the emergence of increased regulations governing the work but increasingly precise definitions of a 'child in need of protection' and the roles of caseworkers as agents of the state in this regard. These trends are not surprising given that contemporary child welfare practice has evolved largely as a result of major legislative reforms – mandatory reporting laws, clarified definitions of child maltreatment in its various forms, and the principles of least intrusion, support for children in families, and family preservation.

Such reforms have given rise to a child welfare system that faces a swell of reports of suspected child maltreatment. As a result, the bulk of child welfare practice is now occupied with responding to reports of maltreatment and engaging in activities related to protection: identifying abuse, investigating and assessing risk, policing families, and providing involuntary/coercive protection services. What we see is a shift from a concern for the general welfare of children and families to a preoccupation with the appropriate legal bases and means to intervene in some – assumed to be 'failed' – families (Boushel, 1994; Parton, 1992).

Alongside increased reports and investigative activities, we have witnessed a transformation in the philosophy, principles, and practices of how to procure the best interests and protection of children. A perusal of the key principles upon which child welfare practice is based reveals an emphasis on maintaining children in their families versus removal or rescue. This emphasis reflects beliefs that the best place for most children to receive care is in their own families, and that families might need guidance, counselling, and support in caring for their children. Though current trends show that fewer children are taken into state care following child welfare investigation and assessment, concomitant essential resources to aid parents are far from forthcoming. In other words, while child protective agencies have allocated considerable energy and funds to investigating more and more allegations, this focus is pursued without adequate resources for prevention, support, and protective services for families to care for their children (Callahan, 1993a; David, 1991; Hutchison, 1992; Hutchison, Dattalo, & Rodwell, 1994; Kamerman & Kahn 1990; Parton & Parton, 1988/1989; Pelton, 1990; Trocmé, McPhee, & Tam, 1995; Wells, 1994).

Have these shifts in protection services improved the welfare of children? Are children better protected with clarified definitions of abuse and protocols for reporting and investigation? Are the problems that led to state intervention or interference ameliorated?

Based upon an analysis of the costs and benefits of mandatory reporting, Hutchison (1993) concludes that the path taken in child protective services has been less than ideal. For one, the reporting and investigative foci separate child abuse from issues of income distribution and poverty. This is problematic given that child protection agencies most often become involved with the poor – a disproportionate number being single mothers and visible minorities – and deal primarily with the results of poverty and marginalization (Armitage, 1993; Bala, 1991; Gelles, 1992; Lindsey, 1994).[5] Second, while the reporting and investigative emphases create a perception of a moral mission in that the state is seen to protect children, little empirical evidence has been found to support the notion that the shift in direction of resources has either provided increased safety for children or reduced overall child abuse. 'If such evidence existed, we could be satisfied that child welfare in its current manifestation as child protective services, is going in the right direction' (Lindsey, 1994, p. 123). Third, we might consider the costs to families and children. 'Professional rhetoric,' suggests Hutchison, 'posits that current [child protective services] are family based, aimed at strengthening the family' (1993, p. 60). This assumption suggests that the benefits of reporting and investigating child abuse outweigh the costs of state intervention. Unfortunately, the epidemic of child maltreatment reports and ensuing investigations has occurred in an era of social welfare reform and repeal marked by massive erosion of social services. These include cuts in financial assistance programs, intensive family support services, programs for mothers and children, child nutrition, daycare programs, and the like. With a decline in family-strengthening services, it is hard to imagine that children are being protected or families aided (Hutchison, 1993). This transformation is not without consequences for women as frontline workers and mothers. It is the frontline worker who bears the contradictory demands of investigating and judging while aspiring to provide service in an impartial, helping manner, and of promoting family preservation without the necessary tools to ameliorate the problems they encounter daily (Pelton, 1990). For mothers, the scarcity of resources becomes all the more devastating when the mandate to protect appears to be shifted onto their already full plates.

The contemporary child welfare system has been criticized for being overly intrusive and underprotective, underfunded, and overburdened. The current manifestation of child welfare presents workers with the most overwhelming – if not impossible – task of ensuring that children do not suffer in their families. This responsibility runs parallel to respect for parental rights and the privacy of families and is in concert with principles of least intrusion or disruption and consent. Not only are workers expected to investigate troublesome circumstances where children are at serious risk and 'where parents are often equally distressed,' but 'they are expected to work with families in these difficult circumstances and ensure that children remain with their families if at all possible' (Callahan & Attridge, 1990, p. 2). Though child welfare workers have the legal authority to remove children from their homes, this power must be exercised with great caution. As Callahan and Attridge (1990) observed, child protection work is frequently accomplished with few resources other than the worker's ingenuity and practice wisdom, and support from colleagues in the field. Added to this observation is an appreciation that caseworkers must sustain high levels of ambiguity and an ability to live with responsibility for acting decisively while unsure of the outcomes of their interventions (Armstrong, 1995).

Interestingly, there seems to be an expectation that social workers can save children from conditions of abuse. This expectation, simply impossible to meet, speaks to the way in which child welfare work has been 'invested with an omnipotence not given to other occupations' (Valentine, 1994, p. 78). This omnipotence goes hand in hand with the structure and delivery of child welfare services. Here responsibility for a child's well-being is assigned to one social worker. Here the range of emotions experienced by workers – from compassion and affection to dislike, disgust, fear, anxiety, uncertainty, confusion, and conflict – is rarely acknowledged beyond private discussions with colleagues or occasionally a supervisor. Here there is an expectation that social workers remain objective, detached, guarded against manipulation, and that they avoid excessive involvement and overidentification. The emphasis is on collecting the facts – the juridical versus therapeutic issues. Here official documents – legislation, standards and guidelines manuals, and accompanying protocols – streamline assessment and intervention and promote decisive action, while the subjective is diminished if not dismissed. Given the context within which child protection practice takes place, if and when problems arise in a case, workers are often left to feel as though they have failed, as though they are responsible (Valentine, 1994).

Rarely are we given an occasion to peer into the child protection workplace, particularly from workers' perspectives. One notable exception is Callahan and Attridge's (1990) exploration of female child welfare workers' appraisals of their work and workplace, with a specific focus on their experiences of power and powerlessness. What emerged was a characterization of child welfare work as challenging, complex, emotional, and fast paced. The workers, embroiled in complicated situations with no easy solutions, often found themselves isolated, insufficiently supported, and inadequately advised in their pursuits to unravel and respond to the needs of at-risk children and their families. The delicate balance between the contradictory roles of policing and helping, the sensitive negotiations, and the many hours of comforting and counselling undertaken in protection work materialized as central to child welfare practice and yet remained invisible in official organizational records of the work. Sprinkled throughout workers' accounts of the trials and tribulations of their work were references to the significance of youth protection. 'In the end, it is work with the potential to make profound differences in the lives of children and their families' (Callahan & Attridge, 1990, p. 45).

There is another layer of invisible work in child welfare – the work of mothers in the protection process. Although concealed in the gender-neutral statutory discourse, the centrality of mothers screams loud and clear in the therapeutic discourse. To this subject I now turn.

4

Understanding Child Sexual Abuse: Highlighting the Inadequacies of Women

At 11:30 P.M. on Thursday, 20 January 1994, Lorraine Dutil drove her 11-year-old daughter, Sarah, to a friend's apartment to babysit the friend's children. The following morning, when Sarah's 16-year-old boyfriend arrived at the apartment to pick her up, he was told that Sarah was no longer there. Having apprised the girl's mother of this situation, Lorraine made a missing persons report to the police and began a foot search through the neighbourhood where Sarah had last been seen. She found her daughter's body in a dumpster on Friday, 21 January.

The next day, Saturday, 22 January 1994, the following newspaper headline grabbed our attention: 'Mom finds child in dumpster.'[1] Beaten in the face, stabbed through the eye, sexually assaulted, her throat slashed, asphyxiated, stuffed in a gym bag, and thrown in a garbage dumpster – this is how Sarah Dutil died.

Timothy Cobb, the boyfriend of the woman for whom Sarah was babysitting, was charged with first-degree murder in Sarah's death. Newspaper coverage of the story revealed Cobb's psychopathic tendencies and extensive criminal record, including a string of murder charges. As a reader, I was appalled that the most recent trial for murder ended in a mistrial and Cobb's release. According to the news reports, Lorraine Dutil and her boyfriend knew Cobb and helped him find a lawyer to defend against a previous murder charge.

On Tuesday, 25 January, the Montreal *Gazette* headline read: 'Slain girl led turbulent life, friends and teachers say.' The opening line of the story read as follows: 'Long before her body was tossed into a dumpster in LaSalle last Friday, 11-year-old Sarah Dutil had been screaming for help.' According to teachers and officials, Sarah was a 'troubled child' and 'mature beyond her years.' At one time she had told school staff 'nobody loves me.' Sarah frequently complained of headaches and stomachaches. She was often locked out of her own home and sought refuge and a warm meal from neighbours. She described 'drug paraphernalia' seen at her home. Although child welfare authorities had investigated allegations of abuse and neglect, according to the press, Lorraine denied the allegations and the case was closed.

The 27 January edition of the Montreal *Gazette* offered front-page coverage of Sarah's funeral. In his sermon, the reverend observed that while 'many children all over the world die violently,' those left to mourn must try to 'forgive the perpetrators of the violence.' In another column published in the same edition, the writer grappled with the complexities of the Dutil case. Entitled 'Imperfect love: Painful, unavoidable questions about Sarah,' the article described Sarah's troubled family, her somatic ills, and the drug-related items found in the Dutil home. The columnist noted that it might be 'easier, more polite and more comfortable to lay all the blame on the killer ... or the justice system.' He pointed out that while it never seems to be a 'good time to ask critical questions about Sarah's life which are disturbing and pertinent,' certain questions must be asked. 'Why was an 11-year-old girl allowed out at 11 P.M. to babysit two preschoolers overnight?' 'What 11-year-old girl has a 16-year-old boyfriend?' 'What parent lets a child spend the night at an apartment where one of the tenants has been accused of murder – something the mother knows because she helped him get a lawyer?' Anyone can parent, the columnist asserts, 'but parenthood carries consequences and responsibilities. Doing it right means making sure your child is fed and clothed and loved. It also means putting their interests above your own and keeping them out of harm's way.'

One week after the first report of Sarah Dutil's death, two final stories appeared in *The Gazette*. Whereas one article presented the Dutil tragedy as an instance of a mother's neglect, the other wondered whether blame ought to rest on the deficiencies of the justice system or on the failures of a single mother of two children, surviving on a welfare cheque in a world where there is nothing particularly strange about 'Uncle John sleeping on the couch after he gets out of jail.'

The story of Sarah Dutil is indeed devastating. It is a story that awakens moral outrage at the abuse of children, provokes passion for the rescue of children, and calls for a search for sensible explanations for horrific instances of child maltreatment. But I see another kind of tragedy in Sarah's story, one that focuses not on the cruel, premeditated death of a child orchestrated by Cobb, but on the inadequacies of the criminal justice system in dealing with Cobb the 'psychopath' and on the shady lifestyle and negligence of Sarah's mother Lorraine. Here, the mother's inadequacies enter into the discussion and remain central to the extent that Sarah's ultimate death seems to be the logical consequence of failed mothering. As readers learned of Cobb's unsettled youth and disturbing list of criminal activities, his behaviour came to 'make sense'; his actions were put into perspective. However Lorraine Dutil's actions and inactions as a mother were found to be disturbing. After all, it was she who failed to keep her child out of harm's way. It is this pervasive, taken-for-granted, and culturally and historically specific construction of mother as idealized and blameworthy together with the simultaneous disregard for social location and the material objective conditions for mothering that connects this story to theory, research, and practice in relation to another form of child maltreatment – child sexual abuse.

Child Sexual Abuse: An Overview

In the last quarter of the twentieth century, the sexual abuse of children and youth became a profound child welfare problem. Estimates on its prevalence vary. According to the annual reports produced by the Canadian Centre for Justice Statistics (CCJS) and the fact sheets published by Prevent Child Abuse America (2000), establishing the extent of any form of child abuse is fraught with difficulty. Variations in definitions, sources and methods of data collection, underreporting, underdetection, and the dynamics of abusive relationships all affect the accuracy of prevalence estimates. As a result, completely accurate national estimates of the prevalence of child abuse cannot be made. Bearing this context in mind, researchers have suggested that the problem of child sexual abuse is considerable in scope. In Canada, a nationwide investigation into sexual offences against children found that 'at some time during their lives, about one in two females and one in three males have been victims of one or more unwanted sexual acts' ranging from exposure to threats to sexual assaults (Badgley, 1984, p. 1). Most of these incidents were first committed when the victims were children (Badgley, 1984). When acts of exposure and exhibitionism were excluded from Badgley's findings, 25 per cent of the female respondents and 10 per cent of male respondents were sexually victimized during their childhood years. According to the Uniform Crime Reporting Survey (UCR) of the Canadian Centre for Justice Statistics (CCJS) (1998), a total of 6474 victims of child sexual assault were reported to 154 police agencies in Canada. Of these, 5009 were girls and 1465 were boys. These findings reveal a ratio of 3.4 female victims to 1 male victim. A similar ratio is found in the United States. A 1996 national incidence study conducted by the U.S. federal government revealed that girls are sexually abused three times more often than boys (Sedlak & Broadhurst, 1996, cited in Prevent Child Abuse America, 2000).

In a recent Toronto-based study that employed in-depth interviews with 420 adult women, more than 50 per cent reported an intrusive sexual experience before they reached the age of 16 years; 17 per cent reported at least one experience of incest and 34 per cent had been abused by a nonrelative, all before the age of 16 years; 96 per cent of the perpetrators were male (*The Gazette*, Montreal, 30 July 1993, p. B3). In the United States, Russell (1986) also discovered prevalent child sexual abuse wherein 38 per cent of women sampled had at least one experience of abuse before the age of 18 years, and 28 per cent before 14 years.

It is estimated that between 2.5 and 8.7 per cent of males have been sexually abused as children (Finkelhor, 1984). Regardless of the gender of the child, the offenders are most often male and known to their victims. Retrospective surveys suggest that between 25 and 29 per cent of abusers are relatives, about 60 per cent are known to the victims but unrelated, and between 11 and 16 per cent are total strangers (Badgley, 1984; Russell, 1986). UCR statistics are strikingly similar: family members comprised 32 per cent of offenders and 62 per cent were nonfamily perpetrators; data were unavailable for the remaining 6 percent (CCJS, 1998). In Russell's (1986) study, of the 29 per cent 'relatives,' uncles were identified as the most common perpetrators (25 per cent), followed by biological, adoptive, step- or foster fathers (24 per cent). A recalculation of these findings reveals that abuse by a father or father figure accounts for about 7 per cent of the total population of child sexual offenders identified by Russell's respondents. These findings challenge the myth that children are sexually assaulted by strangers lurking in dark corners and confront the misconception that the vast majority of child sexual abuse is perpetrated by a family member, commonly assumed to be a father or father figure.

The offender is most often known to and trusted by the child and holds a legitimate power position over the child. He often exploits acceptable societal patterns of authority to engage the child in a sexually abusive relationship (Sgroi, Blick, & Porter, 1985). Sgroi et al. (1985) suggested that because the power and authority of adulthood are accepted by most children, and because the offender presents his behaviour as being sanctioned, little else is required to induce the child to comply. Having engaged the child in an abusive relationship, the offender sets up conditions that eliminate his accountability and enable him to repeat the abuse and thus meet his needs. Such conditions include isolating the child, intimidation, bribery or force, and subtly or overtly imposing a veil of secrecy over the abuse (Sgroi et al., 1985; Summit, 1983). Many children are ambivalent about telling anyone of the sexual abuse. Feelings of helplessness, entrapment, or fear of disclosure force many children to keep the secret. Few report the abuse to authorities. Russell (1986) suggested that from 2 to 7 per cent of cases are reported. As many as 90 per cent of cases go unreported to child welfare agencies in Canada (CCJS, 1998). When children do disclose, they are more likely to tell their peers rather than adults (Boushel, 1994). Researchers have found that while mothers are informed of a higher number of incidents than agencies, friends or sisters are informed of a higher number still (Hooper, 1992).

Though many incidents continue to remain undisclosed, mandated agencies have witnessed an unprecedented number of reports in the last fifteen years. Considerable controversy surrounds the origins of increased reporting. Carter (1999) suggests that social support for children to disclose and improved responses to reported cases have contributed to this increase. According to Finkelhor (1984), the upsurge in attention to the sexual abuse of children has resulted neither from increased prevalence nor because reporting suddenly mushroomed, but primarily because of the efforts of the women's movement and the children's protection movement. While these two groups have had a significant impact on our current conceptualizations of and responses to child sexual abuse, their analyses and recommended responses are fundamentally different.

Child protectionists locate child sexual abuse within the context of other forms of child maltreatment. Like their involvement in cases of abuse and neglect, child protection agencies tend to deal with incidents of child sexual abuse that are intrafamilial, including incest and abuses perpetrated by surrogate parents or caretakers. As noted in the last chapter, child welfare agencies also respond to allegations of sexual abuse by nonfamily members, such as a baby sitter, teacher, or recreation worker, when such persons have charge of that child, meaning they are responsible for caring for or supervising that child. Not surprisingly, given the overrepresentation of reported cases that are intrafamilial, child protectionists understand the etiology of sexual abuse in terms of the characteristics of family systems and the roles and interactions of family members (Dawson, 1982). Ontario's *Sexual Abuse Training Manual*, used in the 1980s to prepare child protection workers to assess and intervene in these cases, reveals this emphasis.[2] The manual advises child welfare trainees to avoid 'fixation with the abuser' or preoccupation with 'parent/child' problems because both support the 'myth' that 'mothers are generally unaware of the sexual abuse. Clinically, this is not the case' (Dawson, 1982, p. 33). The construction of the problem in the context of the family provides a foundation for interventions that emphasize the protection of the child and the amelioration of dysfunctional family dynamics. Along with cessation of sexual abuse by the offender, the manual identifies such goals as ensuring that parents accept responsibility for the sexual abuse and restructuring family and marriage relationships (Dawson, 1982). This focus for intervention is clear in the outline of treatment principles in the manual: child sexual abuse is unacceptable and harmful to children; protection of the child is of primacy; and all family members need treatment (Dawson, 1982).

Though intervention often entails involvement of the criminal justice system, some child protectionists in the late 1970s and early 1980s questioned incarceration of the offender. At this time, the sexual abuse of children is regarded explicitly as a criminal offence and a child welfare matter, and effective protection requires cooperation between these two systems. This position is clearly spelled out in Ontario's revised sexual abuse resource manual for training protection workers in the province. It is accompanied by the following principles for intervention: separating the offender and child to enable the child to disclose more fully; supporting the victim with access to therapy; believing that while the offender is fully culpable, all family members are responsible for change; and rebuilding the family gradually with the aid of therapeutic interventions focused on restructuring 'pathological dynamics' (Institute for the Prevention of Child Abuse [IPCA], n.d.). These principles weave a child and family focus into intervention and highlight the inadequacies of women as mothers in both problem and resolution.

In 1999, the Ontario Association of Children's Aid Societies

(OACAS) and the Ontario Police College joined forces to update training materials once again. They produced a training program entitled Investigating Sexual Offences Against Children, which aims to build and strengthen the knowledge and skills of child sexual abuse investigators in responding to allegations (OACAS, 1999). Like its predecessors, the philosophy behind this manual is both family-centred and child-focused. This emphasis is seen in a number of the competency goals established for investigators. As stated on page 1, hand-out 1, day 1 of the training program, a worker is expected to recognize 'the patterns of interaction in families that maintain intrafamilial sexual abuse' and know 'how to identify family strengths that can mitigate risk and protect the child.' A worker is expected to understand 'the individual and family dynamics of sexual abuse and ... elicit and identify these dynamics during sexual abuse assessment interviews.' A worker is expected to recognize 'problems resulting from stress, disturbed relationships, and low self-esteem in offenders, spouses, and other family members, and make appropriate referrals for further assessment and therapy.' As will be discussed, the implication of women being inadequate wives and mothers is less overt in the newest OACAS training program.

In contrast to child protectionists, activists in the women's movement envisioned child sexual abuse in the context of the broader problem of male violence against women and children. Though differences are apparent, child sexual abuse resembles other forms of male violence in that the majority of offenders are known and trusted males, an abuse of power is evident, and society's indifference towards victims is manifest (Finkelhor, 1979).

By locating child sexual abuse within the context of a range of interpersonal abuses experienced by women and children, the women's movement focused on the power of men over women and children. In this light, child sexual abuse and incest appear not as an aberration but as an exaggeration of 'normal power relations of gender and age' in patriarchal society (Hooper, 1992, p. 2). Coupled with the notion that incestuous abuse is not the most prevalent form of child abuse, feminists have attempted to redefine child sexual abuse from 'a family problem' to primarily a problem of masculinity, the eroticization of male dominance, and the sexual objectification of women and girls (Hooper, 1992).

In general, women activists advocated for increased criminal justice system involvement to protect victims, deter future abuses, and reinforce public standards of the unacceptability of offender behaviour. Despite successes in promoting the criminality of child sexual abuse, some feminists have observed that formal legal prohibition has done little to alter the occurrence of male-perpetrated abuses against women and children (MacKinnon, 1987). In the interests of women and children, feminists also advocated for the removal of suspected offenders from the home. These changes in response to child sexual abuse have worked themselves into the mainstream of policy and practice in this field. Unlike child protectionists, feminists held reservations about family reconciliation treatment (Finkelhor, 1984).

Dominant Explanations

Dysfunctional Families (Read: Mothers)

Numerous theories have been offered to explain child sexual abuse. While no one fully satisfactory theory exists, an emphasis on dysfunctional family dynamics is a theme that dominates in cases of 'repeated' child sexual abuse (Glaser & Frosh, 1993). This understanding has acquired the status of common sense in both lay and professional discourse (MacLeod & Saraga, 1988). It shapes and informs child welfare practice given that CAS cases most often involve sexual abuses perpetrated within a family or by a caretaker.

The analysis of child sexual abuse in the context of family pathology emerged around the mid-1960s. One of the earliest and most widely cited studies of 'family constellation' in incest was published in 1966 by Lustig and associates. Based on six cases of father–daughter incest, Lustig et al. envisioned incest to be 'one of the many socially deviant behaviour patterns ... employed by a dysfunctional family in the maintenance of its own integrity and existence' (Lustig, Spellman, Dresser, & Murray, 1966, p. 32). The incest served to reduce the father's sexual tension that stemmed from an impaired sexual and emotional relationship with his wife. Lustig et al. implicated all members of this isolated and closed family, including the daughter. By assuming maternal roles, the daughter became the central figure and satisfied her father's needs. These needs were assumed to be denied by the man's wife, who was seen as inadequate on many fronts. All family members feared potential abandonment and disintegration of the family and thus maintained the incest. However, the mother was identified as the 'cornerstone' in the 'pathological family system.' She consciously or unconsciously orchestrated and sanctioned the incest (Lustig et al., 1966).

The dynamics identified by Lustig et al. (1966) have been noted many times in more current writings on child sexual and incest abuse. This is not to suggest that variations have not been made in thinking about incest since Lustig's pivotal article appeared in the 1960s. Much theorizing has taken place to distinguish family types and detail individual participants. However, just as there have been developments in thinking about child sexual abuse in the context of the family and its dynamics, so have pejorative and androcentric conceptions of mothers prevailed wherein their inadequacies are implicated, even featured, in theorizing about the problem. A quick glance at practice and professional discourse since the 1960s substantiates this observation.

Kate Rist (1979), for example, describes father–daughter incest as a 'perverse triangle' in which the mother's collusion is of primary importance. In this triangle, initially, there is a rejecting mother who has often been deserted by her husband. She has a dependent daughter who becomes involved in incest with the father. The father is portrayed as an 'adolescent courting his daughter'; he is hostile to his own mother, 'who was seen as neglectful and absent during childhood'; and he is 'highly sensitive to abandonment' by his own wife (pp. 686–7).

Rist described mothers as colluding, dependent, and infantile, and their own mothers as cold and rejecting. Apparently the influence of fathers is irrelevant for either spouse in the perverse triangle. Like Lustig et al., Rist concludes that the mother is 'consciously aware' of the incest but fails to call the authorities out of her own need to preserve the 'pathological triangle' (p. 687). She deserted her husband sexually and reversed roles with her daughter. She sends ambiguous messages to her daughter to assume sexual functions with her husband. She refuses to engage in sex with him, sets the daughter's bedroom next to the husband's, is absent from the house, and asks the daughter to 'comfort' her father (p. 687).

Another example is derived from Ontario's *Sexual Abuse Training Program*, used in the 1980s, wherein the typical characteristics of incest families are delineated. These include marital and sexual distress, mother–daughter role reversal, fear of family disintegration, and maternal sanction of a 'special' relationship between father and daughter (Dawson, 1982). In these families, the mother is said to be 'incapacitated' or 'routinely absent.' The father is said to have experienced a 'crisis' or 'multiple change and stress,' and the daughter is a 'physi-

Understanding Child Sexual Abuse 67

cally maturing' teen who 'lacks attention and affection from both parents' (p. 96).

The training program presents the father as engaging in sexual 'relations' with the daughter around 'mid-life'; he may feel inadequate and impotent; he may view his wife as aging and less attractive; his marriage is stressful. At this time, the eldest daughter enters puberty and may be 'sexually attractive' to the father. He does not exhibit 'symptoms of overt deviance,' nor is he 'promiscuous'; rather, he is described as 'monogamous.' He engages in a sexual relationship with his daughter because she provides a conflict-free relationship, and she is accessible, less demanding, and more compliant than his wife (Dawson, 1982, p. 86). The manual notes that the father may be motivated by hostility towards his wife due to a deteriorated marital and sexual relationship. He engages in sexual abuse as a way to express unresolved problems and meet nonsexual needs such as self-worth, power and control, attention and recognition, or the need to 'compensate for feeling abused and neglected by the spouse' (p. 90).

A more forgiving presentation of the father and his needs is hardly imaginable. One need only consider how the sexual violation of his daughter comes to be seen as a nonsexual relationship by a father who is not promiscuous, or how a midlife or any other crisis (e.g., an aging wife, marital distress, abuse and neglect by his wife, or sexual estrangement) can explain, excuse, justify, or rationalize a father's incestuous abuse of his daughter!

In the training program, mothers are characterized as passive and dependent types with low self-esteem and poor social skills. Their needs are unfulfilled in the family. They are isolated and depend upon the husband financially and psychologically. While the training program notes that the extent to which mothers knew or colluded remains questionable, the reader is reminded that 'these mothers fail to limit the behaviour of their spouses' (Dawson, 1982, p. 91). Such collusion may indicate the mother's immaturity, dependence, jealousy, or powerlessness and ineffectiveness (p. 92).

Dawson described the mothers as being regularly absent from the home, 'thereby not only failing to protect the child but also providing opportunity for the sexual activity to take place' (p. 92). It is also said that these women have poor sexual relations, including 'frigidity':

However, dissatisfaction and withdrawing from sexual relationships is considered more common ... The mother may be unavailable for sexual activity due to real or imagined illness. Depression may also be a reason for sexual denial. Some mothers have been described as keeping themselves tired and worn out and so limit their sexual activity. (p. 93)

Apparently the mother fails to meet her husband's and children's needs. Apparently male prerogative to seek and obtain sexual gratification is a given. Absent from this analysis is any exploration of the mother's needs, depression, hostility, and fatigue. Also lacking is an appreciation for the disproportionate division of labour in which women tend to domestic needs and chores, including care of the infirm, children, and elderly. Absent is serious consideration of the relationship between wife assault and child incestuous abuse (Deblinger, Hathaway, Lippmann, & Steer, 1993; Dietz & Craft, 1980; Truesdell, McNeil, & Deschner, 1986).

In Ontario's revised training manuals on child sexual abuse (IPCA, n.d.), the centrality of mother as villain or victim not only perseveres but soars to new conceptual heights. The manual consists of a series of current writings on child sexual abuse, including an article entitled 'Mothers of incest victims' (James, n.d.) in which mothers are categorized into mother types such as 'the passive child-woman'; 'intelligent, competent, distant'; 'rejecting, vindictive'; or 'psychotic or severely retarded.'

The passive child-woman mother is dependent and immature. She relies on her husband and others to make decisions. She likely doesn't drive a car or balance a chequebook. She appears helpless and avoids conflict. She 'chooses' authoritarian and abusive men and 'embodies the victim role.' She was likely physically and sexually abused by her father, and her relationship with her mother was likely poor because her own mother was emotionally and physically unavailable to her and provided a victim role model. The passive child-woman mother relates to her eldest daughter as a peer and delegates 'maternal responsibilities' to her (role reversal). In the case example provided, sexual disinterest is noted in the marriage, in keeping with the family dynamics framework. Also noted is the father's extrafamilial molestation behaviour, though no discussion of this feature of the case is undertaken by the author.

The intelligent, competent, distant mother type is 'manipulative' and 'seductive' of professionals; she excels in blocking interventions 'aimed at uncovering her role in the incest' (p. 27). Her husband is not as well educated as she but is seen to be 'warm and nurturing' (p. 27). With the mother active and away from home regularly, her husband is caretaker and nurturer of the children. This lifestyle apparently affords the husband ample opportunity to molest the children. Her own mother was assertive, competitive, and distant, and her father was the nurturer in the family. Portrayed as nurturing and caring, men's molesting behaviour is eclipsed. James notes that families with a passive child-woman mother or intelligent, competent, emotionally distant mother have the greatest potential for change.

Next is the rejecting, vindictive mother. She denies the incest, disowns her child upon disclosure, and threatens her to retract. She is 'glad' that her daughter took on some of her responsibilities. She 'openly expresses disgust with sex' and dislikes her husband, who is a 'passive, meek man who is more afraid of her than he is of jail' (James, n.d., pp. 28–9). Like her own mother, she is aggressive and controlling. The author suggests that 'the best way to protect children of mothers like this' (not fathers like this) is to 'avoid returning them home until the treatment contract has been signed, although this is difficult, since these women are clever manipulators of people and systems' (p. 29).

Psychotic or severely retarded mothers may participate in the molestation at worst and fail to protect at best. Like rejecting, vindictive mothers, they hold little promise for treatment (James, n.d.).

To borrow Paula Caplan's words (1989), the issue that emerges through this discourse is not whether mothers cause particular problems but how they actually do so. This undercurrent is seen in the scholarly endeavours in the 1980s that sought to distinguish incest 'family types' and understand incest in family systemic terms. Furniss (1984), for example, identified conflict-avoiding and conflict-regulating patterns of family pathology that underpin and sustain intrafamilial child sexual abuse. In conflict-avoiding families, the daughter is delegated to take the wife's sexual role. Fathers are said to be emotionally immature and threatening; mothers overmoralistic, emotionally rigid, and neglectful of daughter's emotional needs. Conflict-regulating families are viewed as 'more openly disturbed,' disorganized, argumentative, and even violent; the daughter is 'sacrificed' to avert the father's aggression from his wife (Glaser & Frosh, 1993, p. 47).

In this conceptual framework, the mother's demeanour is emphasized in order to explain the father's behaviour and the children's vulnerability. Curiously, MacLeod and Saraga (1988) comment that the mother in a conflict-avoiding family is portrayed as being emotionally distant from the daughter. Mothers in conflict-regulating families are presented as deficient in meeting children's practical and emotional needs and as collusive by sacrificing the daughter. In both cases, father fades from the fore. His 'behaviour is discussed only as a response to the mother's rejection or withdrawal' (p. 34).

In the 1980s, family systems theory was popularized as a way to understand the workings of incest. Zuelzer and Reposa (1983) offered a synthesis of how mothers are understood and described within a family systemic perspective. The authors reject the notion that incest mothers are either innocent bystanders or victims themselves and instead suggest that they are the 'pivot' in establishing incest. According to Zuelzer and Reposa, incest mothers tend to function 'at a pregenital level.' They have 'a pervasive and childish need for nurturance and warmth,' given the absence of 'mothering and protection' in their own unstable and deprived childhoods (p. 101). They elaborate as follows:

> Mothers are frequently presented as dependent women who have adopted a masochistic stance and whose self-image is extremely low due to undifferentiated relationships with their own mothers, characterized by rejection and hostility. Maternal grandmother, in many cases, has been sexually abused herself. (p. 103)

Deserted psychologically or physically by their own mothers, these women are anxious, fear family disintegration, and may even withdraw from their own children and spouse to alleviate their anxiety (pp. 101–2). In their 'experience,' the authors describe these women as lacking 'psychological investment' in their children and as needy and demanding rather than giving and caring.

To recapitulate, insufficient psychological investment in children is associated with the mother and not the abuser/father, and her actions rather than his are regarded as needy and demanding. Again a shift in focus from the actions of abusers to the in/actions of women as mothers (and wives) can be seen.

Likely having suffered incest in her own childhood, the mother may fear intimacy, which may 'cause long term problems with sexual identity and sexual responsiveness which frustrates and deprives the husband' (Zuelzer & Reposa, 1983, p. 104) and renders her an 'incest carrier' (Meiselman, 1978, p. 217, cited in Zuelzer & Reposa, 1983, p. 104). Mothers are seen to collude. They ignore or deny the disclosure or punish the daughter for attempting to disclose. They 'unconsciously' use

Understanding Child Sexual Abuse   71

illness or absence from the family, or 'blatantly' ignore 'inappropriate and provocative sexual behavior in themselves and their family' (p. 105) in order to maintain the marriage and family bonds (Zuelzer & Reposa, 1983). The mother's collusion, awareness, failure to protect her child or limit her spouse's behaviour – along with an acceptance and understanding of male sexual prerogative – are, with few exceptions, recurring themes in the dominant literature on child sexual abuse in the 1980s.

Sgroi et al.'s (1985) discussion of the profile of mothers in incest families provides a graphic example of just how central mothers are in the problem:

> Mothers of incest victims fail to protect on several levels. Sometimes mother is physically absent on a regular and predictable basis, thereby affording the opportunity for incest to occur. The classic example of this situation involves a mother who works a night or evening shift. Sometimes mother is psychologically absent, often ignoring overt seductive behavior between the incest participants that she should be curbing and redirecting and setting limits on at a very early stage. Some mothers fail to protect in a very direct fashion by deliberately setting up situations in which the incest participants are encouraged to engage in sexual behavior. (Sgroi et al., 1985a, p. 28)

The authors offer the case of a mother who regularly encouraged her husband to cover up their four children at bedtime. One night, though aware that their 14-year-old daughter was sleeping in the nude, the mother sent her husband into the teen's room 'to be sure she doesn't get cold' (p. 28). This example, the authors state, 'illustrates a mother's intentional maneuver to encourage sexual behavior between her husband and her daughter' (p. 28). One could easily infer that the example illustrates the father's obvious failure to exert sound paternal/parental judgment and self-control: rather than removing himself from his nude daughter's bedside, he pursues his objectives; hence, he is responsible. The shift in focus – from perpetrator to mother – is apparent again.

Sgroi et al. (1985) note that not all mothers deliberately encourage the incest. A mother often 'escapes responsibility by being ill or complaining that she does not "feel good" ' (p. 29). Regardless, most mothers are 'consciously or unconsciously' aware that the incest exists (p. 29). While the authors explicitly portray the father as powerful and at times tyrannical, though appearing 'quiet, unassertive, [and] emotionally colorless' to the outsider (p. 27), mothers continue to be ascribed a central role in the abuse.

As the 1980s came to a close, scholarly writings in the field continued to present 'mothers as collusive, thereby shifting much of the responsibility for incest from the offender to the mother' (Elbow & Mayfield, 1991, p. 78). According to Elbow and Mayfield, explanations continued to emphasize the mother's personality over the perpetrator's behaviour. In the 1990s, the topic of the mother's role was rendered more complicated. Empirical investigations designed to describe personality profiles of nonoffending mothers and incestuous fathers, and their intimate relationship and family dynamics, permeated the discourse (see Muram, Rosenthal, & Beck, 1994; Smith & Saunders, 1995). Marital relations, particularly male sexual satisfaction, were of foremost concern in the research undertaken by Lang, Langevin, Van Santen, Billingsley, and Wright (1990). Their study suggested that incest offenders experienced satisfactory sexual relations with their wives in comparison with married, noncriminal male volunteers. However, sexual gratification was mediated by unmet emotional needs. Incest offenders reported loneliness in their marriages and spent little time with their wives; both parties isolated their children from each other and thus provided ample opportunity for the sexual abuse to take place. Lang et al. found emotional estrangement from their wives to be central to incest offenders' actions.

Dadds, Smith, Webber, and Robinson (1991) pursued a similar line of inquiry. Comparing members of incest families with fathers, mothers, and daughters recruited from a variety of sources, the authors sought to 'assess the extent of psychological problems in fathers, mothers, and daughters from father–daughter incest families, and their perception of the family system' (p. 576). The researchers found that incestuous families were not marked by frank psychopathology. However, they seemed to be

> characterized by low cohesiveness and a lack of openness and expression of feelings. They were slightly higher in conflict, and family roles and responsibilities were quite structured and rule bound. Family members were not encouraged to be independent and assertive and they tended not to participate in outside social activities. (pp. 583–4)

Dadds et al. did not find any difference between clinic and control couples on martial adjustment and satisfaction. They concluded that the 'results ... go a little way in supporting the idea that incest families ... can be reliably discriminated from nonincest families on the basis of personal and familial adjustment' (pp. 584–5). The authors also suggested that the varying perceptions of the family environment reported by fathers, mothers, and daughters are 'tentatively supportive of models of incest that draw attention to family systems that, in the least, allow the incest to occur' (p. 585). In other words, the absence of adequate cohesion and effective communication may well set the stage for incestuous abuse.

Individual, couple, and family characteristics captured the attention of other researchers in the 1990s. When compared with normative scores, father–child incest families reported greater-than-average social isolation and a high level of familial control of individual family members, and suffered from clinically significant couple relationship difficulties and substantial sexual discord (Saunders, Lipovsky, & Hanson, 1995). Furthermore although certain personality characteristics were said to be representative of perpetrators and nonoffending mothers, Smith and Saunders (1995) found that such characteristics do not stand up to empirical test. According to these investigators, no personality profile of the typical perpetrator exists.

Parallel with this line of inquiry, researchers began to vigorously investigate earlier claims of mothers' roles in establishing the conditions for the abuse. These included women's assumed failure to provide sexual gratification for their partners, seeming encouragement of daughters to take the mother/wife role, and physical absence from the home, thereby setting up the conditions for incest to occur. Also under scrutiny came assumptions around the relationship between the woman's history of abuse and her choice of (an incestuously abusing) partner, and the relationship between the mother's financial stress, social isolation, and substance abuse and incestuous abuse. Finally, researchers called into question assumptions about mothers' failure to adequately protect their children after disclosure (see Deblinger et al., 1993).

Though the dominant scholarship of the 1990s made no explicit mention of mothers' particular contribution to setting up or maintaining the incest, she is implicated by virtue of her membership in the dysfunctional family. In that decade, the subtle treatment of mothers' role is open to dispute. A snapshot of this theme is seen in a 1993 issue of the *Journal of Child Sexual Abuse*, in which a number of scholars engaged in debate about how professionals ought to think about and respond to child sexual abuse, particularly in relation to mothers' cul-

74 What's Mother Got to Do with It?

pability. Garbarino, for example, takes issue with Birns and Meyer's (1993) emphasis on male dominance, power, and privilege. He suggests that a broad range of factors must be taken into account. These include family dynamics, 'dysfunctional men and dysfunctional women, sexist ideologies and normal child behavior, normal personality development and psychopathology, culture and ideology' (Garbarino, 1993, p. 140). Garbarino elucidates:

> Acknowledging a causal role is different from assigning moral or legal responsibility. If a child offered her- or himself sexually to an adult male, the reasons would in no way diminish the culpability of the man for accepting the offer. If a woman is so demoralized by her ... culture that she colludes with the sexual abuse of her daughter, the man who abuses the child is no less guilty. That there are family systems issues that help explain why men violate the incest taboo does not absolve the fathers from blame. (p. 140)

The implication of mothers in the sexual abuse of their children, evident in the formal scholarly writings of the 1990s, is no longer apparent in Ontario's latest version of the *Sexual Abuse Training Manual* (OACAS, 1999). In fact the manual repeatedly cautions trainees to confront popular myths regarding intrafamilial child sexual abuse including assumptions about the mother's awareness of the abuse or failure to protect, her personality profile, and her childhood and adult relationships. When trainees are prepared to interview the mother, they are warned that 'interviewers must be careful of their biases towards the alternate caregiver based on myths or on the alternate caregiver's reaction to the disclosure and the child' (OACAS, 1999, p. 201). Trainees are reminded that 'people are innocent until proven guilty'; after all, 'she may be hearing this information for the first time' (p. 201).

Such illustrations mark a change from the earlier manuals. Nonetheless, the mother is implicated by virtue of her presence in the family. A major theme throughout the training program is the importance of understanding sexual abuse and protection in the context of family dynamics. Trainees are expected to 'recognise the patterns of interaction in families that maintain intra-familial sexual abuse,' understand 'individual and family dynamics of sexual abuse,' and identify 'these dynamics during the sexual abuse assessment interview,' and to acknowledge 'problems resulting from stress, disturbed relationships, and low self-esteem in offenders, spouses, and other family members, and ... make appropriate referrals for further assessment and therapy' (OACAS, 1999, page 1, handout 1, day 1). As well, trainees are taught to identify family strengths that can mitigate risk and protect the child (OACAS, 1999). To this end, the manual cautions trainees that 'frequently the mother is blamed for being absent emotionally due to mental or physical illness or use of drugs and/or alcohol.' The reality is that 'offenders re-molest if they feel they can get away with it; however, the mother may just be away and the father plays on secrecy and [the] power of his role as parent' (OACAS, 1999, pp. 200–1). The manual makes it clear that 'an aware and empowered mother is important' for the protection of the child. However 'an assertive mother/family is a deterrent' (OACAS, 1999, p. 30). The manual recommends caution against blaming mothers for establishing and maintaining the sexual abuse; however, the centrality of mother for protection is emphasized.

Perpetrators in the Context of 'The Family'

In their review of theories concerning child sexual abuse, Glaser and Frosh (1993) indicate that a comprehensive explanation is a complex matter that includes elements related to broad social processes, intimate relationships, and personality. The authors suggest that although one might consider broad social elements, it is probably more useful to attend to microsocial factors for clinical and social work purposes, particularly those concerning 'the psychology of individual protagonists (especially the abuser) and the interpersonal networks in which abuse occurs' (Glaser & Frosh, 1993, p. 26). Merging an understanding of the family with a knowledge of each 'protagonist' appears to be the direction taken in understanding child sexual abuse.

Within the last two decades, research on male violence has come of age. The writings of Groth (1985) and Finkelhor (1984) have made great strides in advancing an understanding of why and how child sexual abuse comes about. Both works were included in the revised training package for frontline workers in Ontario (IPCA, n.d.).

A. Nicholas Groth has written extensively on sexual offenders, popularizing the categorization of offenders as either fixated or regressed. Briefly, the fixated offender displays an early sexual orientation toward (usually male) children, often beginning in adolescence. His behaviour is compulsive and premeditated and results from maladaptive resolution of life issues. The regressed offender is primarily oriented to heterosexual age-mates. His behaviour represents a 'maladaptive' effort to cope with specific life stresses, particularly dissatisfactory adult intimate relations. His first offence was likely 'impulsive' and his victims are female (Groth, 1985, p. 217). Groth concluded that most incest offenders are regressed (about 90 per cent) and are sexually involved with their own child as a result of a disintegrating marriage relationship or life crisis. As he put it, '[w]e have yet to encounter a case in which the incestuous activity was an exception to what otherwise was a stable, harmonious, well-functioning family. Instead the incest always constituted only one issue in a multiproblem family' (p. 218).

According to Groth, while it is important to address dysfunctional marriage and family dynamics, it is even more crucial to 'avoid being distracted from the responsibility that the offender must bear for creating and contributing to the family dysfunction' (p. 218). In contrast to this rhetoric, case illustrations offered by Groth reflect an emphasis on family relationships and serve to explain offender behaviour, its onset and motivation. Excerpts from Groth's presentation of the case of 'Jack,' a regressed offender, substantiate this point.

Jack and Rita, married for eight years, have three children. They married when Rita became pregnant. 'She demanded they marry and he felt this was the right thing to do.' Jack 'expected Rita to run the household' and look after his and the children's needs, but she was a 'spendthrift' who put herself first. The marriage became displeasing and unstable. Rita separated and reunited with Jack on six different occasions. Jack suspected she saw other men and reported that their sexual relationship 'steadily deteriorated' due to her sexual inattention to him. He felt impotent. 'He admits to a couple of extramarital one-night stands involving underage adolescent girls' but feels he was not unfaithful to Rita while they were living together.

Jack admitted to being incestuously involved with his 8-year-old daughter for six to eight months. 'He found himself attracted to her.' He fondled her and 'on four occasions inserted various objects (Q-tip, a pen cap, a .22 caliber bullet) into her vagina.' He can't explain these acts other than to say that they were 'impulsive.' When Rita discovered the incest, she apparently confronted Jack and he denied it. They separated and he has since entered into a new relationship with a 19-year-old. Though sexually active with his new partner, 'he found he could not stop the sexual activity with his daughter.' Rita 'finally pressed charges' and terminated his contact with their children. Jack's situation is somewhat gloomy: 'Because of his wife's spending habits and the expenses involved in the current legal proceedings, his financial resources have been seriously depleted and his plans to go into business for himself have been set back. Currently he is paying Welfare for the support of his children' (excerpts from Groth, 1985, pp. 220–1).

The case of Jack exemplifies androcentricity. The rise and fall of the marriage and the incestuous activity are seen through Jack's eyes. Jack is passive: he 'found himself' attracted to his 8-year-old daughter; he couldn't help but penetrate her with various objects; he cannot pursue business ventures because of his spendthrift wife and legal expenses. In his analysis, Groth states that 'the inappropriate sexual activity appears to be in part the result of and a symptom of family dysfunction' (p. 221). It is 'a reaction to stresses and frustrations encountered by Jack in his marital relationship.' 'When faced with adult life demands he sought a sexual relationship with his daughter to fulfil unmet emotional needs and to cope with unresolved life issues' (p. 222). Jack is effectively excused.

Finkelhor's (1984) model for explaining child sexual abuse is also widely accepted. It incorporates explanations of perpetrator behaviour at both individual and sociological levels. Briefly, the model sets out four preconditions that have to be met in order for child sexual or incestuous abuse to occur. The first precondition concerns the offender's motivation to sexually abuse a child, which may include a feeling of emotional congruence with a child, sexual attraction to a child, or the unavailability of alternative sources of sexual gratification. Second, the potential offender must now overcome internal inhibitions against acting on his desires. The third and fourth preconditions are concerned with delineating factors that enable the sexual abuse to occur. These preconditions include overcoming any external constraints and subduing any resistance by the child to the sexual abuse. In these categories of preconditions, Finkelhor (1984) identifies such factors as an ill, absent, unprotective, distant, or dominated mother; social isolation of the family; improper supervision of the child; opportunities to be alone with the child; unusual sleeping conditions; an emotionally insecure, deprived, or unusually trusting child; a child's lack of knowledge about sexual abuse; and coercion.

Finkelhor's model grasps the multifaceted nature of the problem of child sexual abuse. It includes but is not limited to the psychodynamics of the offender and family system dynamics. It takes seriously the mother's failure to protect or the child's vulnerability as contributing factors which come into play only after the offender is motivated to abuse and has overcome his own internal constraints. It accounts for abuses perpetrated by family and nonfamily members, and abuses of girls or boys (despite the fact that 'father–daughter incest' case illustrations predominate in discussions of the model). According to Finkelhor, the model integrates theories and guides assessment and intervention.

Finkelhor's 'four preconditions' model appears in Ontario's latest training manual (OACAS, 1999), though in a nuanced form. For one, readers are cautioned to recognize that this model offers one theoretical framework for understanding the occurrence of child sexual abuse (intra- and extrafamilial, fixated and regressed pedophiles). At the same time, no other models are offered. Regarding the factors associated with overcoming external inhibitors related to 'other people and situations that protect the child,' the latest training manual suggests a rethinking of automatic mother blame, including any conclusions made about her presence or absence from the home, or her health or ill health. It is further noted that the field is now more aware of the prevalence of family violence 'and how that awareness can cause an otherwise protective parent to be unable to protect' (OACAS, 1999, day 1, overhead 30).

Despite an apparently multifaceted understanding of child sexual abuse, there exists a common tendency to emphasize father–daughter incest in general and the inadequacies of women as mothers and wives in particular. Preoccupation with family dynamics is troublesome for a number of reasons. Most notably, an emphasis on understanding cases of father–daughter incest comes at the expense of understanding most configurations of the problem of child sexual abuse. Furthermore, an obsession with family dynamics creates an all-too-sharp distinction between intra- and extrafamilial child sexual abuse (Glaser & Frosh, 1993), and implicitly assumes that fathers do not abuse children outside the family. This assumption has been challenged by Conte (1985). Preoccupation with father–daughter incest is problematic in that incest emerges as a symptom of deviant behaviour in exceptional families, meaning that families are for the most part safe and loving places. Given the pervasiveness of male-perpetrated abuses against women and children, adherence to deviance and the notion of families as safe havens for women and children are questionable. Finally, placing offender behaviour in the context of conflicts and misfortunes serves to shift the focus away from the perpetrator and onto features of his life – his family, job, finances, and especially his wife and her inadequacies. The issue of how women as wives and mothers are presented throughout the scholarship has come under considerable review and criticism of late, most notably by feminists.

Inadequate Women as Wives and Mothers: Contemporary Challenges

In the literature on child sexual abuse, mother blame has a long-standing history. As has been reviewed, the dysfunctional or pathological family analysis accords mothers the cornerstone or pivot position in incest families. In this discourse mothers have been implicated in establishing and maintaining the sexual abuse of their children, colluding as accessories to the act, or failing to protect their children.

In her review of literature on mothers of sexually abused children, Johnson (1992) found that mothers of incestuously abused children have largely been categorized as collusive, on occasion powerless, and sometimes as protective. According to Johnson (1992), the collusive mother emerged through judgmental clinical statements made primarily by male physicians. These statements gained credibility over time as subsequent authors referred, footnoted, and reproduced them, despite the absence of empirical referents. Whether cold, frigid, withdrawn, or ill, the woman was seen over and over again to have abdicated her obligations as selfless wife and all-knowing mother.

The extent to which mothers know or aid and abet is an issue that continues to occupy clinicians' interests. Ontario's revised training manual (IPCA, n.d.) acknowledges a range of positions on this very issue from blatant statements of mothers' collusion to questions about mothers' 'role.' In his discussion paper in IPCA's training manual on the subject of mothers' role, Roland Summit indicated that 'folklore seems to exaggerate the negative contributions of the mother' (IPCA, n.d., p. 1). Summit states that most mothers of sexually abused children do not know about the abuse, though he notes that they should have known. Although mothers have been 'carefully excluded and protected from the secret,' they should have picked up 'hints or clues' (p. 1).

Recent feminist investigations have sought to shed light on the assumption of mothers' awareness and collusion. Hooper (1992) found that women ranged in awareness from not knowing to suspecting to knowing. Carter (1990, p. 163) revealed how experts, professionals, and mothers internalized expectations that mother 'should have known.' Hooper (1992) argued that 'knowing' must be placed in the context of 'meaning.' In other words, not only are events ascribed meaning and meanings change over time, but naming an event of child sexual abuse, for mothers, may entail specific meanings, such as loss.

In addition to the collusive mother type, Johnson (1992) found an identifiable category of the powerless mother. 'Many of the same clinicians and researchers who saw the collusive mother recognized her powerlessness in the "overwhelming patriarchal" incest family' (p. 3). From a feminist perspective, Johnson argues that these women – helpless, defeated, and victimized – could hardly protect themselves let alone their daughters. Despite recognition of the pervasiveness of male violence against women and children, an appreciation for mothers' powerlessness has generally been concealed under descriptions of and obsessions with her 'collusion' (Johnson, 1992, pp. 3–4).

The final type of mother described by Johnson is that of protector. She protects her daughter from incest before it progresses or takes a protective stance following disclosure. Although some efforts had been undertaken to identify factors related to maternal protection, Johnson (1992) noted that such studies were based on professional assessments, clinical records, case files, and the like. More recently feminists have undertaken research, based on firsthand accounts, into mothers' experiences of their child's sexual abuse. These studies have been added to the knowledge base in a brave effort to reshape what has been known or assumed about these women (e.g., Carter, 1990; Faller, 1988b; Hooper, 1992; Johnson, 1992; Krane, 1994; Myer, 1985).

For example, Myer (1985) examined incest mothers' ability to protect their children, accept help, and maintain their families. She identified three mother types. The majority were 'protecting mothers' (56 per cent), a few were 'immobilized' (9 per cent), and some seemed to be 'rejecting' (35 per cent). Protecting mothers tended to accept the allegations, showed empathy to the child, expressed anger about the abuse and toward the abuser, and took some form of action. While many of these women were ambivalent at first, they eventually 'sided' with the child (p. 51). Immobilized mothers denied, were passive, and took no action. They had histories of neglecting their children. Their children were taken into state care. All were classified with borderline personality disorder. Rejecting mothers showed more concern for themselves than for their children. They supported their mates, who dominated, battered, and frightened them. They tended to be dependent on their partners for emotional and economic support. None of these women separated from her husband. Myer's study challenged assumptions about mothers as collusive, passive, and unprotective, given the variability documented in her research. It also revealed that mother's initial response cannot be equated with her ability and willingness to accept the allegations, support and protect the child, and engage in treatment.

A similar finding emerged in Johnson's (1992) study of six mothers of incest victims. Based upon in-depth interviews, she reexamined the constructs of collusive, powerless, and protective mothers. She found that regardless of their outrage at the incest and position that it was wrong and horrible, mothers' protective efforts varied. Protective efforts were influenced by the state of the marriage before disclosure, support and pressure from outside authorities, and the women's individual problem-solving and coping skills. Though mandated service providers often expressed concern that interventions may contribute to family disruption, Johnson (1992, p. 74) found that 'support and pressure from outside authorities may have helped the mothers to initiate and sustain their protective action.'

Despite research findings that demonstrate a range of responses by women to the discovery of the sexual abuse of their children, conceptions of mothers as blameworthy and collusive continue to infiltrate practice. The domain of protective service work is no exception. Today, almost 70 per cent of frontline child protection workers and sixty per cent of social work managers hold a professional social work degree (Carter, 1993). While one cannot assume to know the extent to which individual students critically evaluate course materials, Ruffolo, Sugamele, and Taylor-Brown (1994) found extensive mother blame in core foundation social work practice textbooks. Having analysed sixty case studies from core texts, the authors observed mother-blaming patterns 'in the information gathering phases of case study presentations, in the attribution of blame for problems in the family system and in the intervention plans developed in the case studies' (p. 124). Here, mothers were 'the solution finders and those most responsible for the problems and changes. Intervention planning centered on the mother taking action in most cases' (pp. 124–5).

Susan Kelley (1990) actually examined professionals' attribution of responsibility, case management strategies, and perceived impact of child sexual abuse. Using vignettes with 228 child protection workers, police officers, and nurses, Kelley found that only 12 per cent of the participants held the offender fully responsible. The nonoffending mother was given some portion of blame by 84 per cent of the subjects.

These findings held true regardless of the features of the case, for example, whether the abuse was intra- or extrafamilial.

Similarly, Kalichman, Craig, and Follingstad's (1990) investigation into psychologists' perceptions of culpability in child sexual abuse found that fathers (offenders) were not held solely accountable and that mothers were centrally implicated. In this study, also using vignettes, Kalichman et al. manipulated fathers' responses to abuse, whether it be admission or denial. 'When the father admitted the abuse, he was blamed more; when he denied the abuse, the mother was blamed more' (Kalichman et al., 1990, p. 74). The mother was seen as a collaborator and thus responsible, and 'a belief that mothers should be aware of what occurs in the home' permeated the responses (p. 74). This is in keeping with the idealized expectations to which mothers are subjected.

Over two decades ago, Dietz and Craft (1980) explored protective service workers' perceptions of the relationship between incest and other forms of family violence and their impressions of mothers' collusion. While they found a significant relationship between wife abuse and child physical and sexual abuse, they also reported extensive mother blame: 'The hypotheses that workers believe that mothers condone the incestuous relationship and that they believe that the mother shares equal responsibility for its occurrence were confirmed by the data' (Dietz & Craft, 1980, p. 606). In fact, 87 per cent of the respondents believed that mothers gave their 'unconscious consent' to the incest, and 65 per cent held her equally responsible for its occurrence. Dietz and Craft linked the formation of these attitudes to derogatory conceptions of incest mothers that permeated the sparse professional and practice literature at that time. This discourse saw these mothers as 'passive, dependent and submissive, chronically depressed, overburdened, and unable to protect their daughters or exert a restraining influence on their husbands' (p. 603). They were also seen as unloving, rejecting, sexually frigid, and aware of the incest. Tongue in cheek, the authors concluded that 'the real abuser ... is the mother' (Dietz & Craft, 1980, p. 603).

Such perceptions of mothers' culpability have hardly changed despite the emergence of a much-expanded sexual abuse literature. The processes by which women may well be rendered central and blameworthy as wives and mothers in contemporary child welfare practice in cases of child sexual abuse unfold in the next series of chapters.

5

Shifting the Focus in Practice: Women's Deficiencies as Wives and Mothers

As discussed in previous chapters, researchers and practitioners alike have come to appreciate the multifaceted nature of the sexual abuse of children. Though the dominant discourse has constructed sexual abuse as a complex individual, family, and social problem, interviews with workers reveal how the mother has become the focus of attention rather than the offender. This shift in focus, I will suggest, is an integral part of the process of transforming mother into protector.

Workers Talk about Child Sexual Abuse

The 'Dysfunctional Family'

Discussions about cases of child sexual abuse, despite their individual particularities, revealed that workers invariably located the problem in the context of family dynamics. As one worker put it, 'These are not straightforward, one-problem, families' but multi-problem or dysfunctional families. Anne Wade, from her frontline perspective, noted that 'in our agency, we look at family dynamics of course. The family is usually so dysfunctional.' Wade's co-worker Barb Wayne indicated that when she begins an investigation into child sexual abuse, she explores 'the family dynamics that contributed to the abuse.' Fay Winters elaborated that 'the sexual abuse is a symptom of a much larger problem in the family, problems mostly between the mother and the father, and the father as an individual.' Repeatedly the label of 'dysfunctional family' was employed to signify that the family experienced problems other than the sexual abuse, and that those problems included marital difficulties and problems unique to specific members.

84   What's Mother Got to Do with It?

Periodically workers made reference to the parents' own dysfunctional families, which might have contributed to the problem of child sexual abuse or to the dysfunctional 'personal history' of one or more individuals in the family. In the case of Fiona Maye, whose former husband (Eldon) sexually abused two of their five children (daughter, age 11, and son, age 10), the worker, Fay Winters, considered a broad range of current and past family dynamics that might have accounted for the sexual abuse. She began with an overview of the marriage that ended in separation after years of assault on Fiona by Eldon, and connects that relationship to the sexual abuse of the children:

> They had a very unstable marriage. Actually, it was a violent relationship ... The marriage was not satisfying for either of them. He was controlling, and he met his needs through the kids. I'm not talking about sexual needs, but needs for power and control and nurturing. Maybe because of this dysfunctional relationship with Fiona, it was easier to look to his children, especially his daughter. I understand that she was his special daughter, daddy's little girl, and she got a lot of attention from him. (FW)

As Fay Winters continued, she shifted her focus onto Eldon:

> He grew up in a dysfunctional home. He had a low self-esteem and poor employment history. He married young, had five kids and a lot of responsibility. The violence started almost right away, and he abused alcohol and was highly addicted to prescription drugs, which may not cause abuse but do lower his inhibitions.

Winters stated that Fiona also came from a 'chaotic family,' has had 'kid after kid,' and 'at the ripe age of 30, she has a 14-year-old son.' The worker assessed that Fiona 'doesn't have good parenting skills' and is 'overwhelmed by all these kids.' 'There are chronic hygiene problems, the house is filthy and smells, the kids are dirty and mom is unkempt, and I wonder about her self-esteem because she is also grossly overweight.'

In the Miller case, also discussed by Fay Winters, similar features were factored into an understanding of the sexual abuse. The case was described by the worker as 'chronic.' It began years earlier when Harriet Miller's two granddaughters were placed with her and her husband Chuck following gross abuse and neglect. Having resided with their grandparents for over four years, the children displayed progress in their developmental milestones but began to flounder. Within months the children disclosed sexual abuse by their grandfather Chuck. 'Looking back,' the worker remarked,

> Harriet and Chuck didn't do such a good job with their own daughter, so realistically, what kind of care were they able to give to these grandchildren? Chuck has been chronically unemployed due to poor health and has a low self-esteem as a result. Both Chuck and Harriet had failed marriages before this one and I wonder if he gets his needs met by Harriet and so he turned to children instead.

Fay Winters's comment about the extent to which Chuck's 'needs' were met by his wife refers to a desire to feel 'powerful.' Workers frequently mentioned a 'need for power and control.' Carol West's discussion of how she approaches a case of child sexual abuse incorporates this theme:

> In these families, the dad needs to feel masculine and has needs for control and power. [It's not] sexual gratification ... [but a need] to be nurtured and supported ... It is obviously an abuse of power and control. But it is also a passive way for dad to work things out with mom. It is his way of expressing anger in the failed marriage relationship.

Emma Webber, too, asserted that sexual abuse is 'a power and control issue.' However, the rhetoric of offender's needs for power and control is washed away as workers couched these issues in the context of failed intimate relations or women's unavailability or unattractiveness:

> Though most of the mothers are unwilling to admit that there are sexual problems, when mom is working the night shift and dad is working the day shift, they're not getting together too often – they are like ships that pass in the night.

> If mom would get up and get with it, then dad wouldn't need to do this. If she feels crummy about herself, he can justify his behaviour and blame her – she's a lazy slob, she sits in her housecoat all day, why doesn't she get dressed and look nice? (BW)

As can be seen, oral discourse mirrors the written in that a deteriorating or failed marriage is considered characteristic of the dysfunc-

86 What's Mother Got to Do with It?

tional family in which child sexual abuse takes place. These dissatisfying marriages are said to involve 'damaged communication' between a passive and weak woman and an inadequate and controlling male partner-cum-perpetrator whom she had 'chosen.' Anne Wade elaborated:

> All abusers are wimps, and come across as helpless, helpless, helpless. They are real losers and very angry at women. Inside the home, they are very, very powerful and controlling but these women are passive and weak and need the husband. Now he didn't make her that way; she was always that way. These women just seem to find controlling men.

In addition to describing the key players in the dysfunctional family, this passage provides insights into this worker's understanding of how the relationship came into being and, more importantly, how the worker constructs the problem. Through her assertion that 'these women just seem to find these controlling men,' the worker rules out coincidence and mutual responsibility; simultaneously she shifts the focus onto the woman's deficiencies. The McKay case exemplifies this shift in focus.

Family Services became involved with Eve McKay in response to allegations of sexual abuse of her teenaged daughter, Jade, by the child's stepfather, Fred. The investigation established that the abuse had begun two years earlier and, at the time of the inquiry, was no longer occurring. The abuse consisted of sexual comments, nudity, masturbation, and verbal threats to ensure that it would remain undisclosed. As a child, Jade had witnessed her stepfather's abuse of her mother; she continued to be afraid of his violent temper. The intake worker, Anne Wade, recalled that Jade trembled during the first interview, fearful of her stepfather and the possible consequences of the disclosure.

Following the interview with Jade, Anne met with Eve to advise her of the allegations. Eve believed her daughter and took appropriate protection measures. Entries in the case file show that Fred admitted to the abuse, said he knew it was wrong, and claimed to have stopped primarily because his wife had 'changed shifts and was home in the evening.'

Anne described the case as a 'classic' one, containing all the elements for abuse: an 'all-powerful and manipulative father,' a 'very passive mother,' 'communication problems' between the couple, a 'daughter who can't assert herself,' and 'role reversal between mother and daughter.' She portrayed Fred as 'totally inadequate' and as an 'introvert with a poor self image.' Physically and emotionally abused by his own father, he developed into a socially isolated, odd, and angry man. 'He tended to get into rages and needed to control others, so he found Eve who was willing to be controlled.' Fred was described as 'overpowering and powerful ... [To] a large extent, this caused the abuse.' 'Fred conditioned Jade from an early age to accept nudity, and that's his abuse of power, but you see, Eve never said anything except "I think you should put on some clothes" and that is all she did.' Anne was taken aback when she first met Fred during her investigation. Knowing about his assault on Eve in years gone by and Jade's fear of him, Anne Wade 'expected this monstrous and frightening man to walk into the office. Instead what I got was this pipsqueak! Skinny and scruffy. Eve could floor him if she really wanted to!'

In this example the worker could have suggested that, given the cessation of abuse when Eve changed her shift-work schedule, Eve was not aware of the abuse and hence could not have been responsible for its development, maintenance, or termination. Yet the worker's analysis of the case makes assumptions about Eve's capacity to identify, regulate, and correct any misconduct – assumptions that serve to shift the focus onto Eve and implicate her in the abuse. It is assumed not only that Eve should have known of the abuse but that she could have protected her daughter and controlled her husband. A contradiction emerges: on the one hand, the perpetrator is seen as being powerful and controlling and his wife as weak and passive; on the other hand, she is assumed to be capable of wielding great power, of being able to predict any misconduct and act accordingly. This theme of implicating the woman surfaces over and over again as workers talk about their cases.

With conviction the intake worker knew 'one thing for sure, and it is that your treatment goals are pretty clear; it's just a question of how to do it, to shatter his power.' Dina Ward, the caseworker, observed that 'Eve is not a strong person. I need to empower her.' Elaborating upon her vision of intervention, Dina stated that 'Eve has got to learn to present as the mother, not the child. I have to teach her to be responsible for protecting her daughter because these mothers abdicated that responsibility a long time ago, and this is a problem with all the mothers. This is classic.' In other words these women are inadequate mothers. This conclusion can only be reached when one assumes that good mothers predict and protect; inadequate mothers fail on both counts. As will be detailed in chapters 7 and 8, interventions into mother's inadequacies are often disempowering.

Women Who Set Up the Abuse

In keeping with the theme of implicating women in the sexual abuse of their children, workers offered an abundance of examples of how mothers set the family up for abuse. Because not all controlling men sexually abuse their children, this factor alone cannot fully explain the problem. The missing link is the mother; her inadequacies facilitate his abuse of power and control. As co-leader of the treatment group for mothers of sexually abused children, Barb Wayne observed that 'every mom in [every] group seemed to provide the setup for her child to be sexually abused.' She elaborated as follows:

> Working late or ... [working] outside the home; not being aware of the stuff that goes on, not putting enough importance on things like when dad makes teasing remarks about her daughter's boobs. So, she's not setting appropriate limits on her husband's behaviour and not realizing that dad makes grabs for female parts.

Barb presented a case that serves as a prime example of how mothers enable the abuse to take place:

> Mrs Miles left her husband alone with the child on a regular basis, and he encouraged her to do that. He gave her money to go out and play bingo and it was too good to be true. He gave her money to go and play bingo! Well, did she not stop to ask what's going on?

Absent from this example is any critical examination of the husband's conduct. Though he sexually abused his daughter, his behaviour is overlooked. Simultaneously, the mother's actions are emphasized: she left her husband with the child; she failed to question his motives. While it is not so incredible that a husband might encourage a wife to enjoy herself, it is remarkable how the mother is held responsible for the abuse. Even more incredible is that the mother is expected to have translated his actions (i.e., encouragement to play bingo) into a warning sign.

The above case example illustrates the problematic nature of mother's absence. Equally troublesome is mother's presence, of which the most common complaint is her unawareness of possible indicators of abuse. Fay Winters, familiar with the popular notion that a 'mother consciously or unconsciously knew what was going on,' described a case in which the mother 'left the kids with the dad, despite the kids' pleas for her to stay home.' This woman, too, apparently failed to properly interpret the meaning of her children's pleas. Workers frequently assumed that the mother was exposed to warning signs, denied them, and purposefully maintained the status quo. In the Miller case, the worker was suspicious of the mother. 'I'd love to be a bug on the wall to find out if she knew, in an overt or covert way, or if she was ever suspicious.' In the case of Fiona Maye, the worker wondered 'Did she have any sense about what was going on? Were there any warning signs, or any red flags? It is not that she's a bad person, but you have to wonder if she could have known.' To suggest that women naturally suspect, inspect, and patrol their partners for child sexual abuse is to reinforce the idea that women are responsible for achieving and maintaining the stable, healthy, and well-functioning family and to deny the notion that warning signs emerge as indicators of abuse after they become known.

The extent to which mothers know of the abuse has occupied clinicians and scholars alike. Preoccupation with this issue itself illustrates how the problem is conceptualized and, further, how child welfare operates to protect children. As will be seen next, mothers' awareness of and responses to the abuse appear to be integral features of the problem and logically necessitate a particular kind of state intervention. The Main case facilitates an examination of the nature and extent of mothers' knowledge of the abuse.

Abby Main

Abby Main's young adult son sexually abused her husband's two young daughters, Betsy and Mildred. Barb Wayne saw this case as atypical. For one, it involved the victims' stepmother. Second, the offender was a stepbrother and had not been removed from the home. While the case may be unusual for these reasons, telling similarities with the other cases become evident with respect to: expectations of women to protect; women's experience of state interventions as intrusive and controlling; and women's inability/unwillingness to discuss their experiences of state intervention for fear of repercussions. These common features will be seen throughout this and the next chapters.

The Main case was activated in response to allegations of child sexual abuse. As written in the Service Intake Record, which details the initial report of allegations, Betsy and Mildred had been sexually abused by their stepbrother Charles Flogg approximately two years previously. The disclosure, made to a security guard at a local department store, prompted a call to the police. The girls' father, Joe Main, and the CAS social worker were notified and called to the police station.

Barb Wayne interviewed both sisters individually. From the Service Intake Record in the case file, the disclosure appeared as follows:

> Betsy stated that she and her sister Mildred were intending to run away, back to their natural mother's home. When they asked a security guard to use the telephone, she noticed that Betsy had been crying. She asked what was wrong and Betsy disclosed sexual abuse. She described an incident whereby her stepbrother, Charles, entered the bedroom she shared with her sister. He stood on the ladder of their bunk beds, unzipped his fly, took out his 'dooey' and asked Mildred to lick it. Betsy stated that her stepbrother was not forceful and did not make threats. After begging Mildred to lick his dooey, she complied. Then Charles went down the ladder to Betsy's bed and made the same request. At first she refused, but then gave in and licked his dooey. While she was doing this, her parents arrived home. Charles ran to his room. About four months later, Mildred disclosed the abuse to her stepmother, Abby Main, who is the natural mother of Charles. Charles was confronted. He admitted to the act and agreed never to do it again. Betsy states that Charles never touched them sexually before this incident and has never repeated the incident. Both of these girls have been sexually assaulted in the past: once by a stepfather and once by a baby sitter. Both were jailed. She [Betsy] does not want her brother to be charged.

The worker proceeded to interview Joe Main. The Service Intake Record states that Joe and Abby Main knew of the abuse and that Joe was 'fearful of losing custody of the girls if the child protection agency and police became involved.' Joe reported that Charles is developmentally delayed. 'Charles readily admitted to the allegations, knew it was wrong and agreed never to do it again.' As 'Betsy stated that she is still afraid to be alone with Charles,' and 'although there have been no incidents since,' the worker arranged for Charles to reside elsewhere until deemed otherwise by the CAS.

The following week, an Assessment and Risk Conference was held in which agency professionals undertook a formal review of the case. Case management decisions were made and formalized in a Voluntary Agreement that stipulated the direction of intervention to be taken without court involvement. It was signed 'on consent.' It is reproduced here:

Voluntary Agreement

(date) This is a voluntary agreement between the CAS and Abby & Joe Main. Charles has admitted to sexually abusing both of his stepsisters, Mildred and Betsy M., when they came to live with their father at (address). He enticed both girls to lick his penis and also licked Mildred's vagina. Both girls disclosed the incident to their parents about four months later. The parents did not report to the agency at that time, but felt that they took appropriate steps to protect the girls. It is acknowledged by all parties that this is a serious incident and subsequently all parties agree to the following:

1. Charles is not to be alone at any time with Mildred and Betsy;
2. Mildred and Betsy be seen weekly or at the discretion of the social worker;
3. the family cooperates in family counselling;
4. Mildred and Betsy take part in sexual abuse treatment groups;
5. Charles be referred to the group for teenagers who have sexually abused;
6. this agreement is for a period of 6 months.

Should parties fail to cooperate with the agency in these steps to protect and provide treatment for the family, the agency will assess the need to make application in Family Court for a Supervision Order. Signed by: Barb Wayne, Abby Main, Joe Main, and Charles Flogg.

The final selection from the Main file is the worker's Assessment and Continuing Service Record, which recounts the worker's assessment and stipulates casework goals to be pursued in the following three-month period. It is noted that the family is very receptive to help and has been meeting on a regular basis for family counselling.

92 What's Mother Got to Do with It?

'Everyone seems quite comfortable with the voluntary agreement, both girls seem to be participating well in group, and Betsy is very clear that she is not being hit or touched.' However the 'family has many problems':

> Abby, the stepmother, feels as though she is responsible for everything. Abby is uncertain how to discipline or set consequences. Betsy constantly loses her temper, and Mildred is very quiet and withdrawn. The family does a lot of fighting. The family has not learned how to problem solve and reacts in a crisis situation with Abby ready to leave Joe and not knowing how to cope with this.

The assessment concludes with the following casework goals:

> The family needs much support to provide safety to the girls. It may be that plans should be made for Charles to leave the home. The situation must be monitored to make sure the girls are protected. It is especially difficult for Abby because the perpetrator is her son and the two girls are her stepdaughters.

The worker's service plan laid out continued assessment of 'the family situation and any indication that the girls may be at risk,' continued participation in the respective treatment groups, and counselling for Betsy, Mildred, and Abby Main.

In addition to providing a sense of how cases enter and progress through the child protection system, this case sparks an examination of the issue of mothers' awareness of the abuse. As will be seen, regardless of the extent to which women knew, their inadequacies are identified and their actions are criticized.

Mothers Who 'Knew' of the Abuse

In the above-noted case, no doubt remains that Abby and Joe Main knew of the abuse. Together they confronted Charles and secured a promise from him that the abuse would not be repeated. Satisfied with their intervention, and swayed by Joe's fear of jeopardizing custody of his daughters, the couple did not pursue the matter with the CAS. Abby Main believed that she 'took care of it.' Like Abby, other mothers also knew of the abuse of their children and also believed they had taken protective measures. For example, Donna Munt persistently confronted the offender. Irma Morgan, aware that her husband sexually

Shifting the Focus in Practice   93

abused their teenaged daughter, confronted him. He 'knew he had done wrong, [said] he was sorry, and said he'd never do it again.' Jane McNab, whose partner's adolescent nephew sexually abused her 7-year-old, 'yelled' at the nephew and 'threatened the creep and his parents' to stay away from the child. In these cases, it is apparent that regardless of the likely ineffectiveness of a confrontation with an offender and the worthlessness of a promise from him that he will not reoffend, these women acted and believed they acted protectively.

However, having suspected or known of the abuse and having made protective efforts without notifying public authorities left the women open to disapproval. When the worker discovered that Abby and Joe knew of the abuse, criticism of Abby was evident:

> She should have contacted the agency to make sure there was adequate protection ... Instead the family kept it a secret ... [Abby] was responsible for not leaving the girls with Charles and it is her responsibility because society sees women as being responsible for fixing what is wrong in the family. (BW)

Clearly, the worker constructed the responsibility as Abby's.

Emma Webber, ongoing caseworker in the McNab case, also indicated that Jane and her partner 'should have reported the abuse to the agency.' Because they did not, they failed to protect. Emma acknowledged that Jane and her partner 'tried to deal with it themselves' by confronting and threatening the nephew, but 'they continued to let him baby sit' and they 'failed to disclose to us' probably because of 'naïvety and ignorance.' While Emma describes 'both parents' as having failed to protect, further discussion of the case reveals a persistent and harsh focus on Jane that is different from her more lenient views of her common-law partner (Chapter 8 details this theme further).

In the Morgan case, the worker recalled how Irma 'was really handling things well' during the investigation with the police. She was 'calm and passive' and 'even offered us tea.' When Irma 'admitted that she already knew of the abuse,' the worker retracted her first impressions: 'Oh, she's not handling things well at all. Where's the reaction – screaming or yelling or something? She's covering up, she knows more than she's letting on. I was angry; she knew her husband had done this!'

Private efforts to deal with child sexual abuse are unacceptable or inadequate as interventions into the problem. These efforts seem to be translated into failure to protect, reinforce women's inadequacies as

94 What's Mother Got to Do with It?

mothers and protectors, and justify state (public) intervention. As will be seen, intervention entails establishing women as mother protectors without helping them carry out the protection mandate. A contradiction appears: On the one hand, women are supposed to 'fix what is wrong in the family'; on the other hand, those very same efforts at taking care of private problems render them failed protectors because the problem was not brought to public attention. When allegations of child sexual abuse come to public attention, women lose control, not responsibility, in the management of family matters, including protection of children. The Munt case reveals this simultaneous nexus of factors: an omnipresent focus on women, scepticism about women's self-initiated protective efforts, and resultant state control. This case features a woman's tenacious efforts to garner support in protecting her children. As will be seen, her determination and motives were questioned.

Donna Munt

Donna Munt contacted Family Services to report that her common-law partner's older brother, James, was 'touching' their two young children. Donna and Greg have two children under the age of 4 years. They live on their farm. James is the paid farm hand. When Donna and Greg became aware of the sexual abuse of their children by James, they talked to him in an effort to deal with the problem. Donna suspected that the behaviour was persisting but Greg expressed no such concern and continued to permit James to function as the farm hand. Donna reported her concerns to the agency. When the case was investigated by intake, a 'promise from the perpetrator and Greg that this would never happen again' was made and the file was closed. Within weeks, Donna made another report. The file was reopened and a voluntary agreement was drawn up to restrict James from the farm in order to ensure the protection of the children. The case was transferred to Emma Webber for ongoing service. Emma continued to get 'calls from the girl [Donna]':

> It might be mud slinging because she doesn't like James and she and Greg are fighting again; he accused her of sleeping around and she accused him of not supervising the kids and keeping them away from James. Maybe she's got good reasons to be upset because her common-law keeps inviting James for drinks and she says no one listens to her and she doesn't have any control in this situation.

In the face of repeated reports to the authorities regarding concerns about James, Emma Webber questioned Donna's motivation. Is this another instance of mud slinging? Does Donna have any particular reason to dislike James aside from the alleged sexual abuse of her children? As ludicrous as it seems, the protective efforts of the woman were doubted:

> How much of her concern was genuine and how much of it was her way of getting back at Greg because of marital conflicts? ... Everything she says is right but how protective a mother is she, instinctively? To this day I'm not 100% sure because she seemed rather careless about the kids' physical safety.

When asked to identify essential factors in the case, Emma Webber noted that the perpetrator had 'pedophilic tendencies' and 'easy access' to children, and that the 'parents ... closed their eyes to it all.' Her elaboration had much more to do with the mother:

> Now, you've got a really young mother who is probably very ignorant of how addicted and devious these guys are and how at risk her children were. Her partner convinced her that James would never touch the kids again and he even got the first social worker to believe him and close the case! Way back, James spent 14 days in jail for sexually abusing another kid, so I'd say they colluded since they let him have access to the kids.

An inconsistency is detectable. Though Donna made her protests known to her partner, the offender, and the agency, the worker not only insinuated that both parents closed their eyes to the abuse and colluded, but then proceeded to emphasize how Donna's youth rendered her ignorant about child sexual abusers.

The extent to which Donna was unfamiliar with perpetrators is a relevant factor but not primary, and yet it is considered pivotal here. A focus on the offender should be apparent yet it is not. Distress with the nonoffending father's behaviour should be outstanding yet it is not. An emphasis on the perpetrator and his nonoffending brother is overshadowed by the woman's inadequacies. An underlying assumption about mothers comes into view: women, as mothers, are responsible for protecting their children at all times and at any cost; men (as perpetrators and nonoffending fathers) consistently fade from view in the construction of the problem and its resolution.

Donna Munt sought help to protect her children. When she ultimately refused to let James have access to the kids, she was reprimanded for taking matters into her own hands:

> I could tell that mother is teaching the kids to hate [uncle James] and she says her son now knows that uncle James is bad. When mother takes the stance of hating the perpetrator and wants no access, it is unrealistic. (EW)

Mothers Who 'Did Not Know' of the Abuse

Eve McKay, Fiona Maye, Bella Mews, and Harriet Miller indicated that they did not know of the sexual abuse. They first learned of it when informed during the investigations. In describing the initial investigations, each of them recalled how they experienced an overwhelming feeling of blame. Following her daughter's disclosure of sexual abuse, Eve McKay was summoned to the agency. 'I thought, teenagers, maybe she got picked up for shoplifting and of course I went to the agency.' She described her first meeting with Anne Wade as follows:

> After she told me to sit down, she asked 'do you know what's happening to your daughter?' I said no but she was just like a drill soldier, coming after me, and she said 'you have to know what happened to your daughter.' I said no! I asked what was going on and she yelled at me and accused me of knowing. She was very forceful and I got angry and asked her 'why are you blaming me?' I felt like a criminal, as if they thought 'you're guilty lady, see what your husband did, and you knew it was going on.' Well I did not know.

Fiona Maye also felt blamed when her worker investigated allegations of sexual abuse perpetrated by her long-time abusive and now estranged husband. In this case, Fiona arranged private placements for her preadolescent daughter and son, Sandy and Theo, because she was 'having a really hard time coping with all five kids and needed a short-term rest.' While residing at his foster home, Theo disclosed sexual abuse by his father. He indicated that Sandy was also sexually abused by their father and by the teenaged brother's friends. During the investigation, Sandy stated that she told her mother. As a result Fiona was told that she could not see her children.

[The worker also] told me not to discuss the abuse with my son, said she'd call when she knew more and then she hung up. I was shocked. They prevented me from seeing my children and monitored my phone calls. They almost automatically assume that I am to blame, that I must have known, and that I couldn't protect my children ... I developed this fear. If they thought I didn't protect these two kids, would they take my babies from me?

Fiona was aware of the assumption that she must have known, feared being judged as an unprotective mother, and forecast the possible repercussions of any failure to protect.

Turning to the case of Harriet Miller, as described above, Harriet and her second husband, Chuck, have been the legal guardians of their two young grandchildren, Sue and Ben, for a number of years because of gross abuse and neglect the children suffered in their infancy. With extensive psychosocial needs, the children were provided with treatment at a staffed facility during the weekdays and returned to their grandparents on weekends. When Sue disclosed sexual abuse by her grandfather, visits were brought to a halt and an investigation was undertaken. Chuck denied the allegations. Harriet held that the child was confused – having been abused in the past, could she be experiencing a flashback or could she be telling a story? Harriet knew that as long as Chuck denied, and she 'went along' with him, she was 'more or less at fault too.' She also knew that 'as long as he denies it, and doesn't get help, the less chance I have of getting them back.' Without question, Harriet is seen to be at fault because she accepts her husband's position of innocence. She is very much aware of the consequences of this action: either temporary or permanent loss of her grandchildren.

To conclude the examination of cases in which the women indicated that they did not know of the abuse, I next present a detailed look at the Mews case. Bella Mews first became involved with Family Services when the eldest of her five children, Kay, disclosed sexual abuse by her father, Ian Mews. The abuse, which took place over a period of two years, included fondling Kay's breasts under her clothes while pinning her arms and attempted digital penetration. It took place while Bella worked her daily 3:00 to 11:00 P.M. shift. When Kay called her sisters for help, her father claimed they were 'only fooling around.' The intake worker's initial assessment reveals that Ian minimized and rationalized the abuse when confronted. Admittedly preoccupied with his daughters' sexual development, Ian claimed that the agency was 'overreacting.' He said he was merely 'disciplining' Kay and 'teaching her not to fool around with boys.' It was also noted that Bella had 'difficulty digesting what was happening,' 'supports her husband,' and 'puts a lot of blame on Kay's behaviour.' Apparently she advised her daughter to 'keep it quiet and not say anything,' as this is how Bella dealt with her own experience of child sexual abuse by an uncle. The worker's case notes describe the family as 'dysfunctional.' In her elaboration, the worker focuses largely on Bella's inadequacies and shortcomings:

> Much of this dysfunction comes from mother, who was sexually abused as a teenager and hid it. Mother is withdrawn and isolated, and found herself a job that keeps her working afternoon shifts. Kay told me that she has never seen her parents kiss and they aren't affectionate. In one interview with Kay and mom, they said they had never been close.

The disclosure resulted in criminal charges, a sentence of 90 days to be served on weekends, two years' probation, and a twelve-month voluntary agreement between the agency and the Mews. The agreement stipulated that Kay was to reside with maternal grandparents in a nearby city and that Bella and Ian were to attend treatment groups and comply with any interventions deemed necessary by the agency.

The interim worker completed a progress report after sixty days of service. In her Assessment and Continuing Service Record, the worker addressed certain limitations with Kay's placement at her grandparents, in particular the need to provide treatment for her. With great detail, she proceeded to express 'concern' that 'Bella works from 3:00–11:00 P.M.,' not to mention the forty-five-minute drive to and from work. From the worker's perspective, this schedule not only meant that Ian was the primary caretaker of the children, but also that Bella 'will not be able to provide the role model for her two youngest daughters, and will miss the opportunity to feel close to them.' Problematic is the mother's absence, not the father's crime. The worker notes in the case file that, with thirteen years' seniority in her job, Bella was 'hesitant' to explore a day job at a local fast food outlet because of the certain drop in salary and feared loss of the family home. From intake to interim worker to ongoing caseworker, one detects a pattern: the concentration on, even obsession with, mother.

Shifting the Focus in Practice   99

In this 'dysfunctional family,' mother is withdrawn and isolated and purposefully found a job that keeps her working afternoon and evening shifts. Her paid employment outside the home interferes with what is expected of her – her real job of demonstrating appropriate affection with her husband and establishing rapport and closeness with her daughters.

This pattern is evident as Emma Webber, Family Services worker, provided her analysis of the factors said to contribute to the sexual abuse. Emma commenced her analysis by highlighting problems in the marriage, particularly how the couple's 'sex life has deteriorated.' It was her impression that the sexual abuse experienced by Bella as a teen 'has interfered with her relationship with her husband.' She noted that Bella's 'night shifts' caused 'some sexual frustration on his part.' However, because 'not every sexually frustrated male sexually abuses his teenage daughter,' the worker looked to Ian for insights into the abuse. She described him as a 'powerful, controlling, aggressive and rigid man' who had a 'very punitive father.' 'I'd say he has pedophilic tendencies.' Emma viewed this case to be 'typical': 'role reversal,' 'mother absent from the home,' 'a weak mother who lacks an ability to nurture the kids,' 'a controlling rigid man'; in short, 'a dysfunctional family.' Her concluding statement – 'I'll treat it as a dysfunctional family unless I find out otherwise, that he is a pedophile' – speaks volumes in that regardless of the breadth of the problem, it is the 'dysfunctional family' that necessitates state intervention.

The concept of dysfunctional family, as it emerges here, accentuates women's inadequacies as mothers and wives. One need only examine the intervention plan in the case to support this position. Here the worker believed that Ian 'needs to be out of the home' and 'Ian and Bella need to focus on their daughter's abuse and not [on the fact] that the family has fallen apart.' Her 'top priority is that they get treatment' in order to 'reunite this family.' As the worker detailed the treatment plan, a disproportionate share appeared to fall on Bella's shoulders. This emphasis on Bella emerges in the following excerpt, which reveals how she is subject to scrutiny and treatment in a number of dimensions in her life. Her husband, by contrast, need only admit, repent, and comply with treatment regarding the sexual abuse:

Ian is in treatment [for sexual abuse], so now I need to work with mother and daughter. I need to build mother up, improve her social skills, life skills, and self esteem. I'd like her to gain some skills in nurturing and parenting because her mothering instincts aren't strong and she's not good at showing affection and warmth to the kids. She could use a parenting group. I also want to show her how controlling her husband is, and we will have to work on the marriage and communication problems. (EW)

In discussing her first encounters with child protection, Bella stated that she was made to feel incompetent:

> The worker made me feel like I let my daughter down, that I should have been there for her, and because I wasn't there for her, I must be an unfit mother ... I cried a lot after that.

Bella encountered similar blame by her ongoing caseworker:

> EW insinuated that I set up the abuse because I always worked afternoon shifts. Well, what choice did I have? I had to work the shift or quit my job, and I worked 13 years for my house and I didn't want to lose it. I didn't know, how could I know, what went on when I was at work!

According to Anne Wade, 'it is very rare for the mother to admit that she knew it and to say she knew what was going on and the bastard is getting out!' Nonetheless, as will be seen in the next chapter, it is assumed that mother can and will protect by supporting the child and separating from the offender. In the Mews case, Bella initially opted to place her daughter with her parents. This decision did not come without a sense of blame:

> The worker said me and my daughter were never really close and understood why she wouldn't want to stay at home. She judged me and I felt blamed because I wouldn't throw my husband out of the house. The worker said that in all the case histories, the husband has to be out of the house.

Striking is the chilling similarity between Bella's understanding of her role in the problem and the expectations of her as a mother protector and those echoed by her workers. That she and other women felt judged suggests that mother blame is neither absent at best nor concealed at worst. Rather, the condemnation of women in its many forms may well be a central feature of understanding and intervening in these cases. Far from being benign, mother blame bears immediate and long-term consequences for women, as will be seen in practices that require women to 'choose' their children over the offender (see Chapter 6) and compel them to sign voluntary agreements or consent to supervision orders (Chapter 7).

Mothers Talk about the Problem: Male Prerogative

Whereas workers tended to emphasize women's inadequacies in their discussions of these cases, the mothers tended to speak of child sexual abuse in terms of male prerogative in sexual matters and disregard for children:

> I find it difficult to understand how a man could sexually want a child ... I'd say it's got to do with him being a man and being in a society that says men can get what they want. (AM)

> I can't see why any man would turn around and do that to children ... There are enough hookers going around and asking for it, so why pick on little kids? (GM)

> A lot of women are molested by a brother, uncle, or father ... It's ... one of the biggest crimes ... It is a problem with society, with men. Why does a guy turn to a kid? There are so many whores around, I just can't understand it. (JM)

In addition to disbelief, some women expressed a sense of betrayal when they first heard the allegations:

> It was so hard to believe that Charles [son] did it ... Here is this boy that I brought up. Where did he get this from? ... When something like this happens, you feel like you could just choke the guy and yet this was my son! (AM)

> It is a shock. You're angry and you're hurt, and you think 'how could he do this to me' or 'why did he do it?' (IM)

> When I first heard, all I can say is that it's a big shock. I remember saying 'I don't believe it.' Then they showed me the papers and the details hit me – he actually lifted up her shirt! (BM)

102 What's Mother Got to Do with It?

In thinking about the abuse, some women referred to their own inadequacies as wives:

> I'm the kind of person that can survive on less affection. Fred always got a lot of affection. His mother was always there for him, and he needed affection. I couldn't give it to him but Jade could. (EM)

> During the two-year spread when he abused Kay, I was working afternoons and he was working midnights and we had very little sexual contact at that time. My shifts were such that we had little time for each other and the sexual interest wasn't there. I'd say there was sexual deprivation – but wouldn't he look elsewhere, look for another woman not the daughter! I guess I just wasn't there for him as a wife. (BM)

To factor their own inadequacies into their understanding of child sexual abuse is to reflect that a gap has been bridged between the dominant understanding of child sexual abuse in the child welfare context and the understanding that the mothers initially held. Redefining the problem of child sexual abuse as an issue of women's inadequacies as wives/partners/mothers – through the concept of the 'dysfunctional family' – casts women as central to both problem and resolution, as will be detailed throughout the rest of this book.

Worker Discomfort with the Conceptual Model

The multifaceted understanding presented by the workers parallels dominant understandings found in professional and practice literatures. These are skilled workers operating from an up-to-date knowledge base. Their appreciation of the problem, including an emphasis on women's inadequacies, in no way contradicts contemporary discourse on child sexual abuse and women's relation to it. While a dominant conceptualization of the problem of child sexual abuse has prevailed, as described in this chapter, some uncertainty and discomfort with this model have emerged.

From Carol West's perspective, the dominant understanding of child sexual abuse and ensuing intervention are somewhat perturbing. She noted that the dominant analysis:

> let[s] incest offenders off the hook because we let them talk about their wives and financial stress and so on, and in reality, it is a power issue and

he has deviant arousal patterns and these do not result from the family or marriage because they are unique to him.

At the same time, Carol knows that mothers are not 'let off the hook.' 'We seem to think that mothers should always choose their kids over the husband.' Not only is the mother considerably implicated as a key figure in the problem of child sexual abuse, but, as will be seen in the next chapters, she also assumes a central position in the protection strategy, a role that elicits expectations 'because they are mothers.'

Carol West suggested that an emphasis on 'problems in the family and the marital relationship' is predicated on the implicit 'message that if she had been a better wife, then none of this would have happened.' She challenges this message and states:

> Instead the focus should be on the fact that he has a real serious problem, he has a deviant sexual history, and it probably started when he was a teenager, and it existed before he met her, and he has a need to be in control, and she may stay with him but she needs to know that it is not her responsibility and she couldn't have known or stopped it.

In keeping with this concern, another worker insisted that the familiar phrase 'nonoffending mother' was not an accurate way to describe mothers of sexually abused children because:

> it implies that there are offending mothers and we know that there are very, very few ... Now, some of these women have been so passive and unprotective of the child, so yes, they have 'offended,' but that is different from perpetrating a criminal offence. The term nonoffending mother means that she failed to protect and that's a family court offence. (AW)

Though the worker recognizes that women rarely offend by perpetrating the act of sexual abuse, she unconditionally assumes that women, as mothers, have always been and continue to be regarded as the protectors of children. This point was raised by Fay Winters. Insisting that 'child sexual abuse is a family problem and we need to deal with it that way,' she recognized that 'a lot of pressure and expectations are immediately put on the mothers to make decisions and choices. In some ways, it is unfair,' but:

They are traditionally responsible for raising those kids and caring for them, and we tend to be hard on them. We have expectations because they're mothers and they're supposed to protect and that is their role in life ... The mandate says we have to make child protection decisions right away, and if that mother can't protect, then we don't leave the kid there ... We're under pressure to protect.

That children require protection from maltreatment is indisputable. That such protection seemingly falls on the shoulders of the mother, without explicit acknowledgment of this responsibility and with little regard for the consequences for her, is questionable albeit enlightening as an instance of how the child welfare state operates. As Gail Wydell said, 'there's a sense that mothers have to be pushed and shaped into something we need, so we can allow the family to reunite so the daughter can stay at home and the father can eventually return.' The phenomenon of mother blaming – which highlights women's inadequacies as wives and sexual partners and reproduces assumptions about mothers' awareness of or collusion in the abuse – characterizes the process by which the state operates to protect children from sexual abuse. As was seen in the discussion of the tragic death of Sarah Dutil, there is a shift in focus away from sexual offenders to the inadequacies of women and their failure to protect. Failure to protect, once fathomed in a way that features the wife/mother, is a problem that can be dealt with through state interventions. These interventions have had the effect of transforming multidimensional women into mother protectors.

6

Transforming Women into Mother Protectors: The Investigation and Its Aftermath

In the last chapter, I showed how women's inadequacies were featured in the conceptual framework of child sexual abuse. I also exposed assumptions made about women as mothers, not the least of which was that they knew or should have known of the abuse and should have protected their children accordingly.

The extent to which the women knew of the abuse prior to its exposure in the public domain and the nature of their initial responses to their children's disclosures are important because intervention in these cases seems to be all about women as protectors. In this chapter and continuing in Chapter 7, I examine investigative practices and legal and therapeutic procedures in order to reveal a process of intervention that relies heavily on the mother as protector. In exploring how the state operates to protect children from sexual abuse, it might be suggested that protection results from immediately separating the victim and offender and garnering support from the nonoffending parent (the mother in most instances). Beneath the surface, however, protection appears to come about through a transformation of women into mother protectors. This process results from: establishing the protection priority for mother; eliciting expressions of belief and support for the child from the mother; bypassing any meaningful exploration or assessment of the woman's feelings, reactions, and needs; and requiring mothers to protect rather than giving them a 'choice.'

Investigation Procedures: A Focus on Mother

Investigations into allegations of child sexual abuse do not proceed haphazardly. Set procedures and objectives are in place to establish the degree of risk and to ensure the child's safety. These tasks and ensuing decisions are often completed at a fast pace, given the urgency of child protection. 'All major decisions are made in the [first] day, no matter what. You have to protect right away. It has to be quick, no time to fool around' (AW).

When a child is considered to be at risk, protection is secured almost immediately by separating her or him from the offender. Using the example of father-perpetrated sexual abuse, Anne Wade summed up the process by which the child's protection is secured:

> Oh, the father has to leave. If he won't leave, she [mother] has to leave [with the children]. You just don't leave the kid in the same house [as the offender]. The key figure is the mother of course. She needs to be capable of protecting. She needs to watch out so he doesn't come back to the house, and if she can't do that, we have to remove the child. You see, the protection of the child is the most important thing, and if that upsets parents and makes them angry, I don't say 'gee I'm sorry for messing things up and I'll just leave.' I have to protect the child.

In addition to securing the safety of all involved children, another key feature of intervention is to garner support for the victim. 'In all investigations, you go in hoping that you will get support for the kids, and you always hope that the nonoffending parent will support them. When that doesn't happen, it's tough because then I have to remove the kid and she feels like the bad person' (FW). While these actions serve to protect the child while upholding the principle of least intrusion, they simultaneously require a hasty, albeit critical, examination of the willingness and ability of the nonoffending parent to protect. Gail Wydell directly identified 'mother' as the key figure at the beginning of the intervention. She stated that the goal of any investigation is 'to be able, at the end of that day, to get mother to be supportive of that child and the child to be able to remain with mother in the home.' This focus on mother appeared constantly as workers talked about their investigations and their efforts to realize the protection of children. This focus arises in the context of commitment to the well-being and protection of children.

> After a child discloses sexual abuse, she wants help and wants the abuse to stop. The child is vulnerable ... her life will be changed and disrupted.

> The mother's role in the outcome for the child is so important. She has to comfort the child and the family and help them recover. (GW)

> I ask 'Do I see any strengths in mom? Is she an ally? Am I going to get her on side for this kid?' She is crucial. Mother is crucial. You really have to work on mother and make her strong. If you don't have her on side, you might as well take that kid out. (AW)

> The mandate says we have to make child protection decisions right away, and if that mother can't protect then we don't leave the kid there. Mom may need some time, but right now we're under pressure to protect. (FW)

> As intake workers, it is our responsibility to get mothers on track. You can be successful at first, but you've got to be there day after day because you know she's going to slip and stop believing her daughter and you've got to help her stay strong and support her daughter. She may feel sorry for him, but you've got to remind her who the victim is. (AW)

The examples above refer to moulding the mother into a supportive protector. How women are persuaded and enlisted to do so is detailed in the next section.

Establishing the Protection Priority for Mothers: Believe and Support the Child

Workers provided numerous examples of how mothers were persuaded to protect. Most workers acknowledged that hearing of the sexual abuse of their children elicited a range of reactions from the mothers. However sensitivity to the mother's feelings immediately became almost incidental and was understandably overshadowed by a clearly delivered message to protect. A 'protection priority' prevailed.

In the McKay case, the protection priority was established in the first interview. Having just advised Eve of her daughter's allegations of sexual abuse perpetrated by her husband, the worker, Anne Wade, 'allowed' Eve to 'react.' She elaborated:

> You acknowledge her reaction and ask if she believes what her daughter said. Usually says 'yes,' an ambivalent yes, and so you say that it's really hard to believe that your husband could do this. You must get her on side.

You tell her that 'it's really, really important to support your daughter and tell her you believe her.'

I tell the mother that we believe the daughter for these reasons and we believe she's telling the truth, and it's extremely important that you, of all people, believe her. You [mother] may have some ambivalent feelings but you need to put those aside, we'll work on that later. When the daughter comes into the [interviewing] room, you [mother] have to put your arms around her and tell her you love her and you believe her, and say 'I'm sorry it happened, we're going to do something about it and you didn't do anything wrong.'

Anne Wade noted that if the mother is not able to accept and support the child's disclosure, then she must be cautious about allowing the mother immediate access to the child. The worker may need more time to persuade and enlist mother to protect or the worker may be faced with the decision to apprehend the child.

Expressions of belief and support are viewed as indicators of the woman's priority to protect. Eliciting a statement of support and belief from the mother appears to be a most common feature of intervention especially at the investigation stage:

The child and her protection are my first and foremost concerns. We say 'look lady, you're responsible for protecting your child,' 'we all believe your child.' Our job is to get her to say the right things; we'll deal with her issues later. Oh, we don't say it in these words. We call it 'support.' (GW)

We say we support moms but what we really say is 'you need to be here for your child.' Even if she is reeling from the disclosure, we want her to focus on her child. The expectation in the first several hours is for mother to go through all these emotions and come out the other end saying 'I believe my child.' (GW)

We let the mother know 'your child needs you,' 'you need to support your child,' 'your child has done nothing wrong.' These kinds of statements are made with a focus on what is in the best interests of the child so as not to have to remove the child from the home. (CW)

[In the Main case,] the girls needed to feel supported and that was mainly what I was trying to do. If it ever came down to a case of feelings for her son [the offender] or feelings for the girls, the girls have to come first, and I let her know that. (BW)

This first encounter with the mother reveals that although she might be shocked, her needs will have to wait. Regardless of her reactions to the child's disclosure, the more crucial message to impart is that mother will support the victim and will communicate these messages to her or him. Such messages were heard loud and clear by the mothers:

[The worker] told me to support the girls ... that the girls are the victims and my son is the criminal and more or less they say I should side with the girls because they need a lot of love and understanding, but so does my son. (AM)

I was asked by family services to make a choice. Would you rather the kids leave or husband? I said husband. They told me that this was a good choice because then the kids wouldn't feel like they did something wrong. (IM)

It sounds like they want me to believe Sue [child] and kick my husband out. That's breaking up our marriage! (HM)

They told me to take the kids and get out of the house. It's a good thing I had a place to go or they would have taken the kids from me that night. (JM)

These passages leave little doubt about the intensity and potency of the message for mothers to support and protect the victim.

In establishing the protection priority for mother, workers called upon their expertise and authority. Recall how Anne Wade reiterated for Eve McKay that 'we' (child protection experts) believed the child. Fay Winters told Harriet Miller that 'in all [her] years at the agency,' she had never faced such a 'graphic disclosure of sexual abuse.' Appeals to knowledge and expertise appeared throughout case discussions, fortifying protection of the child as a supreme priority for mothers if not an expectation of them. Not surprisingly, references to workers' authority during the investigation were common in interviews with mothers:

> When CAS found out, they wanted him out. I felt that he should be allowed to stay at home and we could get help but they are the bosses and this is how it is done and you got no say. (IM)
>
> She was very forceful, like she had control of me. They threatened that they'd take [the daughter] if I didn't get out of the home and they told me that my husband wasn't supposed to see her. Basically they told me what I had to do. They tell you it has to be this way or that way. (EM)
>
> I couldn't say much. I didn't feel like I had the right. I'm here to listen and they and the police say the way it is going to be. (BM)

References to workers' authority were also apparent as the mothers spoke of ongoing interventions:

> She's very forceful in what she believes. It's like she was taught something, this is what an offender looks like so there can't be anything else or this is what the mother is like and that's it. (AM)
>
> Social workers think they know it all and you know nothing. They treated me like a half-wit ... People without education deserve respect but [the worker] comes across as the expert; we have to do things her way. She took control. It was as if I didn't have my own thoughts or I couldn't understand. (JM)
>
> It's like she's this machine, this is the way things are done. Her way is the right way. (FM)
>
> [The worker] wants me to think that she is perfect, objective, and she knows everything and the way it should be. (JM)

This disregard for the women's thoughts and feelings saturated mothers' accounts.

Expressions of support and belief in the child are viewed not only as signs of a woman's priority to protect but as indicators of mothering capacities. Such a conclusion is evident in instances where expressions of support and belief were not readily apparent to the social worker. When Harriet Miller refrained from believing the allegations, the worker stated disappointingly, 'I thought she was capable of having more insight. I thought she was more supportive and nurturing and pro-child but she isn't any of these things.' In the Mews case, the daughter was initially placed with the extended family. The worker thus questioned Bella's 'mothering instincts':

> Bella is a closed and pathetic woman. She was very angry, said she had been abused too and talked about her own hurts from the moment I met her. She seemed hooked into her husband and complained a lot about her daughter. She's not good at showing affection and warmth to the kids and I don't think her mothering instincts are real strong.

Dina Ward also commented on Irma Morgan's maternal caring skills:

> Irma was crying when I first met her. All she wanted was for her husband to return home. This was the extent to which she was able to feel. She had no idea how these kids felt. They were angry and she was completely oblivious to their needs and feelings. She wasn't very intuitive or caring at all. And she's the mother!

In these passages, the women were identified as being more concerned about their partners/offenders than about their children. Not only support for the partner but failure to respond appropriately to the allegations were considered to indicate an absence of the priority to protect. In the case of Jane McNab, whose common-law partner was identified as having sexually abused her daughter, there was insufficient evidence to pursue criminal charges or find the child to be in need of protection. As a result, the sexual abuse investigation came to an uneasy closure from the worker's perspective. In discussing her impressions of Jane during the investigation, the worker (EW) indicated that she 'hoped Jane would have doubted Alan [partner] and I was rather surprised by the extent to which she shielded him. She chose never to have any doubt, and personally, I was expecting her to be more rational and more concerned about her daughter.'

The mothers were no strangers to these kinds of impressions. Bella Mews felt 'judged and blamed' because

> I would not throw my husband out. The worker said that in all the case histories the husband has to be out of the house. She kept coming back to these case histories, but never sat down with me to explain exactly what that meant or what she was talking about. I'd ask a question and she'd say 'according to the case histories.' Well that doesn't tell me anything!

Refusing to accept the veracity of her daughter's allegations of abuse against her common-law partner, Jane McNabb also spoke of having been made to feel inadequate:

> I felt that my daughter was lying. I fought and I fought for CAS and the police to listen to me. I can be quite boisterous. It made me look as if I didn't give a shit about my daughter and I was only concerned about Alan. They made me feel like I was a rotten mother.

Having been perceived as an inadequate mother adversely affected the relationship between Jane and her social worker:

> At first, they were really nice to us, they wanted to help with the kids. Before she treated me fine, she was there to help. But after the allegations were made, our relationship switched. Boy did it switch. From that point on, they thought he was slime and they treated me like scum.

In addition to challenging the offender's denial, other appropriate reactions to the disclosure (e.g., anger at the offender) were viewed as signs of mother's protection priority. The absence of anger called mother's protective abilities into question. From her investigation into the Morgan case, Carol West recalled that:

> Irma was shocked, no shut down. There was no reaction. She was very passive ... there was no anger, no real questioning. At the same time as she was saying that she believed [her daughter's allegations of abuse], she was holding Bob's hand and telling him that it would be okay.

In Carol's words, Irma 'sided with her husband' and demonstrated 'more concern for him than the children.' Although Carol stated that she 'would have preferred if Irma blew up,' she denied expecting a particular response from this or any other mother during the investigation:

> I don't have a vested interest in the mom saying that she supports or believes the child. If the mom says the kid is a lying bitch, I think it's the right choice for the child to be placed away from her.

> I feel better when moms say they're angry or scared or guilty, as long as they're in touch with their feelings. We can work on their feelings later.

Some workers have a set way of dealing with the mothers. Not me. I think there are high expectations that mom should support the child and if you just pushed hard enough you could get mom to be that way, but since quite a few cases have blown up in our faces, we realize there are some moms who just can't.

The workers' observations and the women's responses to the disclosure, investigation, and ensuing interventions are not necessarily one and the same. The Morgan, McKay, and Main cases provide clear examples of women's different reactions to the disclosure and investigation.

Perceptions of Mothers' Reactions

In the case of Irma Morgan, the intake worker saw 'no reaction.' In contrast, Irma said that she felt 'shocked, angry, and hurt.' She wondered how her husband 'could do this,' that is, sexually abuse their daughters. Following the investigation, Irma described how 'everything was falling apart.' Her husband was gone, her children were 'miserable' particularly with her, and it 'got worse over time.' She recalled how she cried herself to sleep for the year, off and on, until he was home:

> I never knew what to do. Here I am in this situation, my husband is gone, I've got to deal with the teenagers all on my own, and I just don't know what to do! So, I'd cry. It was like someone was coming at you with a torch in your face and your arms are tied and there's nothing you can do, you're trapped.

In the McKay case, the investigating social worker recalled how 'Eve's affect was very flat. You didn't see any emotion at all.' She remembered that Eve acknowledged the abuse and was able to express statements of support and belief. Having advised Eve of how she might best protect her daughter by separating from the offender, the worker was 'amazed at how quickly she got a place to stay.' It was the worker's impression that the investigation and its aftermath 'didn't affect [Eve] one bit':

> Again this is the elusiveness of Eve. You don't get much from her. She moved out, she says she's doing fine, and basically she feels leave us alone. She had a job, she continued to go. They were still seeing each

other, you know, that didn't change, and they were allowed to see each other, so not much changed for her. (DW)

Eve's story is quite different. When she learned of the allegations, she described 'deep anger ... I felt like I was about to blow. I was upset. I cried and cried for two weeks solid.' Eve found the investigating worker to be 'very forceful, like she had control of me.' 'They threatened they'd take Jade if I didn't get out of the home.' She 'never gave them the chance.' For Eve, the investigation was 'the worst thing that ever happened in my life; I can't remember worse.' While the workers reported little change for Eve as a result of the investigation and immediate intervention, Eve's recollection stands in marked contrast:

> They said I had to find a place to live. It wasn't easy because at the time I was working and I had to pay first and last months' rent plus you have to pack and move and pay for the movers. I thought they'd offer a bit to help you out because they said we had to move ... [But] I done it on my own. I had no place to go, and I couldn't stay with my mother because she's in low-income housing and she'd be cut off. I managed but it was tough for a couple of months. They didn't even call low rental and tell them that this was an emergency. It was a lot of pressure on me to get a place.

Despite the fact that Eve 'had' to move – that is, she had to embrace the 'protection priority' in order to prevent the apprehension of her daughter – minimal help was provided to assist her in the move. It seems to be assumed that women can and will protect without assistance. This theme is constant in mothers' accounts.

In the Main case, the worker simply claimed that Abby must have been relieved that the abuse was now 'out in the open':

> I think it might have accounted for her worried, tearful expressions. She always had a worried sound to her. Maybe it was because she knew about it [the abuse] and never told and lived in fear that the girls would tell some day. It must have been a relief to have it out in the open. (BW)

Relief does not capture the essence of Abby's experience. The investigation 'changed my whole life.' Abby was all too cognizant of being 'stuck in the middle' between her son and stepdaughters, of being the protector who must 'watch all the time.' She gave up one of her jobs and spoke of having given up her 'freedom.' She even considered separating from

Transforming Women into Mother Protectors

her husband, taking her son with her, in order to protect her stepdaughters and find some 'relief' from the pressure of protection:

> It was hard for me. How can I explain it? My husband was angry at me and that hurt and [young stepdaughter] blamed me because it was my son and that hurt. It was very difficult for me; I felt bad for everyone and I thought I couldn't take the pressure and I'd have to get out.

The protection priority, presented as support and belief in the child, is obvious during the investigation (and subsequent) interviews with mothers and workers. In a sense, both are responsible for protection. Failure of the social worker to elicit supportive statements by the mother translates into suspicions about mother's ability to protect in particular and her abilities as a mother in general. Failure to elicit supportive statements may also result in apprehension of the child. Anne Wade was clear on this point: 'If the mother is not on side, then that daughter is not going home. It's all part of your investigation and your assessment of the safety of the child. If mom gets on side then the prognosis is really good.'

'Dis'-Regarding Multidimensional Woman

In establishing the protection priority, the worker ends up circumventing any meaningful exploration of the women's feelings or reactions around the disclosure and investigation. Though some workers have insights into the effects of protection practices for women, such insights are often overshadowed by the mother's protection priority:

> Mothers are overlooked in the investigation. They're shocked and the focus is on the child and the perp[etrator]. (EW)

> The investigation focuses on the child and the perpetrator and the mothers are sort of wandering out there in no man's land and they have no support, but it's hard [for workers] to be all things to all people. (BW)

> Because of the child focus, we don't always deal with the mom and dad, and I have to constantly be aware of my feelings, especially towards the perp ... because he has treatment needs, not just the kid. (FW)

> In the investigations, mothers are put through so much more than the

alleged offender. I think that I want to deal with mom's feelings and push past them because there are concerns about the risk to the child and protection of the child. (GW)

Our job is to get her [mother] to say the right things. We'll deal with her issues later. Oh, we don't say it in these words. We call it 'support.' (GW)

Part of me knows that she's hearing something shocking and maybe we've got to allow a period of denial rather than judge her and the safety of her child ... We say we support moms but what we really say is 'you need to be here for your child.' We want to get her to focus on her child even if she is reeling from the disclosure and even though she may not believe it: 'how can it be true?' We want her to focus on her child. (GW)

Mothers seemed to be keenly aware of the dearth of support and assistance beyond the expectations to separate offender and victim and support the child. The case of Bella Mews is a prime example. When allegations of abuse were investigated, Bella recalled her first encounter with the social worker at the police station:

They gave me an ultimatum: either my husband had to leave the house or my daughter had to leave. At the time I couldn't see my husband leaving because I was still working in the afternoon shift and I'd have to quit my job and I'd lose the house. So my daughter volunteered to go live with her grandparents [in a nearby town].

Having experienced financial hardships in the past, and having overcome periods marked by inadequate food and shelter for the family, Bella indicated that keeping her house was extremely important to her. She imagined that someday her children would benefit from possession of this house. She also 'found it very difficult to put Ian [her husband] out; it'll cost him rent and food.' Thus Kay, their daughter, was sent to her grandparents' for protection.

Kay was suicidal within weeks. She wanted to return home. 'Here my daughter is pleading with me and being a mother I wanted her to come home.' Against the conditions stated in the 'voluntary agreement,' Bella 'gave the all clear' and Kay returned. When CAS got wind of these events, the worker threatened to apprehend Kay unless Ian agreed to leave. Bella described feeling 'like an accomplice to a crime' because she allowed her daughter to return home with Ian continuing to reside in the house. Though she attempted to explain the events to her worker, 'it didn't make a difference. The worker said I had no business bringing my daughter back.' Through this process, Bella was denied the right to decide what was in the best interests of her daughter.

Faced with the threat of apprehension of their daughter, Ian left. For Bella, the disclosure, investigation, and immediate interventions entailed the feared loss of her home, removal of her daughter, return of her daughter after attempted suicide, and separation from her husband. Bella was overwhelmed with new trials and tribulations. 'Through all of this, I nearly had a nervous breakdown.' 'All of a sudden I'm a single parent with five kids to raise and that is a big chore in itself.' She described her life as 'pretty hectic.' When her husband was at home, 'it was a bit easier' given that the girls listened when he 'yelled at them.'

Despite the changes and challenges, Bella did not receive support and understanding for her plight. Her daughter did not receive counselling or group treatment, both of which Bella had been requesting for nearly half a year. Not only did her daughter get 'pushed aside' but 'I got pushed aside ... All they do is run after Ian.' 'Now Emma says she's worried about me because I nearly had a nervous breakdown and she's worried about Kay. Well whose fault is that?' According to Bella, CAS did not help out, with the exception of facilitating a welfare application. What she needed, however, was 'a baby sitter when I come to group' and 'daycare to help me look after the kids and the house.' Though workers repeatedly expressed an understanding that mothers' needs and issues ought to be addressed after the crisis, few support or relief services were ever offered. As such there seemed to be an assumption that mothers can assume the protection mandate without tangible aid. Assumptions such as these were apparent as workers spoke of their investigations:

> Originally [mother] accepted the allegations, believed the daughter, and went to the women's shelter but I knew she was not someone who wanted to work with the agency. I knew it because I wanted to do mother/daughter work and she'd come in half an hour late or she'd bring her 4-year-old. Clearly she has got to be on time. Also, you cannot do work with the child there! (BW)

> I made it quite clear that she should come to group but she says she might

have to work on Tuesdays. So I instructed her to ask for Tuesdays off. She says she can't do that, she takes what she gets or she loses her job. It is obvious that she will make sure that she works on Tuesdays. (BW)

I remember she had to cancel one of our meetings because she had to work overtime, so I agreed to see her in the evening. [My supervisor] said I was too accommodating. He said that if it was an appointment with the doctor then she would have been there. I just pulled out her major bread winner and she's got three kids to raise. If she needs to make some extra bucks at night, what is the problem? [My supervisor] ... said it was my problem. (CW)

Similar issues were apparent in the Morgan case: a lack of support for the women and the expectation to separate from offender and protect the victim. Irma Morgan stated:

[The worker] came right out and asked me what I want and I said I want CAS to leave us alone and I want my husband home and the children home but she said 'well you cannot have that.'

Instead, Irma Morgan could have the opportunity to 'make a choice' between supporting her husband and supporting her daughters. Though she wanted to please all family members, she was 'made ... to choose.' The various dimensions of her life were denied in the name of protection. In the following excerpts, Irma refers to the workers' disregard for her relationship with her husband, family, and marriage, concluding that her 'worker didn't give a shit about me or my husband, just the kids':

Bob [the husband] could come over any time to see me and the kids because I was supervising the visits but he couldn't stay overnight. If I had to be there anyway, why can't he sleep over? I know him better than they do. What gives them the right to say he can't be alone with his kids? I see what goes on in the home, they don't!

I always thought [the agency] is there to bring families together, to explain why something happens and to give ideas about how to deal with it. I thought they'd help by talking to the kids and to us as a family. I got nothing for six months and then I got the shaft. I think they should accept your feelings. I wanted my family to be together. My family is MY family.

No one knows my family better than me, and they should see how the woman feels before they do anything.

Although she is the key player in the intervention, Irma is cut out and denied. As mother protector she is required to control, monitor, and protect, though she is not in control and what she has to say has little influence. 'The social worker has a lot of power and you can tell them you don't like what they're doing but it does no good.'

Eve McKay also described a lack of support beyond the expectation to believe, separate, and protect. She found a place to live without assistance. The pressure of protecting did not subside for Eve after she set up home with her daughter. In addition to working full-time, Eve was required to attend more meetings than imaginable:

> I had to go to mothers' group and meet with the social worker and come to the agency with Jade to talk about how it's going and drive Jade to her group too. It is a lot of pressure. It is hectic. It was meetings, meetings and more meetings. I never had so many meetings in my life.

Despite her initial impression that attendance at the 'mother's group' was optional, Eve quickly recognized that she was obligated to attend:

> They said they would like me to go to the mothers' meeting. Fred was supposed to go to his psychiatrist and they asked Jade if she'd like to go to the teens' group. I really didn't know what to expect so I didn't go to the first meeting. The next day, the worker called and said 'Eve you have to be there.' What do you mean I have to be there? I was not prepared for that! If I ever missed a night, they'd call and want to know why I didn't make it; they want to know everything. They do not accept that you cannot make it.

The intrusion extended far beyond the obligation to attend group. As will be discussed in Chapter 7, intrusions into the women's intimate relationships were common.

Having been involved with the agency for over a year, Eve considered that beyond telling her to move out, 'the agency did nothing.' 'All they care about is that the child is sexually abused; they don't care about the parents.' Similar comments were made by other mothers, indicating their awareness of the supremacy of the protection mandate:

120   What's Mother Got to Do with It?

> All she [the worker] wanted to care about was the girls. (AM)

> They believe the child. I told her I want my kids home and I want my husband here but they are not listening to me. (HM)

Jane McNab experienced similarly inadequate support. When allegations of abuse were made by her daughter against her common-law partner, the worker summoned Jane to the agency:

> She never said what happened, just that she was going to interview my daughter and if I wanted to be there I could come. So I asked her for a ride [to the agency] and she said 'if you really want to be here, you'll find a way to get here.' Well give me a break! (JM)

Apparent, again, is the assumption that good mothers can and will embrace and fulfil the protection priority without assistance. Jane made her way to the agency and secured the immediate protection of the children by separating from her partner. However, she did not accept the allegations of abuse made by her daughter and sought to change her worker's mind:

> The social worker thought he was guilty. I thought she was bigoted. No matter what I said, she would not listen to me. I phoned and phoned ... I fight for what I believed in. He is innocent! (JM)

Just as Jane's credibility as a partner is denied – 'she would not listen to me' – so her credibility as a mother is dismissed. For Jane it was possible that her daughter was lying. When she tried to convince her worker of this possibility, she was told that 'a child of [this age] doesn't lie. They made it out as if they knew her better than me.' Following this confrontation, Jane was instructed to refrain from talking to her about what happened. 'I think they were afraid I might tell her that it wasn't true.' More devastating to Jane was the directive to the daughter to avoid talking to Jane:

> [The daughter] was told not to talk to me. Well, SHE IS MY DAUGHTER! You know they listened to our phone calls, and I have every right to say what I want to her, she is my daughter! Once they hung up on me, they treat me like a piece of shit. They act like I didn't love her. I don't believe every little word she says but she's still loved.

Jane reported little if any support following the investigation. In her opinion, CAS 'took over' but did little else. After all, it was Jane who made the necessary arrangements for separating the children from her partner. 'And the other thing was that they never got the kids the help.' When discussing her perception of services, Jane stated:

> First they did nothing for us. Now I'm getting help in parenting because they say I have to, it's part of the [voluntary] agreement, but not because I want it. They moved heaven and hell to try to get us into court but they didn't move the earth to get those kids counselling. They just left them there and gave us a lot of grief. I was the one who got the kids to counselling!

Through the process, Jane believed that she had been labelled 'a woman who takes the side of the husband' given that she held firm to the conviction that her daughter fabricated the allegations.

A contradiction is apparent. Under normal circumstances, women are expected to tend to crises as they see fit. However, following allegations of child sexual abuse as seen here, women are expected to tend to crises as directed by the agency, which defines when and how they can mother.

Just as Jane McNab was prevented from talking to her daughter about the allegations, so were other women subject to controls imposed upon them in relation to their children. Abby Main was not supposed to talk to her son during the crisis period. Harriet Miller was told 'don't discuss anything about the sexual abuse with the kids.' Both Irma Morgan and Abby Main were informed that the children were not allowed to talk about their group treatments. Abby Main asked 'what kind of family is it that you can't talk about what's going on? We used to talk. Now they don't talk to me anymore. How can I help if I don't know what the girls are feeling or how my son is feeling or why he did it?' Instructions to refrain from discussing interventions served to shut Abby Main out. Once again, a discrepancy is evident. On the one hand, mother is expected to monitor, supervise, and protect; on the other, she is denied access to the workings of group interventions for the victims. Such a discrepancy can only make sense in the context of a conceptual framework that emphasizes women's inadequacies as mother protectors as a central component of the problem. As suggested in the last chapter, mothers are assumed to know or have known about the abuse and thus are viewed with suspicion. Blame and suspicion require caution and control, for example, cancelled visits, restricted access, monitored phone calls, and limits to conversational topics with their children.

Imposed controls were evident in the case of Fiona Maye, whose son and daughter were sexually abused by their father. In this case, it was believed that she knew of the abuse. Fiona experienced a loss of control that reflects, at best, having been ill informed and, at worst, having been disregarded as a mother:

> I couldn't understand how they could just, basically, shut me out. They basically took my kids from me and for no apparent reason. It's like you woke up one morning and someone just said 'sorry, you can't see your kids no more.' I had been given no estimate as to when I could see my kids, nothing, and I felt betrayed by the agency. I made private placements. I set them up so I could work on me and on us as a family.

> All of a sudden, I felt like I lost all control, I had no control whatsoever. I developed this fear that if they thought I was unable to protect the kids, did that mean they'd come in and take the babies too?

Fiona was disregarded. Such disregard heightened her fears and altered her behaviour:

> When the disclosure came, the worker changed her attitude toward me. They kept me in the dark and I was kept from my kids. I felt that whatever I said, it would be used against me. For the most part I felt judged and afraid and I didn't feel like I could talk to her because, say, if I told her about problems I was having, would they take my kids? So, you don't show how you feel.

It is ironic that, while women are needed and expected to protect, the way in which protection comes about seems to largely disregard their issues and push them away.

Disregarding mothers' experiences while using them to pursue protection puts workers in an uncomfortable position. Carol West reflected on the Morgan case:

> I tried to tell her that, yes, it is hard to accept that Bob has a serious problem and he has to go for treatment, but as an adult he consciously decided

to hurt his child. She could not hear what I was saying. Oh she said she believed her daughter, but at the same time she was clutching Bob's hand and saying 'dear, it'll be okay.' And she said 'you don't know what this is doing to my husband, you don't know him,' and I said 'no, you are right.' I tried to align myself with her and I tried to listen to her but I said 'you don't know what it's doing to your daughter. Do you know what this is doing to your daughter?'

In this passage, the worker appeals to the mother to recognize the consequences, for the child, of any hesitation around adopting the protection priority. Barb Wayne, a group leader for mothers of sexually abused children, voiced frustration with women who are hesitant about protecting given the consequences for the child:

Can they [mothers] not see that by totally aligning with the husband, they're pushing the daughter farther away? Do they not see what's happening there? I was able to see this but they weren't, and it was frustrating trying to get them to see.

Anne Wade also noted the consequences of mothers who don't believe the child:

I don't rant and rave about it. I confront her very clearly. I ask her 'do you realize the consequences of what you are doing? Your daughter cannot live in your house if you do not believe her, so you are in fact putting your daughter out.' She'll blame us and say it's our fault, but I say 'no, you did this, you made this choice' and I put the responsibility back where it belongs.

Absent from these images of responsibility are the perpetrators' actions. Prominent, instead, is frustration with inadequate women who, for whatever reason, do not readily adopt the protection priority.

This pot-pourri of themes – establishing a protection priority, calling upon worker knowledge and expertise, pursuing the interests of the child over those of the mother – is displayed in the investigation interview in the Miller case. In this case, Chuck (Harriet's husband) denied the allegations of sexual abuse of their granddaughter (Sue) and Harriet supported his position. The worker (Fay Winters) tried to encourage and convince Harriet to support the child's disclosure by relying on her experiences as a child protection worker:

> I told her that in all my years at the agency, I never heard such a graphic description of sexual abuse from a [young child]. I told her that I believe the disclosure is authentic. What did she think of the child's problems at school? Could she understand what was going on with Sue? No. She was firmly behind Chuck and wouldn't budge. Her explanation was that she would have known or Sue would have told her. I explained children often don't tell and, look, she's close to her husband and they live together and could she consider this to be true at all? Not at all. No matter how I approached it with her, she denied it! My G-d, these people took abused kids into their home; they were supposed to care for them!

Fay was disappointed in Harriet for standing 'firmly behind' Chuck:

> She came across as affectionate and maternal but what happened to this caring, supportive lady who had some insight? She's so rigid and unable to see anything else. I am so disappointed in her ...

> If she faces it, she faces the fact that she's married to somebody who abuses kids and the fact that she's a middle-aged woman who might find herself alone and I don't think she's prepared to go through her life alone.

Though she understood this crisis for Harriet, Fay could not 'wait for mom to come around.' She must 'do something right now and hope that, with continued work, she'd support the child.' As a result of Harriet's 'total unwillingness' to accept the allegations of abuse, Fay sought a six-month Temporary Wardship order. She 'talked to Harriet about Chuck leaving the home ... but they firmly believe he is innocent and they've rejected the option.' 'In most cases,' Fay states, 'we get the perpetrator out of the house and go for a supervision order, but in this case, they've rejected that option. There is no compromise here.'

In this first investigation interview with Harriet, a powerful image of negotiating mother protector emerges through Harriet's description of a debate she had with Fay on the veracity of the child's disclosure:

> They [social worker/police officer] said that Chuck exposed himself to Sue and that she said he peed white stuff. How does a [child of this age] know this? I nearly fell over! I was in shock and Chuck was just devastated. I says 'don't you think she could be lying or she might be having flashbacks about the abuse when she lived with her mother or her father?' The kids had nightmares when I first got them. Could it have been one of

the guys [the biological mother] was carrying on with, this guy and that guy, or one of the baby sitters? Fay wouldn't listen, she had her mind made up. I was very upset with her. I found that no matter what I said, Fay always contradicted me. She would not listen, she had her mind made up.

Harriet's explanations are ignored. She is presumed not to know how to interpret her child's or husband's behaviour. This disregard of women's many dimensions – their experiences as wives and mothers – is most apparent in Harriet's own account:

Fay came over to the house after we met at the police station. She said Sue was very specific in what she said. I said how do you know she's telling the truth? I know my husband, I've been married to him this long, I know what he's like. He grew up with children, lots of nieces and nephews, and nothing like this ever happened, not in my family and not in his.

I would have liked them to talk to me, see what I think, take my opinion into consideration. After all I've lived with this guy for so many years, don't you think I know him better than anyone else?

In challenging her worker's expert opinion, Harriet revealed a keen understanding of what was expected of her – to believe, to separate, and to protect:

Fay said kids [of this age] don't lie. Well I beg your pardon [younger children] lie like little troopers! They showed me the tape-recorder and said it was all on tape. I says 'how do you know she's telling the truth'? Fay says we have to go by what she tells us. I was really upset with her and I says 'if my husband was to walk out of our house with his clothes and his belongings, I'd have the kids back just like that' (snaps her fingers), and she said yes.

There is no room for Harriet's explanations for the child's statements. Conversely, no matter what Fay Winters put forward, Harriet 'denied' it. More than being a debate about the disclosure, this exchange is all about negotiating with the mother to protect. The expectation to protect is clearly understood by the mother – 'and I says "if my husband was to walk out of our house with his clothes and his belongings, I'd have the kids back just like that" (snaps her fingers), and she said yes.'

As demonstrated in this case, intervention is predicated on an assumption that this mother can and will 'choose' to protect. The perpetrator's departure from the home is presented as an 'option,' and reference to 'supporting' the child is, from the woman's perspective, a request to separate from the man in her life. The extent to which mother protection is a choice or obligation is the next subject for attention. In addition, Chapter 7 examines administrative, legal, and therapeutic practices that challenge the illusion of choices and options and further reveals the coercive and burdensome features of mother protection.

Mother Protection – Choice or Obligation?

'I am responsible for protecting kids' (EW). 'The protection of the child is the most important thing' (CW). 'My chief concern is the safety of the child. This is my mandate' (AW). 'It is my responsibility to see that a child is protected but it is the parents' responsibility to protect the child and I am responsible for overseeing it, for facilitating it' (BW). As these passages suggest, workers were fully committed to the well-being of children and conscientious about protecting them with the least intrusion. Separating the offender from victim is a central feature of contemporary best practice. While some workers talked about separation of the offender from victim as an option, others recognized the coercion implicit in this aspect of intervention. Emma Webber remarked, 'we proceed with coercion – we almost force the dads out.' Following an investigation, Dina Ward reported that she 'didn't even have to threaten the mother with apprehension of the children' to secure the protection of the children through the offender's departure from the home. Carol West noted, 'we expect dad to get out of the home and mom to be the kid's ally.'

The expectation that mother can and will separate and protect was evident from the onset of the investigation to case closure. As Gail Wydell put it, there are 'enormous expectations for the mother to support the child.' 'The expectation ... is for mother to go through all these emotions and come out at the other end saying I believe my child.' Barb Wayne stated 'there is an expectation that if something happens to a child, the mother is going to protect, and we wonder how could she have let that happen?' Carol West also spoke of expectations. 'There are high expectations that mom should support the child.' She continued: 'They're in a no-win situation of having to choose between

Transforming Women into Mother Protectors 127

their husbands and their children.' Because 'quite a few cases have blown up in our faces,' Carol gives mom 'the choice' to protect the child or have the child placed away from her. As Carol spoke of choice, she alluded to expectation:

> We seem to think that mothers should always choose their kids over the husband. Inherent in that is our message that if she had been a better wife, then the abuse would not have happened. Actually the focus should be on the fact that he has a real serious problem.

The 'option' to protect is not necessarily indicative of idiosyncratic values held by individual workers but rather part of broader social relations, expectations, and structures that reproduce notions of women as unconditionally responsible for the well-being and care of children and families:

> The message that society gives is that if things go wrong in the family, when it comes right down to the crunch, it's mom's responsibility. Moms are expected to be aware, see the red flags and say 'hey that's not appropriate.' (BW)

> I think our work puts pressure on the mothers, a lot, to make decisions and choices, and we say we've got to do something with the kid here, and you've got to make some choices, and in some ways it's unfair ... I think we tend to expect a lot from the mothers because they're mothers and they're supposed to protect and that's their role in life, and yet their whole world has just fallen apart and they're in pain. (FW)

> It's not likely, but it has happened, that a woman will choose her partner over her children because of what we impose on them, guilt. It's not likely that the woman will say 'right now I'm choosing to be with my husband' because we put her in the position of feeling judged that she is not a caring and good mother if she chooses this adult man over this helpless child. The choice is not much of a choice. (GW)

To suggest that children are protected from sexual abuse by separating offender and victim is to state the obvious. Discussions with workers and mothers about the investigation exposed aspects of protection that more often than not go unrecognized. In my examination of investigation procedures, it became evident that the mother of the sexually abused child is expected to protect by reacting and responding appropriately to the allegations. She is expected to support and believe the child and express anger at or doubt about the offender. Absence of such reactions naturally causes concern among workers about a woman's capabilities as a mother in general and as a protector in particular.

Another key element suggested here is the expectation that mother can and will protect. Despite workers' best intentions to allow a woman to choose to protect and their deep commitment to their moral and legal missions, guilt, coercion, and threat permeated the immediate protection process.

Chapter 7 continues to trace the transformation of women into mother protectors by examining juridical agreements and orders to protect, as well as therapeutic practices that reinforce and maintain protection.

7

Enforcing, Reinforcing, and Maintaining Mother Protector

Child protection investigations into allegations of maltreatment and the ensuing interventions reflect the principles of child welfare legislation. In Ontario the chief principle concerns the child's well-being. Respect for the autonomy of families, consent, and use of the least-intrusive course of action also guide practice. As seen in Chapter 6, separating the offender and victim and garnering maternal support for the child are central features of intervention. These practices represent the least intrusion in protecting children from sexual maltreatment. Also apparent in the last chapter was the expectation of women to separate and support the child. As Fay Winters so bluntly put it, 'we expect a lot from mothers because they are mothers and they're supposed to protect and that's their role in life.'

Building upon the theme of establishing the expectation to protect, this chapter explores how the mother protection priority is reinforced and maintained through contractual and legal measures and therapeutic interventions.

Legal Context Revisited: Inadequate Mothers Become Protectors

After allegations of abuse have been investigated and verified, efforts to protect children from further abuse may be achieved with or without court involvement through voluntary agreements, supervision orders, or wardship orders. Like supervision orders, voluntary agreements seek to concretize the protection of children. They are, in essence, protection contracts. Both documents stipulate who does what, when, and where. They differ in that voluntary agreements are negotiated outside the formal judicial system whereas supervision orders are granted by the family court. As such, voluntary agreements are considered to be less intrusive than supervision orders, given the absence of court involvement. Voluntary agreements often stipulate that failure to comply with the terms of the agreement may result in an application to the family court, by the agency, for a supervision order.

If a child is deemed to be in need of protection, a protection application is submitted to the local provincial court (family division) and a request for an order of supervision or wardship is made. Either temporary or permanent wardship of a child is secured through the family court. Wardship orders are a more disruptive protection measure than supervision orders. Wardship orders entail apprehension – that is, the removal of the child from her or his home and parental care – and formal placement by the child protection agency in an approved setting (e.g., with extended family, or in a foster home or group home, as decided by the agency).

Voluntary Agreements

The Main case provides a typical example of protection as negotiated in a voluntary agreement. To recap, the agreement detailed the abuse and delineated conditions of the agreement including necessary cooperation with social work involvement and family counselling, participation in treatment groups, and the assurance that 'Charles is not to be alone at any time with Mildred and Betsy.' In this agreement, the protection of children appeared to be a joint venture between all parties. The agency seemed to be particularly active in providing or making a referral for treatment to the victims, perpetrator, nonoffending parent, and 'the family' as a whole, and monitoring the safety of the victims through social work contact. At first blush, this agreement did not seem to make excessive demands upon the nonoffending 'parent.' However, statements such as 'Charles cannot be alone at any time with Mildred and Betsy' conceal demands upon mothers. Someone has to ensure that an offender 'cannot be alone at any time' with the victims. That someone is often the mother.

The McNab, Munt, and Mews cases also included voluntary agreements. Their contents closely resembled the one in the Main case. In these agreements, statements about protection appeared without explicit mention of maternal responsibility. The McNab voluntary agreement stated that the parents will monitor the children when the offender (nephew) is nearby. In the Munt case, 'parents' were to ensure that uncle James did not have access to the children. Workers' discussions of the agreements echoed the neutral phraseology seen in the agreements, for example: 'they (victims) are not to be left alone with [offender]' (BW); 'they were to keep a complete eye on their children when the nephew was visiting his parents next door' (EW); or 'they must make sure that Uncle James will not have contact with the children' (EW).

Apparent through documentation and case discussions, the responsibility for protection is both indistinct and genderless. To put it another way, the relationship between protection and a particular protector is indiscernible beyond vague references to parents. However, interviews with mothers presented a markedly different picture of the responsibility for protection through voluntary agreements, as can be seen in the Main case.

Abby Main's protection responsibilities began long before the agency became involved with her family. When she was told of the abuse years earlier, Abby indicated that she and her husband would 'take care of it.' She told her son that what he did 'was wrong' and recognized that he should not be left alone with the girls.

> In the back of my mind, I knew I could never leave these girls with him again and I kept asking the girls 'has Charles been around you girls?' They'd say no, it was okay, and I was convinced it was okay. (AM)

When the official investigation took place two years later, no further incidents of abuse were revealed. However, further state intervention was deemed necessary. As Abby described the investigation period, she provided insights into how she was factored into the realization of protection. She indicated that she felt as though she 'wasn't in control' of her son's destiny. 'Barb [worker] called to say that Charles could not be in the house until a decision was made to lay charges so I found a place for him to go.' While Abby experienced a loss of control, she clearly continued to carry out the protection mandate by finding a place for her son to reside until further notice was given.

Mothers in other cases made placement arrangements during the investigation period. Bella Mews suggested that Kay reside with grandparents. Jane McNab arranged for the children to stay with friends though she reported that 'the court papers say the CAS did it.' Donna Munt, too, found refuge with her children at her sister's place while decisions were being made about pursuing more intrusive court involvement. While one might argue that these women failed to protect by refusing to oust the perpetrator, their actions might also be viewed as indications that they took responsibility for protection by making placement decisions for their children.

To return to the Main case, within days of the investigation, Abby was informed that there was an agreement to sign. In her description of her decision to sign the agreement, choice is not apparent:

> [The intake worker] was forceful. She had the girls in mind, and this was her way of protecting the victims, as she said, and if we didn't go [sign], he [son] would have to be out of the house or something like that. As voluntary goes, I'd say I didn't have a real choice. I had to sign this agreement.

Jane McNab and Bella Mews also referred to the absence of choice in engaging in a voluntary agreement to protect:

> Quite frankly, we did not have a choice. We had to work with the agency. We were voluntary and we agreed to work with them. (JM)

> At the police station, I felt a lot of pressure to make a decision. They gave me an ultimatum ... either my husband had to leave the house or my daughter had to leave ... I asked my daughter how she would feel to go live with her grandparents and she said fine. So we signed an agreement that she would live with my parents for the year and my husband would get treatment. (BM)

In discussing how an agreement stipulating that the offender will not have access to the victims is accomplished, Abby provided a most vivid picture of the gendered nature of mother protection:

> I'm the one who always protects them. I arrange for the baby sitter. I worry about getting home on time. I have to be there when they get home from school and I worry about that. Joe says five minutes won't matter but I say it does. This is a big change for me in my life. Joe and I used to go out every so often for dinner after work, and the kids would come home and I wouldn't worry because they are old enough to take care of themselves. Now, it's like they're little 3- or 4-year-olds and I have to be there.

Expressions of accountability and responsibility – for example, 'I have to be there' – were common in the mothers' accounts about protecting their children. Bella Mews indicated that, whereas she used to work long hours, 'now I'm home with the girls all the time.' She noted that she is 'no longer denying what happened' and that she 'will go to moms group' and 'learn the danger signs and what to watch out for' in order to 'protect the girls.' Gina Merton, whose adopted grandson sexually abused his sister (GM's adopted granddaughter), indicated that the abuse is on her mind 'all the time.' She 'keeps the kids close by' and keeps a watch on them. 'Like a mother bear, I gotta know where they're at every ten minutes. I keep a darn good eye on them.' Harriet Miller, who hopes for her grandchildren's return to her and her husband's care in the future, also made reference to 'being there' if given the opportunity:

> If I had it my way, the kids would be home and they'd be safe because I wouldn't go out anywhere and if I did go out, I'd do it when they're at school and I'd be home in time for their lunch or I'd take them with me.

In the process of reuniting with her daughter and husband, Eve McKay asserted that she would protect her daughter and make sure that she is safe. 'It's an awful thing to say but I'll be watching and I will not miss it if it happens again. I wouldn't dare miss it.' Eve is confident in her protection skills now:

> I know the warning signs now – if he starts drinking or smoking again, or he's depressed, like he'll sit for hours in front of the computer, if anything like this happens, I'm supposed to talk to him and I'd call the agency. I'm supposed to look out for him and how he's feeling and he's supposed to look out for himself too.

Workers' comments – 'realistically, these mothers are going to have to do it [supervise, monitor, and protect] for many, many years' (AW); 'this is forever' (DW); and 'she will have to watch him forever' (EW) – leave little doubt about the gendered nature of the protection mandate. Mother is cast as protector regardless of the features of the case, even in instances where the father is a 'nonoffending' parent. That women vowed to remain at home and keep a watchful eye on all members reflects the powerful message that they must sharpen their mothering skills and responsibilities.

Returning to Abby Main, not only did she effect significant changes in her daily life but she was all too aware of the absence of comparable changes in her husband's daily life, a husband whose biological daughters were victimized:

> I used to have two jobs. I worked at a restaurant on weekends and I loved that job. Now I've had to give it up because if Joe has to go out on the weekends, I have to watch the kids. I can't leave them alone ... I [used to like] getting out of the house and meeting people and now I'm forced right back into having to be home on weekends.

> I can't work overtime at work either because I have to be home before Charles gets home from school. My life has changed. I have to be there to meet all of them and I have to watch out when they're home. I have no life of my own.

> I lost my freedom because I have to arrange everything around being at home but I don't find Joe has to. If he says he has a meeting or is going camping with the boy scouts, he doesn't ask 'are you going to be home?' He just expects me to be there and that I know better than to plan things for myself.

Not unlike Deborah Harter, who was court ordered to be tethered to her teenaged daughter, mothers are expected to protect, to always be there. As exemplified in the Main case, there is no recognition of the costs of protection for women, including loss of paid employment outside the home, and the loss of freedom and the right to determine what is in the best interests of self, children, and partner. The costs also include certain acquisitions: namely, increased responsibilities associated with mothers learning and fulfilling the policing and protection mandate.

Arguably, statements such as 'Charles cannot be alone at any time with Mildred and Betsy' are nowhere near as neutral as they appear. Rather, such vague statements of protection hide the expectation of them to become 'mother as protector.'

The next section examines those cases wherein supervision orders were sought to protect children. In addition to legally binding mothers to protect, these court orders reveal the ever-present theme of women's inadequacies as a central component of the protection order.

Supervision Orders

In instances where the child is considered to be in need of protection sanctioned by the court, a request for supervision or wardship is made to the provincial court (family division). Workers revealed that supervision orders to protect are customarily sought in cases of incest or verified abuse, or in instances where agency involvement seems necessary, as in situations where it is suspected that the family will not follow through with treatment unless it is court ordered. My exploration of the experiences of supervision orders begins with the Morgan case.

IRMA MORGAN

In the Morgan case, Bob admitted to touching his daughters' breasts. He was charged with one count of sexual assault and requested counselling for this problem. A twelve-month supervision order was sought because 'the children remain at risk for further abuse until the father receives treatment and demonstrates an understanding of the harm his actions caused' and until 'mother is able to demonstrate her ability to protect her daughters from further sexual abuse.' Obtained on consent, the order specified living arrangements and access: daughters were to reside with Irma; Bob was to live elsewhere; and visits between Bob and his daughters were to be supervised by a 'CAS approved person,' who, the case file reveals, was Irma. In addition to specifying treatment needs and CAS involvement, the supervision order also identified 'supportive counselling for mother' as a needed service. Irma was very much a part of the protection application and treatment plan.

Just as mothers indicated an absence of choice in engaging in voluntary agreements to protect, so too did Irma feel compelled to consent to the supervision order and its terms of support and separation. 'I didn't want to make a choice [between husband and children] but they made me do it. I wanted to make things better for everybody.'

EVE MCKAY

Anne Wade recalled that Eve McKay was 'very supportive' upon hearing the allegations of abuse perpetrated by her husband against her daughter. Eve believed her daughter and arranged to move out of the house that night. She also vowed never to take her husband back. By the next day, Eve had spoken with her husband. He apologized, 'said how depressed he was and how he'd commit suicide,' and asked her to return home. According to Anne Wade, Eve began to 'waver': 'I told Eve that we would be very concerned if she returned before we felt that enough treatment had taken place. I explained that we will probably want a supervision order to carry out the treatment plan, and that the order will help Eve protect her daughter.' Anne elaborated on her rationale for securing the twelve-month supervision order obtained 'on consent':

> I knew that Fred was very manipulative and controlling of Eve and I knew she would have a hard time standing up to him to say no, she won't return home. I got a court order so the onus will not be on her because the court order says she cannot return with Jade. It's like the police laying a charge against a wife abuser – she can't withdraw it because she didn't make it. So we obviously needed a protection order simply because there wasn't the confidence that mom could protect and Jade is still at risk.

In this case, then, the child was at risk because her mother might not be able to say 'no' to a husband who tried to convince her that he is sorry or he is innocent or he will change. In this case, mother is weak and cannot protect without a court order. While the worker claimed that the court order took the onus off mother, it is possible that it actually legally bound her to protect and took the onus off father. No comparable order restrains him from pleading with his wife to reunite or from badgering her for visits with the child.

As in other cases, Eve's portrayal of the process of securing the supervision order reveals a lack of consensual relations. Rather, intimidation and criticism are apparent: 'She acted like she had power over me and I was worried about that. When she said to take Jade and leave or else they'd take her, I never gave her the chance to take her ... I felt threatened. She was the judge and the jury and I could be hung.'

CHRIS MACK

The Macks became known to CAS when their young adult daughter approached the agency for information on a 'survivors group.' She informed the group leader, Dina Ward, that her father had sexually abused her and her older sister when they were children. The abuse had progressed from fondling to intercourse. After further investigation, it was revealed that the older sister had told her mother, Chris, about the abuse during her adolescent years. Apparently, as recorded in the case file, Chris was angry with her daughter and refrained from talking to her for several months after that disclosure. At the time the family pastor was called to offer counselling, the abuse stopped, and the older sister left home.

Enforcing, Reinforcing, and Maintaining Mother Protector 137

At the time of this disclosure to CAS, both sisters agreed to make statements to the police in order to initiate an investigation and aid in the protection of their youngest sister, still living with the parents. Upon police investigation, Harry Mack admitted to the allegations of incest regarding his older daughters and was charged with sexual assault. Investigations into the sexual abuse of the youngest daughter suggested that she had not been sexually abused. However, given the historical abuse and the mother's response, a supervision order was secured to protect her on the basis of 'substantial risk that the child will be sexually molested.' The order detailed living and visitation arrangements and cooperation with treatment.

In Anne Wade's elaboration on the need for a supervision order, Chris' inadequacies outweighed Harry's past abusive behaviour, the latter of which did not even appear in the worker's response:

> Chris knew seven years ago and didn't take any steps to protect or put her husband out or get help. She was totally passive then and she's the same now, very weak. There's no ... ability to protect the young girl. Oh she cries and cries 'I want my husband home' and 'I want everything to be the way it was.' Maybe we can rehabilitate this family but mother is the unknown entity for me. I just don't see any strength in her to support and protect. So by getting a supervision order, you're really saying that this parent can't protect without our involvement.

The worker focuses on Chris, described as weak and unprotective for having failed to 'put her husband out' or 'get help.' As discussed in the last chapter, such an emphasis coincides with gendered expectations of women in families to embrace the protection priority.

FIONA MAYE

The theme of mothers' inadequacies and inability to protect without state involvement was again evident in applications for supervision in the case of Fiona Maye. The first order of supervision was sought in response to a range of problems such as 'physical neglect,' 'running behaviour,' allegations of 'sexual abuse' by two of Fiona's children, 'family violence,' and Fiona's 'difficulties in managing the house and controlling her children's behaviour.' The first order was intended to 'provide Fiona with concrete expectations that will require her commitment to care for her children. Fiona's passive nature has made it very difficult for her to follow through with formulated plans.'

Obtained 'on consent,' the order called for scheduled and unscheduled home visits, abuse treatment for the children, and the following controls: no extended baby sitting of younger children by older siblings; no access by the father to the children unless at the discretion of the CAS; mother to monitor her eldest son's friends in the home and refer any concerns to the CAS worker; and mother to utilize behaviour management counselling and parenting programs as recommended by the CAS worker.

During the period of this first order of supervision, Fiona and her children moved and the case file was transferred to another CAS. Having perused the file, the new caseworker was 'quite impressed' with Fiona, who 'willingly consented' to a supervision order that 'outlined so many of her difficulties.' 'I think it was her cry for help. She saw us as helpers and not intruders.' In keeping with the terms of the order, the worker (Fay Winters) secured behaviour management counselling for Fiona, group treatment for the victims of sexual abuse, and a variety of other services from daycare to subsidized housing. Upon termination of the first order, an extension was sought. Fay Winters remained concerned about Fiona's ability to protect her children, particularly the daughter, who had been assaulted by her brother's friends. She wanted Fiona to 'understand what her kids went through and ... her role in the abuse.' The worker elaborated as follows:

> When the children disclosed the sexual abuse, mom was very cooperative. However the children told the previous worker that mother knew of the abuse. I am concerned about her ability to protect. I think she is overwhelmed with managing these five children, and the breakdown of her marriage, and the violence, and she says she's fully supportive of the kids and believes them but I wonder if mom will follow through without assistance.

> When you have a supervision order, you feel like you have more authority and control in the home, and yes, Fiona meets the children's basic needs but there is such chaos in the home. I can work with the kids to monitor the home and I can get them treatment so they'll continue to be safe.

Even though Fiona complied with the agency during the order of supervision, it is the worker's impression that she continues to require court-ordered intervention on the grounds that she might have known

Enforcing, Reinforcing, and Maintaining Mother Protector 139

or should have known about the abuse of her daughter by her son's friends. Despite a willingness to work with the agency, Fiona is perceived as having failed to protect, thereby justifying further court-ordered intervention. Consent hardly captures the essence of Fiona's experience (the text in brackets are questions I asked during the interviews):

> I know I still have a lot of problems with my daughter, but I'm totally willing to work with the Children's Aid. I don't understand the need for another supervision order. I guess they don't feel like I can protect them. [Protect them from what?] I'm not sure what they're talking about.

> [You saw Fay this morning. Did you ask her?] G-d no. I'm afraid to say anything because it might be used against me and then I'd lose the tiny bit of control I have. [Meaning?] I have some control ... because my kids live with me but there's a fear they'll take my kids and then I'll lose that control. So if something bothers me, I don't talk to her and I'll do what they say to keep my kids.

Fiona provided a number of examples of her fear, loss of control, and inability to communicate with her worker that are well connected to stipulations in the supervision order having to do with her responsibility to monitor and protect her children:

> This Christmas, I can only afford one gift for each of the kids. I thought of taking a job for the month but I don't feel like I can because I was told by Fay that I have to have a proper baby sitter. I want a proper baby sitter but I feel pressure. Do I have their approval? Is the baby sitter proper enough?

> On Sunday, the kids were really acting up and I yelled at them and I felt guilty. So I put the babies down, waited until they were asleep, and called my sister-in-law to come over so I could get out of the house and go for a walk. She's only ten minutes away. I left my daughter and son with the babies and I felt so guilty but it's better to get out than to take it out on the kids with the way I was feeling. In the supervision order, it says they can't baby sit but I needed a break. I would never tell Fay about it because I worry that she'll say 'what kind of mother are you that you need a break from your kids?'

The expectations on this mother to oversee, monitor, and protect are ensconced in the supervision order. Clearly the juridical context contributes to shaping a particular kind of relationship between this woman and her worker, which in this case is one marked by strain and distrust. This theme is revisited in Chapter 8.

DONNA MUNT
In the Munt case, an initial voluntary agreement was ineffective as a protection contract because James continued to work on the farm and have access to the children. Donna's complaints to the agency about his disregard for the agreement compelled Emma Webber to take more intrusive measures. She visited the farm, accompanied by two police officers, and 'threatened to apprehend the children and take the matter to court.' In response Donna left the farm with the children and returned when it was determined that James had gone. Emma proceeded to obtain a six-month order of supervision on the basis that the voluntary agreement was an inadequate means to protection.

As indicated in Chapter 5, the worker questioned Donna's motives for lodging complaints against James. She questioned the sincerity of Donna's protective efforts, given her tumultuous relationship with her partner Greg. The following excerpt reveals how the worker used the 'mud-slinging' between Donna and Greg as evidence for more intrusive protective measures. Not only are Donna's protective efforts rendered invisible but she is pictured in a derogatory manner:

> She accused him of not supervising the kids, and he accused her of not pulling her weight, sleeping around at night, staying in bed in the morning, and not taking care of the kids. I turned this mud-slinging into a protection issue – the children could be endangered by the farm machinery, no one seemed to be watching them. When I discussed his accusations against her, she got real snappy, she was like a clawing cat, and her remarks about Greg were vicious.

This presentation of Donna as failing to supervise and care for the children appeared again as Emma Webber described the couple's reaction to the threat of apprehension:

> He was angry. He knew I was serious and that I'd throw the book at him if necessary. And she transformed into this real slut! She was callous and hard and angry at Greg, and teased the police officers in the most provocative way. I suspect that she does sleep around.

Emma did not apprehend the children but sought a supervision order to secure protection by 'guaranteeing that James will not have contact with the children' and requesting cooperation with treatment plans. One is struck by the way in which Donna is featured in the delineation of risk:

> I really zeroed in on her immaturity and failure to supervise the kids. This is in the supervision order, that I will monitor her parenting. I even tried to add that Donna will participate in child management and parent programs but she got into a rage and was vicious towards me.

Emma noted that 'when Donna is with the kids, she is warm and talks pleasantly and the kids look fairly perky, so I guess she is doing some things right.' At the same time she was 'concerned about Donna's lack of responsibility and common sense. Her mothering instincts don't seem very sound either. She'd rather sleep in than look after her kids. This is a protection concern and a sign of immaturity.' Donna's protective efforts – complaints to the agency and calls for agency aid – are disregarded. Instead her inadequacies as a parent are featured over those of her common-law partner, who demonstrated indifference toward the initial voluntary agreement.

BELLA MEWS

In the Mews case, Ian refused to leave the home when the allegations of sexual abuse made by his adolescent daughter (Kay) were investigated and verified. The intake worker negotiated a twelve-month voluntary agreement which stipulated that Kay would live with her maternal grandparents, and that both parents would attend treatment groups and cooperate with individual and family counselling as recommended by the agency. Having opted to protect Kay by relocating her, Bella 'felt like I was being judged and blamed because I didn't throw my husband out of the house.' Such a feeling again challenges the rhetoric of choice.

Within weeks, Kay indicated that she wanted to return home. Contrary to the agreement and clearly without the caseworker's consent, she was brought home. When the worker became aware of the situation, she threatened to apprehend the daughter. Ian left the home instead. A twelve-month supervision order was sought to ensure protection of the daughters in this family because:

> Ian had made statements that these girls were beginning to act like sluts

like their older sister. He was beginning to show a keen interest in their sexual development ... and stated that he had a fetish for breasts. Adding to the concern in the home is the fact that Bella works from 3:00 P.M. to 11:00 P.M. (Excerpt from the 90 Day Assessment and Continuing Service Record)

The application requesting a supervision order detailed Ian's sexually abusive behaviour and his lack of regard for the seriousness of his actions and their effects on his daughters. For these reasons, 'it is in the opinion of this agency that (the identified children) are not safe in the home with their father.' The order continued:

When she is home, this agency does not consider the mother to be capable of protecting the children. She supports her husband and a lot of blame is put on Kay ... The mother has also stated that Kay should have kept it to herself.

Bella's work schedule and support of her husband rather than her daughter are integral facts in the protection application. The Family Service Plan, filed with the protection application, indicates that when father receives sufficient treatment and 'mother is able to protect daughters,' agency intervention will no longer be required. Ian contested the application for supervision. Correspondence between his legal counsel and the agency revealed a salient change in the 'facts' of the case: Bella resigned from her long-standing job to stay at home 'to care for the children 24 hours a day.'

While all written records in the case documented Bella's work schedule as cause for concern regarding the protection of her daughter, Emma Webber indicated that she did not want Bella to suffer the consequences of Ian's actions:

I just didn't want her to be penalized for something her husband did. She has [many] years on the job and seniority but she said she wanted to leave the job, she felt like a slave to it. When we got into it, she said she felt guilty, she didn't really know her kids and she hasn't been around to see them grow up. She insists it wouldn't have happened if she had been there and she believes it won't ever happen again because she's home now and she can't understand why I still want Ian out. (EW)

A number of contradictions are apparent. Emma does not want Bella to bear the costly loss of employment. However, she seems to be oblivious to the dynamics of intervention whereby women quit their jobs or vow to 'be there' to protect their children. As seen in the above excerpt, Bella acted according to the expectations to protect and she addressed her inadequacy – absenteeism from the home. Given this change, continued separation from her husband did not make sense to her. Instead, as will be seen later, regardless of the changes they make, their workers wonder if the conditions will ever be safe enough and protective enough for family members to reunite. In their pursuits to save children, workers can and do overlook mothers.

To summarize, by separating the abuser from the victim (and siblings), and engaging in voluntary or court-ordered agreements to protect according to specific conditions, mother is legally bound to protect. She is a central feature of intervention to secure the condition of protection regardless of the form of those interventions, whether they be voluntary agreements or court orders to protect.

As heard through these mothers' accounts, agreements deemed 'voluntary' and orders obtained 'on consent,' were actually rife with coercion and threats at worst, and lack of alternatives at best. The mother protection priority, ensured via contractual and legal measures, was also found to be maintained through ongoing group and casework practices.

Maintaining Mother as Protector

Mothers' Support Group

At various points in their professional careers, Barb Wayne and Gail Wydell were leaders of the mothers' support group at the agency. This group, as Barb put it, helps mothers to protect their children, deal with the impact of the abuse on the family, and attend to family dynamics so as to avoid recurrence. The extent to which these responsibilities lie with mother was overwhelmingly clear:

> It seems that the wife has to be aware of the husband's needs. If he feels depressed, she needs to be aware of that. So does he, but there's still the sense that the onus for sensitivity to the child and to the husband rests more with the mother. (GW)

> The men need to recognize the strategies they use to get what they want in a sexual way, and the moms need to be aware of those little patterns,

little quirks ... and how to put a stop to that ... If a father is parading around the house nude in front of his teenage stepdaughter, she needs to ask him to stop and she needs to question if there is something else going on. (BW)

We ask mother to be alert to the nonverbal communication between her child and her husband. We say 'you are now aware of the sexual abuse and understand how this occurred in your family, and you are now the watchdog.' (GW)

She is the central figure. Sure the child and father have to be aware of what's going on ... but there's this expectation that mom will have her radar out for protecting the child. At the same time we say 'it's not your fault, you're not to blame.' Actually so much of what we say is 'yes, you are responsible,' not in words, but we show them how to recognize past patterns of the family or clues they may have had that the abuse was going on, which seems to say 'you are responsible.' I've said it before, we impose guilt on them. (GW)

Both Eve McKay and Bella Mews referred to their involvement in the mothers' support group. Bella identified such learning goals as developing an awareness of 'the danger signs and what triggered the abuse,' 'better communication with my daughter,' 'to become stronger,' and recognizing that her husband is 'controlling me.' Whereas the rationale for learning the warning signs as a means to family reunification seemed to make sense to Bella, the impetus behind goals related to her relationship with her husband and daughter were less apparent to her. She didn't understand the nature of the communication problems with her daughter, nor did she experience control by her husband. 'Whatever education they have' gave the group leaders the right to set these goals regardless of her say. Not surprisingly, such goals are consistent with an understanding of child sexual abuse as a problem of inadequate wives and mothers.

Eve McKay, a participant in the group for over a year, expressed satisfaction with her involvement. The group was 'just like a bunch of women sitting down to coffee and gabbing.' In contrast, meetings with the social worker were 'a waste of my time.' In discussing group sessions, Eve referred to similar goals: 'to look for changes in the household with your child or in your husband'; 'we talked a lot about ... the situation and what to watch for and how to cope if it ever happens again.' As well as learning about monitoring family dynamics, the group experience allowed Eve to realize how her inadequacies contributed to establishing the conditions of abuse. She spoke favourably of having garnered this insight:

> We talked about my family, my parents ... There was no love shown. I had a hard time showing affection and I think this is part of the abuse because Jade is affectionate. The group brought this to my attention, how I didn't show my affection, and I'd say this has been very important for me to learn.

Women's inadequacies, and the need to address them, were echoed in Barb Wayne's description of the general objectives and philosophy of the mothers' group:

> We aim to move her [mothers in general] to greater levels of insight, to look at what's happening in the home, what are the dynamics in that home that make sexual abuse possible. What are some of the things in her relationship with her husband and how do they contribute to setting the scene for sexual abuse? Obviously not every controlling father is an abuser, so there must be things that set it up.

Casework Practices

Reinforcing and maintaining the mother protector mandate entailed not only dealing with women's responsibilities for monitoring interactions or suspicious dynamics, but also addressing relationships with husbands (offenders) and children through group work and ongoing casework practices. Dina Ward had 'to teach Eve to be responsible for protecting her daughter.' She 'wanted Irma to be aligned with the kids ... and I let her know that.' Emma Webber was 'teaching Bella to see his control.' Barb Wayne sought to help Abby recognize her responsibility 'for not leaving those girls with her son ... [and] for fixing what is wrong in the family.' She also hoped that Abby could show some 'spontaneous affection' to the girls.

While love and affection, support and protection seemed to be part of the mothers' mandate, there were limitations. Barb recalls having had to confront Abby on the rules around her involvement in treatment:

> The girls told their group workers that Charles was bullying them ... He

was confronted in his group ... went home and told his mother and she punished the girls and sent them to their room for saying these bad things. We held a family meeting to set the record straight. What goes on in group is private. Abby has to back off and let the treatment groups do their work.

Given the expectation for mother to assume responsibility for supporting, protecting, and loving these girls, the expectation that she 'back off' and relinquish control for protecting to official treatment providers seems to be a paradoxical set of expectations wherein any move on her part can lead to criticism.

As well as general comments about women's responsibilities, specific casework practices were identified through the interviews that appeared to reinforce and maintain the mother protector priority. Such practices included requiring mother to hear a full disclosure from husband/perpetrator and child/victim (mother 'needs to know'), supervising access between perpetrator and wife and children, and scrutinizing, correcting, and reevaluating women's relationships with these men.

Mother Protector 'Needs to Know'

About four months into the McKay case, the workers discovered that Fred never told Eve how he had abused Jade. Eve's ability to protect was considered to be threatened and obstructed as a result. Eve did not want to hear about the abuse because she feared 'the worst ... intercourse.' Fred did not want to tell. The agency, however, insisted. Eve 'understood that if Fred didn't tell me, if we didn't have this meeting then we would not be allowed to start treatment.' The worker was forced to confront them:

> I said 'Eve you have to know because it is interfering with your ability to believe and get help and treatment.' It got to the point where I simply said 'I guess you people are not ready for treatment, not ready for group.' There was a long silence and then Fred told her ... It was very, very hard for him to do this, but he just felt so much better afterwards. I think it was a real turning point. (AW)

According to Eve, the meeting was beneficial. Knowing that there had been no intercourse, she 'loosened up a bit' and was 'less angry' at her husband than when she imagined 'the worst.'

Bella was also required to listen to her husband recount the abuse and discuss the abuse with her daughter. With 'no direction from the worker,' Bella was uncertain about what to say to her daughter. She reassured her that she neither was angry with her nor blamed her. Given her initial position that her daughter should not have disclosed, Bella's statement of support was endorsed by the worker, though her motivations were questioned:

> She seemed to be intelligent and amenable to reason; that is, she seemed to be. I don't know whether it was respect or fear or what but she started asking us 'what the heck do you want?' She has some potential for change, I think, but I don't know if in fact she is changing or it's just another side of her that is coming out. (EW)

In both cases, the women's anger is affected. Eve's anger at her husband was reduced, and Bella's anger at her daughter for disclosing was withdrawn. This practice of confronting mother with the details of the abuse appears to be a progressive feature of best practice in that the offender must detail his behaviour, and thus his responsibility for the abuse is reinforced. At the same time, however, this practice aims to rev mother's protective engines, reinforce her protection mandate, and point the case in the direction of 'family' reunification.

Access

When an offender is separated from a child, issues of access and visitation arise. The mandate to oversee access, in the accounts generated in this book, frequently resides with mother protector. In the Mack case, the supervision order stipulated that father 'cannot be alone with child at any time ... unless mother is present' but he 'may go home when daughter is not there, i.e., in school.' According to the worker, supervision by mother makes her responsible for protection. It 'tells her that we think she can do this.' Jane McNab was also given the supervision mandate. The worker was 'reasonably comfortable with it because Jane and [partner] are anxious not to have him accused again. So we turned it around so it's for [his] protection just as much as it is for [JM's daughter]' (EW on JM).

Monitoring access was effectively assigned to mother in these cases. While such was the situation with Eve McKay, problems with access led to doubts about Eve's abilities as a mother protector. Several months into the case, Eve's fulfilment of the protection mandate was under question when the worker learned that Fred had 'unapproved' access to Jade. 'He is not supposed to see the child unless we set it up' (DW). Despite Eve's reports that her husband and daughter were not seeing each other inside the home, the worker found out that Eve gave Jade the choice to see her father outside the house, after an outing for groceries:

> Mom asked Jade to bring in the groceries. She said she gave Jade the choice. I said to her 'You are the mother! You do not give the child the choice because she will feel obligated to walk past her father, who she is not supposed to see, to get the groceries.' Probably Fred asked Eve to ask Jade to get the groceries, so he is controlling her but she let him. (DW)

Even though Dina Ward suspected that Fred controlled Eve to gain access to her daughter, she holds Eve responsible for upholding the protection mandate. Anne Wade, who knew of incidents like this one through her dealings with Fred in the Fathers' Support Group, saw the situation not only as an instance of Fred's 'manipulation of Eve' but as a reflection of Eve's 'strong tendency to keep things from us. She covered up for him and made it hard for herself.'

From the workers' perspectives, a mother cannot make decisions that are seen to jeopardize the protection of the child, regardless of how those decisions came about. Put differently, she cannot be a good mother protector and good wife at the same time. In the McKay case, allowing access resulted in the apprehension of Jade and her placement with the extended family for a short period of time. Eve was expected to oversee access as set out by the agency; she was not granted the right to decide upon the nature and extent of access. She was aware of this dynamic:

> We wanted to do more but they said Jade could not be around Fred. I didn't agree with that because I'm there and I don't see what is so wrong about the three of us going out for supper but they said no. (EM)

In the Morgan case, the father was allowed to visit the home when the children were at school. According to the worker, father's removal meant that 'he no longer functions as a parent,' nor as a marital partner:

> He had such generous access. There were certain days they could be together for the whole day and that was not proper ... They are supposed to start all over again, date, get to know each other, and develop better

communication. We are supposed to discuss it weekly. This is the proper way to do it. But the whole impact of our intervention was lost – he had all this access and no consequences. (DW)

The consequence of separation from wife and children for the offender is obviously unsatisfactory from the worker's perspective. At the same time, however, she doesn't seem to consider the consequences of the marital separation for Irma as a wife. Irma was confused on the subject of access. Given that she knows 'him better than they do,' and given her responsibility for 'supervising' access, Irma could not understand why her husband was prohibited from sleeping over. When asked about her husband's full access to the children, Irma's worker responded, 'not until we tell you it's alright.'

In these cases, women lose control around access and all that it entails (for example, their ongoing relationships with their husbands) as the state intervenes and regulates in the name of protection. At the same time, women are expected to control and monitor access. These responsibilities have, in effect, been transferred to mother. As was apparent in the Mews case, any move on mother's part to alter access renders her open to criticism and penalty.

Access in the Mews case was 'a mess' (EW). Whereas the initial voluntary agreement granted 'supervised' access by Ian to his daughter, the terms of the supervision order denied him such access. Bella understood this decision to be a response to having allowed her daughter to return home and having 'lied' about her whereabouts. The worker viewed the denial of access as a necessary protection strategy given the failure of the previous attempt; it also coincided with insights she acquired from a workshop with a child sexual abuse specialist:

> We changed our supervision order [to] ... no access because they [offenders/fathers] continue to control the kid. This request is more than we ever made in other cases, and they're contesting it, well, maybe just Ian is contesting it. He wants access to Kay and a six-month assessment.

In this case, activities concerning access and its management were effectively removed from mother, who was deemed to have failed to protect.

Scrutinizing, Correcting, and Reevaluating Relationships

With an understanding of child sexual abuse that features women's inadequacies as wives, it should not be surprising to find casework practices that scrutinize, correct, and reevaluate women's relationships with their partners. While such practices represent measures to reinforce and maintain the mother protection priority, they also reflect workers' heartfelt concern for the women on their caseloads. Notably, mothers were much more vocal on this subject matter than their workers, possibly suggesting that attention to the marriage or intimate relationship was seen by the mothers as being incomprehensible and intrusive, and by the workers as matter of fact, requiring little mention and even less explication.

Direct reference to scrutinizing and correcting the marital relationship was made in Dina Ward's discussion of Irma Morgan. Dina expected Irma and her husband to 'date, get to know each other and develop better communication.' She expected to discuss this dating relationship 'weekly' and perceived this intervention to be in keeping with 'the proper way to do it' – that is, treat cases of child sexual abuse. Irma held quite a different view, suggesting that such intervention was irrelevant and confusing:

> We had quite a few interviews with Dina, almost every week or every second week, but she wasn't helpful. We were supposed to work on our 'communication problems.' She thought we had problems but we always talked about things. To be honest, I'm totally confused as to what she was trying to do. She'd tell us we were handling things perfectly, so why couldn't Bob come home? That really bugged me.

Interventions into intimate relationships were by no means overlooked by the women, regardless of their reactions to such interventions. For example, after Ian separated, Bella experienced quite a loss. She was 'miserable' and lonely with him gone. Aware of the expectation to 'date' and improve her relationship with Ian, Bella described that feature of intervention as 'weird':

> We're more like boyfriend and girlfriend. He drops by to visit, he buys me groceries, we talk on the phone. It's like we're dating. This is what the CAS wants ... After all these years I'm supposed to date my husband again.

Eve McKay resented intrusion into her marriage. Committed to protecting Jade through separation from Fred did not, in her opinion, give licence to pry into her intimate affairs or to suggest alternatives:

> They want to know everything, like how's your sex life. It is not right to ask ... There has to be a limit to what they can ask. They say 'I should go out and meet new people.' Well come on ... You're not running my life. They can ask how I'm feeling and how I'm coping but that's it.

The extent to which Eve is in control of her life as a woman, mother, and wife is questionable.

In the Main case, the worker identified the marriage as being problematic given Abby's tendency to 'deal with crisis by threatening to leave or by breaking down and crying.' Abby explained that the thought of leaving had nothing to do with her relationship with her husband. Rather it had everything to do with the stresses she experienced as a mother protector. 'Yes I thought of leaving with Charles so I wouldn't be stuck in the middle and there would be no conflict between him and the girls, not because of conflict between me and Joe. [The worker] was judging our marriage and that is not right.' The pressures and expectations of mother protection again seem to be denied. This theme was captured in Anne Wade's discussion of the Mack case. According to the worker, Chris Mack was 'totally dependent on Harry.' 'She's passive and needs him and that's her role' (AW). Given these impressions of mother, Anne sought to 'reinforce anything that is positive':

> I tell her that I think she can ... protect [her daughter]. I reinforce how terrific it is that she believed Tammy and didn't deny that it happened. However she became absorbed with her husband, totally, and was crying a lot and I'm not sure if what I said registered with her.
>
> I try to be supportive. I say 'I'm sure you'll be able to manage and there will be a social worker to help you.' I appreciate what she's going through and how difficult it is, and we will help.
>
> I'd like to see Chris get angry at Harry, take a stand. I don't want them to separate if they have a good marriage. He doesn't abuse her but he has to allow her to have some strengths. I have to diminish his power so they can function better. (AW)

Not only is the marriage scrutinized, but the many dimensions of Chris' life are denied. She is seen as a mother protector. Implicit in the declaration that she 'can' protect is a failure to understand the conditions of mother protection for women, seen in Anne's continued discussion of the case:

152   What's Mother Got to Do with It?

> This past summer, there was a little spark in the case. Harry told fathers' group that he wasn't sure if Chris would take him back. I was really surprised. I didn't think she'd consider separating. I asked Harry about it in the next meeting and he said ... Chris doesn't feel that way any more. It's not that I don't want him to return home but it would be ... very encouraging if she was even thinking that she didn't have to take him back if she didn't want to and that she was showing concern for the kids.

Encouraging women to reevaluate their relationships with their partner/perpetrator was evident as Gail Wydell discussed the case of Lucy Mann, which included wife assault, verified child physical abuse, and suspected but unfounded child sexual abuse perpetrated by the father/husband. At the time of the investigation, Lucy and her children separated from the abusive father/husband. They stayed with friends until Lucy was able to establish a home for herself and her children. Over the course of several months, she began to speak of reconciliation. Gail could not understand how this woman could have a change of heart given the husband's psychological and sexual abuse of her and violent abuse of his children. Gail was angry that Lucy considered a reunion over the safety of her children. Gail struggled with her disappointment in Lucy:

> The child protection part of me sees that these kids have been severely abused and do not want to live with this guy. But there's a part of me that wants her to leave him. Lucy is bright and intelligent and this man pulls her down and she would be better off without him. I didn't tell her this but I wonder if it came across to her because I pushed her to leave her husband in the first place. (GW)

Gail encouraged Lucy to leave her husband and wished for continued separation. She was driven not only by her sense of responsibility for the well-being and protection of the children but also by her belief in what was in the best interests of the woman herself. Just as Gail hoped for something 'better' for Lucy Mann, so did other workers try to make sense of women's relationships with men that appeared to be unsatisfactory:

> He was drinking heavily and she was going to leave him anyway so I wonder why she wants to go back to him. Why doesn't she try it on her own? She's dependent on him, she has so few friends, and yet she is such a likeable person. It doesn't make sense to me. (DW on EM)

Enforcing, Reinforcing, and Maintaining Mother Protector 153

Irma was almost like his mother. She took care of him, protected and nurtured him. He came first, the kids came second, and she came last ... He jerked her around. They had financial problems, he was drinking and spending money on rye. He told her he was sober and he was not. It really bothered me ... I always thought she deserved a lot better, she deserved someone to take care of her and treat her special. (CW on IM)

Alan is not sure if he wants Jane or not. I haven't confronted her with this but I see her as a slave. She does all the housework, she puts a lot of effort into his kids, she cares for them, and what does she get back from him? Not much. He takes her goodness, he takes her offer to parent his kids, he takes her affection and I wonder what's in it for her? I guess it is better than nothing. (EW on JM)

She's been through family violence, an abusive husband, she has all these kids and she's trying to raise them under adverse conditions. She's got a lot on her plate and she gets no support from her family. I know she's feeling down and she wonders if she did the right thing to leave DM. I remind her of what she's done ... She booted him out of the house, she took charge ... and she showed him just how strong she is. I keep telling her what a strong year she's had! (FW on FM)

Encouraging women to reevaluate their intimate relationships reflects workers' feelings about women not only as mother protectors but as multidimensional women who deserve 'better' in their intimate relationships.

Rarely did the women offer evaluations of their relationships that were similar to their workers' understandings. One exception was Jane McNab, who recognized, for a fleeting moment, that her partner took advantage of her and refused to commit to the relationship. For the most part the women spoke of their marriages as integral features of their lives and of family reunification as their main objectives:

I always wanted to be a wife and mother and a companion for my husband. We planned on having four children – well, we have five! (BM)

I think it's just a natural instinct to look after your kids and your husband and make sure they're happy. (EM)

You have to be pleasant with everyone and keep things calm between the kids and the husband. A woman doesn't take sides; that is unfair. I try to hear both sides and I try not to choose sides. (IM)

What I want is to make sure the family gets back together, to put back together what was torn apart. (AM)

What my kids want, what I want, even what the workers want is that we get back together as a family again. (BM)

Coupled with a commitment to oversee the safety and protection of children, the goal of family reunification was echoed in the workers' views of their responsibilities:

My chief concern is the safety of the child. It is my mandate, written in law. But I am also definitely responsible to the family, to be as constructive as I can be. (AW)

We have a mandate to keep families together and we have reunited families if they are all committed and willing to work. Sure the victim comes first, but you cannot lose sight of the other family members. We try to do voluntary services, but it is a dilemma to balance the officer role with the helping role. (FW)

In this last excerpt, Fay Winters talks about the difficulty of balancing authority functions with helping functions. In contemporary child welfare practice, authority functions seem to outweigh helpful services, and, as suggested here, they do so on the shoulders of women. This theme is taken up more fully in the next chapter.

8

Critical Reflections: Workers' and Mothers' Thoughts on Mother Protector

This chapter presents workers' and mothers' critiques of intervention as well as their impressions of each other. As will be apparent in the pages that follow, the relationship between worker and mother is often experienced as conflict: intervention appears to work against the very women needed to secure protection.

Challenges of Child Protection Work

The characterization of child protection work as 'critical, complex, fast-paced, risky, solitary, invisible, contradictory, and potentially divisive' (Callahan, 1993a, p. 73) coincides with the struggles identified by workers in this study. In response to questions about their responsibilities and practices, social workers spoke about the significance of their work in relation to opportunities to protect children. Simultaneously they made reference to the ways in which the nature of the workplace affected their protective efforts. Intake workers, for example, must assess a child's safety as a priority. This means that they do not have adequate 'time to do a full assessment and document everyone's concerns' (DW). Intake is 'short staffed and overworked' (DW). Good investigations rarely happen 'because of our jobs and our caseloads' (BW). Barb Wayne leads groups, performs back-up, and has twenty cases at intake. 'If a sexual abuse comes in, it can take a full day. I get upset with myself because I fall behind or I don't do the job the way I'd like' (BW). Carol West expressed 'real conflict in this job' between what she viewed were agency constructions of her tasks and her own professional conceptions. The agency sees her as being responsible for investigating, completing the necessary paperwork, and moving on. 'As a professional I should be doing a proper assessment and plan of action. I should decide who is best suited to get the case. We should be accountable to the client.'

Such reflections of their work coincided with mothers' descriptions of the investigation as a whirlwind. As one mother put it, 'they rushed after us and after a few days they forgot about us. As quickly as it came up, it died.' Not surprisingly, mothers came to resent an intervention plan that '[moved] heaven and hell to get the husband out and then nothing' or 'opened up a can of worms and then nothing,' meaning, nothing by way of help.

Workers also spoke of barriers to protecting children that emanated from the network of professionals affiliated with this task. Variation in law enforcement officers' discretion to lay charges, the effects of a lack of corroborating evidence, or questionable credibility of children as witnesses affected protective efforts. Anne Wade spoke of the effects of uncooperative police practices. When she attempted to convince an officer to lay charges for the sexual abuse of two siblings, she was told, 'We don't need to nail him for both.' She described this attitude as 'pervasive. My experience is that there are certain police officers who you know will not charge and if you push them, you may get the minimum charge.' In another case with insufficient evidence and very young child victims, Emma Webber asked 'why do we bother to investigate with the police and bring it to court to see it get thrown out? The system favours adults and doesn't know how to deal with child sexual abuse.'

The 'why bother' question was rhetorical. Workers expressed deep commitment to victimized children and their families. They believed in the goodness of their work. Emma was proud to be engaged in 'valuable' work, 'even if I say we use coercion.' 'I have some leverage to work with the family system. What motivates me is that I work with the family and I feel like I'm helpful.' Carol West summarized her impressions as follows:

> I don't think we always know what we are doing or how valuable our efforts are, but I know we have a real desire to help people with their difficulties and their pain. I have a real strong sense of fairness, right and wrong, and I try to advocate for the client.

Within the context of such challenges, workers raised questions about their interventions in protecting children from sexual abuse. The following section elucidates some of these concerns.

Workers' Thoughts on Their Interventions

Chapter 5 outlined some of the consequences of conceptualizing child sexual abuse in terms of women's inadequacies. This concept not only 'let incest offenders off the hook' but reinforced mother's culpability and hooked her into the ensuing protection strategy.

The protection process of transforming women into mother protectors disregards the many dimensions of women's lives while casting them in the role of mother protectors (see Chapter 6). Workers spoke of how mothers were overlooked in the process. From Emma Webber's perspective, after the crisis of disclosure and investigation, 'the moms are angry at the agency and they are much, much harder to reach.' Given the centrality of women in the protection of children, such a consequence can hardly be dismissed.

In talking about her work, Gail Wydell realized how she 'pushes past' mothers' feelings in order to address risk and protection concerns regarding the child:

> Intake workers want to be able, at the end of that day, to get mother to be supportive of that child and the child to be able to remain with the mother ... This expectation is probably very unrealistic and if there's some other way we can support her and protect the child, not remove her, then I'd like to see that happen.

Gail was not alone in her critique. Carol West described how 'mothers are in a no-win situation of having to choose between husbands and their children.' Carol noted 'I'm not always sure if it is best for dad to leave the home.' She thought of one case wherein she believed the child and father could have remained in the same home. 'That would be seen as severely radical, almost crazy. The way we proceed is with coercion; we force the dads out and even the police tell him that he'll have it easier if he leaves and cooperates' (CW).

Emma Webber also had doubts about whether her intervention was helpful or destructive. 'Can you take a family and pull it apart without destroying the people?' Emma worried that Bella Mews 'will have a nervous breakdown.' 'I thought I would destroy her by having her leave her job. I thought I was putting her in a completely impossible predicament.' The workers find such predicaments personally troublesome:

> I feel as though I'm personally hurting these people: I'm putting them in a horrible place. I try to hold on to my belief that this is going to be good for them. It has to be! In another case, a lady works afternoons, and when she gets home from work at 11:00 P.M., she claims she can only fall asleep at 3:00 A.M., and then she has to be at group for 10:00 the next day. She's a wreck, and I feel guilty making her do that. The other group leaders just say 'so, she'll get a little less sleep that day' but I feel personally responsible for making her life difficult.

Apparent in these passages are ambivalence, guilt, and a sense of responsibility for uneasiness in the progression of the case rather than a critical examination of the nature and structure of interventions that identify mother as problematic or intervene according to assumptions about mother's daytime schedule and availability. Whereas Emma Webber did not 'have' Bella Mews leave her job, she feels responsible.

Remarks of personal responsibility were not uncommon. Emma felt 'so responsible' for having placed the Merton children with their grandparents. After all, she 'did the adoption work' and saw the children in weekly play therapy. Having been involved with the family regularly, she was aware of the son's bowel control problem, which was 'a real clue to sexual abuse and I never figured it out.' Emma berates herself for failing to suspect: 'I have to deal with my failure and my guilt.' Faye Winters was 'devastated' and 'felt sick' about the Miller case. How could she 'have failed to pick up on clues of abuse? What did I miss?' Similarly, Dina Ward questioned her 'skills' when attempting to understand her strained relationship with Eve McKay. She did not, however, look critically at the context of intervention.

In reflecting on everyday interventions, Emma Webber recognized the coercive nature of the practice of separating offender from child and the ramifications this had for the mother, for herself as a worker, and for the child:

> There are a lot of times when your client isn't happy with what you do, especially in sexual abuse cases. You turn the family upside down and they go crazy and feel like they'll never get their feet back on the ground. A woman has operated all her life a certain way; she may be subservient.

To ask her overnight to stand on her own two feet is devastating. She needs a lot of support and we use coercion. I try to be helpful and show them that our goals are really the same, but I feel like I have to do things I'm not happy about because of the agency policy, to get the father out and so on, and then I am coerced.

The McNab case came to Emma's mind. Despite insufficient evidence to pursue court involvement, Emma was 'given a strong message [from co-workers] that he [alleged offender] was guilty' and directed to act accordingly. This directive posed 'a real struggle. I felt there was no ground to be gained by treating him punitively.' She found herself debating the pros and cons of intervention. Though she believes in the importance of her work, she wonders if 'we play G-d and interfere in these families.' Sometimes she feels she has 'too much responsibility,' and other times 'not enough power.' Ultimately she questions, 'do we do more harm than good?' 'Does the kid hurt more being separated from the father?' 'Have we done something wrong from the start for the mother to support or collude with the father? When this happens, I feel guilty. I messed the kid up. We think we know what they need, but do we?'

Carol West also questioned the extent to which interventions make a difference in people's lives. When Carol's supervisor viewed her as 'too accommodating' and directed her to schedule appointments with clients much like doctors do, she was disturbed by the uncertain outcome such disruptions have in the mothers' lives:

We say that if they can go to a doctor, then they can come to us. I find it hard to accept this argument ... You go [to your doctor] because you are in pain and you believe he [*sic*] will take care of it. We believe that we can do the investigation but do we really take care of them? We have no evaluation system where we can monitor our work ... We expect the dad to get out of the home and for mom to be the kid's ally, and I don't know if that works. I'm not convinced.

Gail Wydell, who considered that she supports mothers and protects children, recognized that coercion and judgments are often used. While she believes in separating offenders, she wonders if any further support could be given to the mother. Ultimately Gail sympathizes with the child: 'I think [mother] should hear what [her] child is saying. I feel angry when she's not able to meet the child's needs or hear the child.'

Though workers may support and seek to understand the mother's plight, the mandate to protect the child takes precedence. As a result, a mother's hesitation or failure to protect is troublesome for workers.

Frustrations with Mothers Who 'Won't' Protect

Workers spoke of their disillusionment with women who did not believe the allegations, offer immediate support, or provide an appropriate reaction to the offender – in short, mothers who did not protect:

> 'Can you not see that by totally aligning with your husband, you're pushing your daughter farther away? Do you not see what's happening there?' I was able to see this but they weren't, and it was frustrating trying to get them to see. (BW)

> You get really angry at the mother who won't protect because the kid needs a nurturing mother at that time. Some mothers start off protecting the kid and then fall into supporting the father and you really try hard to stop this from happening. (EW)

Frustration and anger are apparent. When Carol West realized that Irma Morgan knew of the sexual abuse and 'did nothing,' she felt 'angry.' Fay Winters was 'disappointed' in Harriet Miller and 'felt anger' toward her for failing to support the children. 'I thought she was capable of having more insight, I thought she was more supportive and nurturing and pro-child, but she isn't any of these things.' Anne Wade, too, indicated that when mother 'doesn't protect and doesn't believe' she feels angry and wonders 'how can she do this to her kid?' Anne identified one of the most difficult features of her work as having to deal with 'mothers who don't believe' and who protect accordingly. Carol West voiced difficulty with women who fail to believe and protect:

> We have a hard time with assertive women or women who are not nurturing towards their kids. We have a hard time with those women who are oppositional to what we want, so we don't deal with them, we ignore them, or go on expecting that we will make them nurturing, we will make them protective of their kids, we will make them buy what the agency says the problems are. The child welfare system gets angry at dependent and weak women, we get angry at them.

Gail Wydell referred to failed mother protectors as 'weak' women:

> In terms of the mothers, I think there's a sense that they have to be pushed and shaped into something that we need so that we can allow the family to reunite, whether that be for the daughter to stay at home or the father to eventually return. I sense that so much is put on the mother, and we make derogatory comments about the 'weak' mother.

Any perceived opposition to effective mother protection warrants critical appraisal of mothers and their inadequacies (e.g., weak Chris Mack, assertive Jane McNab, or tenacious Donna Munt), justifies intervention, and ensures worker frustration with them. Workers' frustration and disappointment in any mother's unwillingness to protect offer support to the contention that mother protection is obligatory and expected, not a matter of choice.

Workers' Explanations for Mothers Who 'Won't' Protect

Anger, frustration, and criticism pervaded workers' discussions of mothers who were assumed to have known or should have known of the abuse, or were perceived to have either hesitated or failed to protect following awareness of the abuse. They understood this failure to protect in a number of ways:

> No woman wants to believe that the man she trusted did this to her kid so she has to believe differently in order not to destroy her whole life. (EW)

> The mothers I deal with really believe and have convinced themselves that it hasn't happened even though they have had warning signs. That's because they not only love the husband but they love the children and it's too dangerous and too scary for them to think that their child has been victimized. (CW)

> Most often mothers waver because they talk to the husband and they feel sorry for him but you've got to remind her who the victim is. (AW)

> There may be intimidation by some of the husbands, and this is where we assume that these men have some control over their wife. (EW)

> Maybe it has to do with income and security and ... life is too scary

> another way, to move out, to be on their own. Most have never been on their own, ever, like Bella. (EW)

> Looking at it from a systems perspective, I think that she's a [middle-aged] woman and this is her relationship and she's already had a failed marriage, and maybe she needs him as much as he needs her. (FW)

> She loves and trusts this person and he betrays her and that betrayal is really, really tremendous and the only way she can deal with it is to deny it happened. (BW)

> There's the stigma: her daughter is the 'other woman' in her life, and that's hard to deal with, the jealousy and stigma. (BW)

> It's a dilemma for these mothers but ... (FW)

These explanations enabled workers to make sense of the seeming contradiction between a mother's awareness of abuse and any hesitation or failure on her part to offer immediate protection.

Fathers and Mothers – A Brief Comparison

Whereas workers dwelt on how mothers frustrated them, they tended to view fathers as more apt to change. With years of experience in such cases, Anne Wade concluded that 'mothers are harder to deal with than the fathers.' She elaborated:

> Sure I find it hard to deal with men who totally deny or call the daughter a slut. That's tough, but mothers who don't believe, that's really hard. When she doesn't protect and doesn't believe, this is terrible. This is one of the hardest things for me to cope with and I feel angry. How can she do this to her kid?

Anne's exasperation rests with mother's failure to believe and protect rather than with the abuse committed by the offender. She seems to be more willing to understand the offender/father than the mother. She 'feel[s] for the fathers.' 'You need to give them hope, to help them feel like this is not the end of the world, and it can be resolved, and you need to care for them. If you let your anger become too strong, you can't help them.'

These sentiments were by no means unusual. Gail Wydell, once angered by such men, now 'see[s] them as whole persons.' Over time Gail 'was probably more prepared to see the evil perp [perpetrator] as a whole man than ... to see the mother in any other way than she's supposed to believe.' Dina Ward's feelings towards offenders also changed: 'I used to feel like they were bastards; well they're not bastards and I don't hate them. After all, the adult perp has a whole history to him, and that doesn't forgive him, it just makes you see him as a human being.' In her work with abusing men, Dina came to view them as capable of change, of 'getting in touch with their feelings' and confronting their actions. 'Somewhere, they begin to look at the poor communication with the wife, and they begin to realize that this is why they needed someone else, and they chose a child instead of another woman.' According to Dina, 'it doesn't seem that the women move as far.'

Other workers expressed compassion towards offenders. Emma Webber was 'trained' to appreciate that the perpetrator is 'likeable' and 'not all terrible.' In fact, 'the perp is always a victim. My training is that ... his self-esteem is low and I try to help him' (EW). Carol West stated her position succinctly. 'We see them as fathers first, who have committed a criminal act.'

Fay Winters knows all too well the potential effects of failing to empathize with an offender. Through her professional practice, she has come to understand his plight:

> Just a few days after [an] investigation, the father committed suicide. I was blown away. I felt so responsible. I realized that these men need help. Yes the child has to be safe but we can't forget about the father. I'm quite committed to working with these men and I assess how the father is coping. I can help despite my anger because something has been going on in his life that has led up to the abuse. He has treatment needs, not just the kid.

Whereas fathers were portrayed as 'whole persons,' 'human beings,' as 'likeable' and capable of change, mothers were characterized by frustration, disappointment, and doubt about their capacity for change.

Barb Wayne described Abby Main as 'usually close to tears when you talk to her.' She is 'enmeshed with her son,' 'a very emotional person and a very tense woman, stressed out, and she deals with crises by threatening to leave or by breaking down and crying.' In contrast, she spoke of Joe Main as 'a pleasant sort of person; doesn't seem to get as upset as his wife.' Abby's life was dramatically altered as a result of the intervention into the sexual abuse, unlike her husband, whose daily routines were reportedly virtually unchanged. Such divergent portrayals reflect a failure to appreciate the impact of interventions on women and the absence of any protective expectations for fathers.

In the McNab case, Jane was described as 'hysterical, pretty emotional, and volatile.' 'She can be nurturing but I really need to work on her parenting skills.' Jane 'intimidates' the children, 'yells,' and 'locks the kids in their bedrooms to keep them quiet. She even takes the light bulbs out of the sockets because the kids melted crayons on them.' Emma Ward noted that 'Jane is trying to set limits, but her instincts are wrong.' She is 'very defensive' about her parenting and her parenting is not very good'; 'she does not take feedback well, at all!'

Jane's common-law partner was seen in a more positive light. He was described as 'passive-aggressive but he's got a soft side.' Despite her knowledge of his history of drug abuse, wife assault, and verbal abuse of Jane, the worker saw him as being 'committed to the kids,' 'nurturing,' 'genuine,' and 'more reasonable and rational.' After all, 'he took the locks off the doors and the noise didn't seem to bother him that much.' 'He takes feedback quite well, much better than Jane.' That her partner's tolerance and cooperation are accentuated over his abusive behaviours is noteworthy. It is even more telling given that Jane fulfils child and home care responsibilities. In fact, the worker recognized that she scrutinized Jane's competence as a parent for this very reason: 'she is doing most of the parenting, and not very well, so I have to look at her actions.' The theme of mother's responsibility is again evident through descriptions of clients. Such descriptions reinforce expectations of women to 'parent' (mother), and ensure that mother's competence and 'instincts' will be scrutinized and criticized while any gratuitous efforts from the father/father figure will be applauded.

Emma Ward described Donna Munt as 'soft and motherly, with a flip side that's a hard prostitute, street-type person.' She's like 'an acting out teenager' whose 'mothering instincts don't seem very sound.' Though Donna 'can sound very nurturing,' 'she's not always a very protective mother.' She's 'rather careless' and 'immature.' She lacks 'responsibility and common sense.' As seen in Chapter 7, Donna's immaturity and 'lack of supervision of the children' formed the core of the protection application despite the fact that it was her common-law partner who regularly placed the children at risk for re-abuse. His instincts, lack of responsibility, and immaturity go largely unnoticed by the worker.

In Emma Ward's opinion, Bella Mews is 'a very needy lady,' 'emotionally flat,' and 'talked about her own needs and hurts long before her daughter's hurts'; she is 'closed,' 'pathetic,' 'whined when she talked,' and she too 'lacks maternal instincts.' No analogous criticism is made of Ian's lack of fathering instincts or his preoccupation with his own needs when he sexually abused their teenaged daughter.

Emotionally flat, weak, and unchanging – these words are consistently used to describe mothers. Eve McKay was described as having a 'flat affect.' During the investigation, she 'showed no emotion at all.' Her ongoing social worker identified her as 'the elusive one.' Though both workers spoke fondly of her, they referred to her as weak. 'Eve is a really likeable person' but 'she can't handle that Jade was abused.' 'She would have a hard time standing up to him [husband] and saying no, you can't come back.' Her weaknesses, too, formed the core of the protection application.

Similarly, Anne Wade described Chris Mack as 'very, very weepy' and 'weak.' She was 'frightened about what would happen when we asked her husband to move out'; 'she didn't think she could cope'; and 'she wanted her husband to be home again.' Anne Wade indicated that 'from the moment I met them, Chris was totally dependent on him. I believe we may be able to rehabilitate this family but mother is the unknown entity for me. I don't see any strength there, no strength to support and protect Tammy.'

In stark contrast, Dina Ward depicted Fred McKay as a 'gentle man' who is 'really trying to understand and get into his feelings':

> Sure there's the manipulation and control, but he comes with good stuff and we work on it. We do straight clinical work. I don't get that sense from Eve. With her, it is straight protection work.

Anne Wade described Harry Mack as 'very handsome, well built and charming.' He appeared 'remorseful.' 'He's so apologetic, like a grovelling dog, and begged for forgiveness.' Anne 'couldn't get angry at him because he's just like an affectionate little puppy and he's really trying and you have to appreciate that.' Clearly, men can change.

166   What's Mother Got to Do with It?

Making Sense of Frustrating Mothers and Encouraging Fathers

When confronted with seemingly ambivalent or unprotective mothers, workers expressed frustration, anger, and disappointment. These frustrations can be understood in different ways. One explanation begins with a recognition that workers must secure the immediate protection of children from sexual abuse. This goal is achieved, first and foremost, through a nurturing and supportive mother protector. Time constraints faced by the worker, women's feelings about their partners (offenders), or their ambivalence around the veracity of the child's disclosure are therefore obvious obstacles and hence a source of frustration for workers in the protection process.

This frustration can also be understood in quite a different way. Frustration, anger, and disappointment make sense not because of obstacles to protection but because of the way in which protection seems to be operationalized in practice – as the responsibility of the mother. As I have suggested throughout this book, intervention appears to be based on an unrelenting expectation that multidimensional women will, without question, embrace and comply with the mother protector mandate. Women are expected to react appropriately to the disclosure, cast any ambivalence aside at least temporarily, and 'choose' her relationship with the child as mother over her relationship with the partner (the offender in many instances) within a period of hours or days.

This translation of protection to mean that children need a nurturing and supportive mother is so natural and acceptable that it is almost beyond any question. In fact it is rarely articulated. At the same time, this realization of protection ensures that women will be investigated, inspected, evaluated, adjusted, and transformed. Not surprisingly, while workers revised their understandings of offenders and saw potential for change, the women (mothers) continued to frustrate them and seemed less capable of change.

Protection is all about women; they are central to both problem and solution. This transformation of the problem is in concert with dominant contemporary discourse on motherhood in which women are assumed to be located in the private sphere as self-sufficient nurturers and carers and as the natural, instinctual, and logical protectors of children. These women, then, must be defective. When she fails to protect, mother necessitates repair and is positioned as principal subject of the state. This shift in focus onto mother ensures that the presence or absence, actions or inactions, of men – except for their sexually abusive misconduct and its treatment – fade from the fore. Here he must admit to having sexually abused a child, repent for having done so, and accept criminal and therapeutic responsibility. Should he separate himself from mother and child – best practice outcome – she is faced with having to survive differently. With mother now preoccupied with providing food and shelter, her life is altered, though she did not perpetrate the offence.

As well, she must always be seen as performing: supporting, believing, protecting, improving her marriage and her parenting/home skills, tuning into her children, and monitoring and identifying warning signs. Therapeutic interventions into her life extend well beyond protection skills in that having failed as a protector itself implies that she hasn't done such a good job as wife and mother. On the other hand, he is not expected to perform. In this light, it is no wonder that men appear as amiable, understandable, and encouraging, and women as unpleasant, incomprehensible and frustrating. 'In a culture which sees children as mothers' business, any participation by fathers is thought remarkable' (Pascall, 1986, p. 84).

These differing experiences of fathers/perpetrators and mothers/women are almost inevitable. Interventions that expect women to protect, that fail to recognize how dramatically their lives are changed, and that ensure that the costs of protection are borne by mothers are interventions that will, at once, feature and negate women in the name of 'protection.'

Mothers Speak Out

Having looked for respect, information, help for their children, and access to alternative practices, and having received few of these, it is no surprise that mothers expressed dissatisfaction and criticism:

> CAS is responsible for making sure Kay gets the proper counselling, which they have not done ... How much emotional damage is being done to Kay because she's sitting with this guilt and anger and she needs group counselling now! I told Emma this but she is not listening to me. They have done nothing for her. (BM)

> What I wanted was help for my daughter and they could teach me how to cope. I guess that's all I wanted. Dina said she'd see us as a couple, but

she hasn't done that yet. We were supposed to get family counselling, and I asked her for it but there has been none. (EM)

The kids need help right away, and because you don't know what to do, it gets worse, and they just blame you. I worry about my daughter ... You know ... there has been no counselling on the molestation. (JM)

CAS should prosecute anybody that needs to be prosecuted and get help for the kids. No charges were ever laid in this case and the kids didn't get help and I should not have been kept in the dark. My daughter should have been given one-to-one help from the start with someone who is specially trained to help her. I don't know how to help my kids cope; I needed help! It falls on my shoulders. I'm the one who has to cope and I don't know how! When you have a problem, you go to a specialist, but they have a lot of questions and few answers if you ask me. (FM)

They should sit down and tell you so you understand what's going on and why you have to do things their way and could they possibly give you alternatives? Could the husband stay in the home and could they monitor the situation on a weekly basis as long as he is going to father's anonymous group? They should also try to be more understanding of the wife; they treat her like she's an accomplice to a crime that she had no knowledge of. At least this is how they made me feel. They didn't listen to me, they tell you what to do with no explanations, they don't tell you what's down the road and that is scary. (BM)

The dearth of help is undeniable as is frustration with the few services rendered. There was mention, however, of some satisfaction with some services. Fiona Maye received child management help to teach the children to 'clean their mess.' Bella Mews has 'been helped a lot in mothers' group.' Eve McKay received guidance in how to better 'control' her daughter. She also learned to engage in activities with her daughter. As Eve prepared to reunite with her husband after a year of treatment, she recognized that their relationship was improved during the year of 'treatment.' At the same time she was hesitant about reuniting for fear that not enough change had been made:

I wonder if he'll do it again ... I hope I'm not going back to the booze and pot and stuff like that. But I do miss him and being a family again and not being alone. I realize that Jade has control over this and it is up to her.

Even though she expressed hesitation, Eve believed that she had done what was required in order to win approval of her plans to reunite as a family. When such approval was not forthcoming, Eve was confused. '[Worker] says we're not ready but I don't know why and it doesn't make sense to me.' The caseworker was concerned about protection. As she expressed it,

> Eve doesn't live with Fred right now but they want to get back. Jade said she doesn't ever want to go back, and that means Eve can never go back until Jade leaves home, and Eve has accepted that, but they still see each other, they still date.

The worker's scepticism about the effectiveness of the intervention cannot possibly make sense to women who engaged in interventions that supposedly sought long-term protection of their children. In fact, when the women spoke of interventions regarding their relationships or parenting, much of what was provided did not make sense to them. Fiona Maye went to child management classes but wondered why. 'I think they expect me to change but I'm not sure why.' Jane McNab received counselling as stipulated in the voluntary agreement but she 'didn't know what for. We never talked about the abuse at all; more of it had to do with our relationship.' Irma and Bob Morgan worked on their 'communication problems' as defined by the worker. Irma was 'totally confused as to what she [worker] was trying to do. She'd tell us we were handling things perfectly so why couldn't Bob come home?' This made little sense to her.

One of the most potent themes was that of wanting to be recognized, heard, and considered, as mothers to their children and as partners to the men in their lives (see Chapter 6). Repeatedly they indicated that their desires were ignored. Some of the women asked for an alternative to separation from the offender. Regardless of the features of the case, they experienced numerous and diverse costs associated with the intervention, costs which remained largely hidden. Not only did the services rendered seem to disregard the women and fail to address their needs, but they also resulted in feelings of loss, burden, and distress. As such, the effect of agency intervention was not to strengthen women as mother protectors but to disempower them in various aspects of their lives. Bella Mews 'nearly had a nervous breakdown. They come in and break up the family and leave you hanging ... They make you feel negative about everything – your family, your marriage.' Harriet Miller felt 'lost,' as though her 'life has gone down the drain, there's not much hope in it'; she felt as 'if everyone is against me.' 'They've interfered' with Abby Main's life, though she 'didn't think there was anything wrong with it.' Now her 'independence has been taken away and I have to be the guardian for everybody.' Irma Morgan believed 'they ask you to give up a piece of your life, they just cut off a chunk of your life.' It was her experience that her worker 'was working against me.' Jane McNab's perception was that 'our whole lives were shattered and then we were thrown to the wind. I don't think they realize what they do to people.' Considering workers' and mothers' markedly dissimilar understandings of the problem of child sexual abuse (Chapter 5), it is not surprising that mutual frustration and dissatisfaction existed.

Mothers' Frustrations with Their Workers

Powerful, forceful, inflexible, judgmental, and firm best describe mothers' impressions of their social workers, though some changes were noted over time. Abby Main found Barb Wayne to be 'nice to talk to but firm in what she believed.' While in the process of pursuing a voluntary agreement, Abby described Barb as 'forceful,' given the need to protect the victims or consider removal of Abby's son from the home.

Eve McKay was 'immediately turned off' by the intake worker. 'I remember thinking, oh my G-d, I hope she's not a social worker.' Eve recalled how the investigation worker 'screamed' at her; 'she was very forceful,' 'like a drill soldier'; 'she acted like she had power over me, and I was worried about that.' Irma Morgan described her worker as having 'a lot of power.' 'You can tell them you don't like what they're doing but it does no good.' As noted in Chapter 6, mothers were cognizant of workers' concern for the children over themselves and their partners: '[Worker] didn't give a shit about me or my husband, just the kids' (IM); 'all they care is that the child is sexually abused, they don't care about the parents' (EM); 'I called and wanted to talk to her but all she wanted to care about was the girls' (AM); and 'they believe the child and they're not listening to me' (HM).

Bella Mews characterized the intake worker as inflexible and powerful. 'It was their way or no way.' However, she saw the interim worker assigned to her case quite differently:

> She was okay, at least she listened and she didn't make me feel like an unfit mother. She said she understood that I had five kids and I was work-

ing and it must be really hard and she was more understanding, but she wasn't very helpful because she was really only there to fill in for the summer. But Emma [current worker] doesn't seem to understand – all she thinks of is the protection of Kay.

Bella found Emma Webber to be 'so overbearing and authoritative and I could not tell her how I was feeling because I was afraid I'd fly off the handle.' Over time Bella realized that Emma 'was looking after the best interests of my daughter' even though it meant having to 'put my husband out' and risking losing her house. 'I think we have a better relationship now than we had at first.'

Bella's (and other women's) awareness of the protection mandate as interfering with the worker's willingness or ability to 'understand' her is most telling, as is Bella's improved relationship with her worker over time. The former comment challenges the notion that understanding mother is unrelated or antithetical to enhancing the mother protection mandate. The latter comment suggests that once mother is on side, and has accepted and adopted her mandate, the nature of her relationship with her worker improves. Thus mother's protection efforts spark improved relationships with her worker.

Harriet Miller's and Jane McNab's experiences support this speculation. Given their refusal to unconditionally accept the veracity of their children's allegations and their perceived resistance to the protection mandate, both women described unfavourable and almost punitive changes in their relationships with their workers:

> Before, she treated me fine. She was there to help. But after the allegations were made, our relationship switched ... They acted like 'look at her, she's sticking to her man,' and a lot of women do, and a lot of women can't live without their man but they can let the daughter go, and that's how I think they saw me, that was my impression. (JM)

> They hardly tell me anything any more. Why should they? I'm only the lowly mother. (JM)

> Before, I liked Fay, we got along great. We talked and that, she took the kids to play therapy, but when this all happened things changed. They used to call me to report on the kids. I used to know exactly what they were doing, and now they don't call me and the kids don't call no more and the only time I see them is on Fridays. (HM)

Both women were aware that they were perceived and treated differently as a result of their reactions to the allegations. Neither woman appeared to be treated respectfully in the protection process. In both cases, the workers noted changes to the nature of the relationship with these women who supported their husband's claims of innocence and hence failed to protect. As Fay Winters put it, 'our relationship changed. I see myself as the confronter and authority figure more than before, where I was supportive.'

Harriet felt as though 'everyone' was 'against' her. Given that a mother protector declares the perpetrator guilty, sacrifices her marriage/partnership, and complies with the required intervention, Harriet's feelings make sense. She is punished (e.g., cancelled visits), criticized, and left to feel persecuted.

The same dynamic was evident in the case of Fiona Maye. 'When the disclosure came, the worker changed her attitude toward me.' Fiona felt as though she had been 'kept in the dark' and found it difficult to trust her worker. 'I felt that whatever I said, it would be used against me, and I just didn't feel comfortable.' 'I just didn't feel like I could talk to her.' Other mothers spoke of an inability to trust, talk with, or relate to the assigned worker:

> She's decent, I like her but I don't trust her. We can sit and talk about things about the kids, and things are running smoothly and we're keeping up our end of the bargain, and so she's acting decent. But I can't talk to her! Heck no! (JM)

> I don't think I can trust her ... As far as talking to the social worker, you've got to watch what you're saying. It's hard to know what to say or if you're saying the right thing. When I go to talk to her about Chuck and the things that never happened, she either goes on another subject or she contradicts what I say or she challenges it. To me, she's pointing a finger right at Chuck and she's going to get what she wants and forget about us. (HM)

> I can't talk to her because [of] fear ... For example, if I told her that I felt threatened, I was afraid they'd think I had something to hide, why should I feel threatened? So, you don't want to show how you feel. (FM)

> I'd like to be able to tell her how I feel, and I'd like her not to judge me ... Social workers have to look at it from their experiences, instead of being

clinical and doing it from the book. It's like she's this machine, this is the way things are done, and it's the right way. (FM)

There are a lot of things I wanted to talk about ... but she can't relate from my point of view, I'm living in it and she's living on the outside of it. (AM)

Such passages are hardly suggestive of a helping relationship. Rather, they speak to an absence of trust and respect, and feelings of inferiority, disregard, fear, and confrontation. Women's experiences of being scrutinized, threatened, and criticized make sense in the context of interventions that feature their inadequacies over those of the offender and seek to transform them into, and maintain them as, mother protectors. The case of Gina Merton closes this chapter. She was the only mother interviewed who consistently voiced satisfaction with her social worker and the services received.

GINA MERTON

Gina has been with her husband, Dave, for many years. Gina raised his children from a previous marriage and more recently his grandchildren. The grandchildren came to live with the Mertons in response to a request by their son-in-law, who had been grossly abusive of the children. When asked about her decision to care for the young children after having raised her own son and her husband's children, Gina indicated that there was no choice in the matter. The abuse and neglect of her grandchildren disgusted her and 'it was just something that had to be done':

I'd be an awful wife if I said I didn't want to raise them. Family is the most important thing to me. As long as I keep my family happy, that's all I need. I don't ask for much, bingo twice a week, and the rest of the time I'm here for my family, cooking and baking and getting the kids treats and that.

Shortly after the children arrived, the Mertons took legal action to adopt them. 'Any mother that gives up her children is no mother in my books'; 'a good mother is home with the children, not running here and there and neglecting the kids the way she did.' Their request to adopt was successful.

Gina learned that the children had been physically and sexually abused by the son-in-law within months of the placement. She also discovered that her teenaged grandson had sexually abused one of his sisters. Gina's involvement with CAS centred on the adoption and help for the children in response to the abuse.

When asked about her relationship with Emma Webber and perceptions of services rendered, Gina gave a glowing report. Emma, whom she respectfully refers to as Mrs Webber, 'helped us and gave us money' to get the children proper wardrobes and braces for her granddaughter, whose teeth were broken when her father threw her down the stairs. 'I have no complaints. If I really need something, Mrs Webber finds a way to help. Oh, she is wonderful.' Gina's only complaint was that her son-in-law had not been charged for the sexual offences, 'but they're working on it.'

In caring for these children, Gina is now the designated mother protector, and, as noted in Chapter 7, she keeps her children close 'like a mother bear.' She described herself as follows:

> Me, I'm just a housewife. Don't get me wrong, I'm not complaining. It's the woman's job to do the housework, look after the kids, and provide for the family. To love my kids, and have enough in the house for my family to keep them good and happy is enough for me.

Unlike other women interviewed, Gina spoke of having been supported not blamed by her worker, and helped not hindered. She made no reference to having been disregarded or to feelings of inadequacy.

Certain features differentiate this case from the others. These features not only provide a possible explanation for the positive mother protector experience, but offer insights into state practices to protect children. To begin with, Gina was not implicated in the abuse. It occurred under someone else's care. Unlike other mothers whose inadequacies were embroiled in the problem and resolution, Gina was explicitly viewed as a resource. As such, she warrants and deserves support not repair. Given that the abuser resided elsewhere, Gina did not face having to 'choose' or 'take sides,' nor did she have to brave the consequences of separating the child from offender, moving or losing her home, or quitting her job. Unlike other mothers, the many dimensions of Gina's life as mother and wife were irrelevant to the protection application and ongoing practices. Finally, Gina's perception of herself as a homemaker, caregiver, and protector seems most compatible with the ever-present albeit hidden expectations by workers that mothers be readily available, unconditional, and selfless carers and protectors.

Summary

Conscientious and skilful workers aim to pursue the safety, security, and protection of children in the least disruptive ways. But the pursuit of protection entails an incessant focus on and transformation of women into mother protectors. This transformation rewrites the problem, denies mothers' construction of the problem, shifts the focus onto mother as failed protector, and responds accordingly, thereby ignoring women's articulation of needs and placing them in a subordinate and often defensive position. While the mother is expected to protect, the activities and relations of mother protection carry burdens, costs, and consequences. These outcomes are often hidden and more often discounted by the best of workers, as heard through such comments as needing to 'push past' the woman to get at the (mother) protector. This results in pushing away the very women needed to protect children. Arguably, then, best practices may well be counterproductive.

9

Protection as Gendered and En/Gendering: Implications for Theory, Practice, and Research

There exists in many parts of Canada a more or less comprehensive and coordinated network of institutions that function to respond to the sexual abuse of children. The child welfare system, the focus of attention here, is entrusted with promoting the best interests and protection of children from actual or suspected sexual (and other) abuse. The activities entailed in protection include investigation of allegations of abuse, assessment of risk, determination of required actions, and provision of guidance, counselling, or other services to families to support their efforts to protect children and to prevent those circumstances that may require more intrusive state interventions.

Underpinning child welfare endeavours to protect children are a collective set of beliefs that speak to the relations between the state, families, and children and suggest that, generally, the care of children properly resides with the family, 'to be carried out in its privacy' (David, 1991, p. 95). As is well known, the state may intervene in the family in response to child mistreatment by parents or caregivers. Such intervention proceeds according to predefined principles and procedures, namely supporting the independence and integrity of families, using the least disruptive efforts, and offering help based on mutual consent.

Protection of children from abuse, support for families, and efforts to refrain from intrusion into autonomous and private families appear decent, just, and impartial goals. The examination of everyday child protection practices undertaken in this book offers a depiction of the activities and relations entailed in the protection of children from mistreatment that is a far cry from being supportive and 'least disruptive.' This book has shown how the mandate to protect children from sexual abuse, while explicitly residing in the public sphere, is seemingly shifted to the private sphere of the family. This shift in the protection mandate, and its execution, are effected by accentuating certain features of the problem of child sexual abuse such that women's inadequacies are both implicated and central and by transforming (and maintaining) multidimensional women into mother protectors.

In this investigation, protection is rendered problematic. Unlike the surface view, protection appears as a complex process of hidden, taken-for-granted, gendered, and 'en/gendering' activities and relations that reverberate, with varying costs and consequences, through the lives of women in families. Protection is seen as women's work, obligation, and responsibility. In the final analysis, child welfare intervention works against the very women needed to secure protection. This chapter explores the theoretical, professional, and practical implications of my examination of protection.

The Social Relations beneath the Surface

The relocation of the protection mandate from state to family and the transformation of multidimensional women into largely one-dimensional mother protectors cast light on the social relations that lie hidden beneath child welfare protection practices. I will speak to three elements in this process: women as the bridge between separate spheres, women as a state service, and the impact of state interventions in women's lives.

Women: The Bridge between Separate Spheres

Defining the conditions that justify state intervention into families and ascertaining how interventions proceed have been central to child welfare discourse. State and family are presented as separate spheres. State 'intrusion' has been constructed as though it were separate from the autonomous and private family. While the state is not supposed to infiltrate the privacy of the family, the statutory mandate of child protection practices to investigate, assess, and intervene in order to protect children infringes on the privacy of the family. The protection mandate, in essence, legitimizes the state's manipulation of the boundary between public and private spheres.

As I have suggested, the protection mandate has been transferred to the mother. This shift speaks to a number of features of the relations between women and the state. First, child protection practices that give rise to protection through mother are by no means neutral or haphazard but clearly gendered and en/gendering. A dependence upon mother for successful protection of children and the assumption that mother is willing, able, and flexible to devote herself to this task are consistent with traditional 'separate spheres' ideology. This ideology imagines women as located in the private sphere of the family and as naturally and primarily responsible for and capable of tending to the physical, emotional, and other needs of the young, the infirm, and the aged. Everyday practices in cases of child sexual abuse also exhibit complementary assumptions about the needs of children for continuous care by their mothers and the availability of mothers to provide such care and protection.

To understand that protection is accomplished through women in families is to appreciate that the state depends on women to protect in the best interests of the child. Clearly, there is no contradiction between operationalizing protection as mother protector and dominant contemporary discourse on women as mothers in the private sphere, nor is there anything that is particularly inevitable about how the state operates to protect children from sexual abuse through mother's labour as protector. As such, everyday child protection practices, even in the best of practice settings, reproduce a gendered division of labour wherein women are relegated to and held responsible for the family.

Second, the pattern of protection by women as identified at this particular agency offers empirical support to feminist theoretical discussions on the ideological split between the public (state) and private (family). Not only is the boundary between state and family porous, changeable, and inaccurate when examined from the perspectives of women, but the manipulation of the borders between state and family pertains to particular persons in the private sphere – women. In other words, it is through women's caring, consuming, and patchworking that these borders are manipulated.

The location of the protection of children from sexual abuse in the family and its allocation to women illuminates women's complex relations with the welfare state as unpaid carers, consumers, and intermediaries. From the identification and accentuation of the problem of child sexual abuse in terms of mother's failure to protect, to interventions aimed at convincing mother to fulfil her mandate, it is assumed that mother is the best, if not the only, unpaid caregiver/serviceworker. It is assumed that, regardless of her relationships to the public sphere in general and wage labour in particular, she can and will patch together whatever service or resource is needed to protect her child. It is also assumed that she will bridge the (state) mandate to protect through her transformation of multidimensional self into mother protector. That women's extensive and complex servicing and patching coalesce to protect renders public and private spheres intimately interconnected. It also calls into question the very nature of state services as distinct from women's servicework and the mechanisms by which resources and services are allocated and delivered.

Mother Protector as a 'State' Service

While the state can be seen as a distributor of benefits or provider of goods and services, the family – more accurately women in families – has been viewed as a producer, processor, and consumer (Sassoon, 1987a) of state resources. Laura Balbo (1987) has suggested that women's cheap (as in free) and flexible (as in available) service work transforms state resources into usable goods. She argues that, in contrast to a conception of an interventionist state as relieving the family, it is women who actually arrange, negotiate, and convert public services for personal need. As such, women in families are far from relieved; rather, their workload is increased, as has been seen throughout this study.

In this exploration of protection practices, the demarcation between state service and women's service has not been entirely unambiguous. As documented here, intervention appeared to be based on the transformation of women into mother protectors; the extensive, expected, and often invisible supporting and believing, monitoring and mediating by women – subsumed under the concept of 'mother protector' – formed the crux of intervention. To be blunt, mother protector appeared to be the state resource, good, or service; she was, at once, serviceworker, patchworker, and labourer (albeit unpaid and unrecognized) for the state. Though positioned as a 'client,' she hardly emerges as a 'consumer.'

That women are positioned as 'clients' – rather than 'consumers' with rights to state services and benefits as outlined by Fraser (1989) – again suggests a gendered and en/gendering subtext in protection practices. As detailed here, the problem of child sexual abuse was rewritten from a child having been sexually abused to a child needing and having a right to protection. This transformation of the problem embroils women as potentially defective mother protectors. Women appeared not as self-determined and determining co-participants in the protection undertaking but as predefined mother-clients whose protective obligations and skills had obviously failed and were thus in need of repair. Being failed or defective mother-clients, their needs were constructed as 'maternal needs' and 'their sphere of activities as that of the family,' to borrow Fraser's wording (1989, p. 153).

The positioning of women as mother-clients and mother protectors must necessarily give rise to tension. Mothering, including protecting, is not supposed to be problematic. 'Mothers are not supposed to need or have the right to need social services or social funds' (Rosenberg, 1988, p. 387). Good mothers cope; mother-clients have obviously failed. As well, because mothering, like mother protecting, is constructed as woman's role, mothers are always expected to remain 'in character' (Rosenberg, 1988). The activities and relations, labour, costs and consequences, and the 'low control'/'high demand' (to borrow Rosenberg's [1988] wording) entailed in mother protecting, however, are eclipsed.

The Impact of Intervention on Women

Feminist scholars have long debated the effects of state responses to women's needs and issues. The extent to which the state is liberating or oppressive for women,[1] supportive of families, and capable of challenging the prevailing distribution of power in general, and traditional gender relations in particular, is central to feminist appraisals of the impact of state endeavours on women. In light of these aspects of the relations between the state, families, and women, what might be the impact of the transformation of women into mother protectors?

In this book, the transformation of women into mother protectors emerged with costs and consequences for them. Highlighting women's inadequacies meant denying their thoughts on both problem and resolution. The scrutiny of women's awareness and immediate reactions translated into feelings of blame and censure. Interventions aimed at transforming women into mother protectors were permeated with expectations – even threats – for mother to protect. As well, interventions aimed at enforcing and reinforcing protection entailed adjustments to women's daily routines and relationships and were experienced as intrusive, disruptive, and nonsensical. The narrow expectation of mother to be the primary protector, coupled with beliefs about children's needs for mother's support and protection, resulted in the disregard for the multiple dimensions of women's lives, not to mention the near-complete exemption of men as nonoffending fathers from the protection mandate. While protection appeared as women's responsibility, its impact on women went by and large unnoticed. One would be hard pressed to view protection by mother as gender-neutral; rather, it sustains traditional gender relations.

The gendered nature of protection practice, however, is implicit. Explicit, instead, are state efforts to protect children from mistreatment by supporting the family and aiming to intervene in the least restrictive ways. From this surface view, the transformation of women into mother protectors promotes the maintenance of children in their mother's care and thus appears to be supportive and noninvasive. However, from the perspective of women in families, 'support' is hardly an appropriate word to describe their experience of child protection interventions. Though considerable energies go into investigating allegations, assessing risk to the child, and securing immediate protection – all activities that involve the scrutiny of women – there is insufficient support to aid mother with the protection mandate; her experience is largely one of intrusion and disruption.

It should be noted that the 'least-disruptive' principle in Ontario's child protection legislation is concerned with preventing placement in substitute care. As such (as was heard through interviews with workers), disruption for women in this regard was irrelevant or invisible. Nonetheless, the near absence of support and women's experiences of interventions as intrusive and disruptive offer insights into the workings of the state. First of all, the main resource in protection is mother. The presence of mother and all that she is expected to be are almost enough to justify the dearth of state support and disregard for her experience. As Sassoon (1987b) put it, only in the absence of women in families does the state provide fundamental service. Second, 'support for the family' entails merging the protection of children with the family. This merger assumes, as if a fait accompli, that women's identities and needs are synonymous with their identities and needs as mothers and with those of their children. Again, the posturing of women as mothers is seen, and the impact of everyday intervention is seen as sustaining traditional gender stereotypes for women.

Feminist analyses of women's relations with the state have suggested that 'support for the family' is really support for family responsibility, and family responsibility is really women's responsibility (Pascall, 1986). While responsible for protecting, women receive little support to carry out the mandate and are accorded no control in fulfilling the responsibility; nor is their existing workload adjusted so that they can protect. By this, I mean that the responsibility for protection is 'added on' to women's already existing obligations, whatever they might be. Simply put, women are expected to protect; only in the absence of successfully procured mother protectors does the state provide protection, and only in an effort to bolster 'mother protector' are supplementary or supportive services available. As Dale and Foster (1986) pointed out, state services often aim to supplement women's expected caring activities. State services reported in this book were, by and large, compulsory (e.g., attending sessions with worker or group meetings, accepting child management services, etc.) and aimed at enhancing the successful transfer of the protection mandate to mothers. This is not to suggest that no benefits were derived from services, nor that the women were definitively opposed to and oppressed by protection. However, costs far outweighed benefits, and benefits seemed to be contingent upon mother's unconditional availability, willingness, and ability to accept, embrace, and fulfil the protection mandate while relinquishing most control over the workings of the mandate. In this sense, Gillian Pascall's (1986) conception of the state as eroding women's control seems appropriate.[2]

The state depends upon and expects women to offer mother protector service. This expectation assumes women's availability, if not flexibility, and thus reflects a relationship between the welfare state, the paid labour force, and the domestic sphere that is 'organized as if women were continuing a traditional role' (Sassoon, 1987b, p. 160). Taken one step further, this assumption seems to deny such significant social and economic changes as women's increased participation in the paid labour force, regardless of the nature and extent of that participation (e.g., occupational, classification, and wage discrepancies; full vs. part-time employment). Today, of course, most women do not function only as 'mother' and 'wife,' dependent upon a male wage. Thus, in considering the extent to which state interventions alter the prevailing distribution of power and traditional gender relations, I would suggest that the mother protection intervention hampers, if not excludes, women's participation in the paid labour force. It assumes that such participation is marginal and thereby reinforces economic and personal dependence on men, if not on the state, and thus sustains women's positions as unpaid labourers in the home.

There are implications in assuming that women's relation to the

Protection as Gendered and En/Gendering 183

world of paid work is marginal. When a woman drops out of the labour force to care for her child or other dependants, the costs to her and her household are not only extensive but often unrecognized. Given that women are assumed to be located in the private sphere, and allocated to protect, patch, and bridge, out of love or duty and for the sake of others, the costs to her of such a sacrifice are invisible. She is depended upon and expected to assume yet another aspect of domestic, unpaid labour: protecting. And she is expected to do so in the best interests of her child, with little regard for what might be in her own interests.

Another set of implications concern the costs, for the state, of reproducing the gendered division of protection and other caring labour. Feminists have suggested that reinforcing women's position as unpaid labourers in the home is an advantageous response to the fiscal crisis of the welfare state and an effective, efficient, and humane means to connect, via women's patchwork, state and family (Dale & Foster, 1986; Sapiro, 1990). This position applies to the transformation of women into mother protectors. It could be argued that the allocation of protection to mothers is a cost-saving measure for the state. While the state expends a certain amount of money on professional services – for example, the social work labour required to investigate and assess allegations of abuse – the allocation of protection to mothers certainly saves the state those expenses related to substitute care for children. Thus, to cease depending on women as unpaid caregivers and protectors could be costly. It should be pointed out that this allocation of finite funds to social work services necessarily means that such money is not designated for the recipients of service – women and children.

However, there is another way to look at this issue: It is possible that mother protection does not actually save costs. Mother protection entails women's marginal or flexible labour force participation or withdrawal from the labour force, requires separation of child from offender, and results in potential loss of at least one if not the only source of income. It thus may actually cost the state by rendering women and children financially dependent on it (e.g., through welfare, Mother's Allowance, subsidized housing, and the like). As scholars have pointed out, families involved with a child welfare agency are usually already disadvantaged, marginalized, and disenfranchised. A look at the women in this case study reveals vulnerability in at least two areas. First, these women were engaged in rearing a considerable number of children (biological, adoptive, and stepchildren) throughout their lives. Of all the mothers, only two had families of one or two

184 What's Mother Got to Do with It?

children. The others were responsible for between three and six children. Second, the mothers in this study had low-paying jobs or were unemployed. Thus, removal of the one, if not only, breadwinner necessarily heightened the costs of the intervention' for these women.

One final point on costs and consequences centres on the contradictory effect of interventions that are aimed at embracing mothers as protectors but result in estranged and damaged worker–client relations. As has been detailed earlier in the book, this outcome appeared both unanticipated and counterproductive. In the end, mothers seemed more alienated than engaged, and both workers and mothers seemed frustrated and tense. This outcome cannot benefit the well-being and protection of children. To study, plan for, and serve children with a disregard for their female caregivers – their mothers – does not appear to be in the best interests of children.

Of course, the child welfare system is not responsible for changing the prevailing distribution of power that maintains the oppression or inequality of women. Similarly, this arm of the state cannot meet 'all of the needs of families and children' but it can and must 'do its part in making change' (Callahan, 1993b, p. 203). Callahan calls for feminists to rethink rather than reject child welfare state services. This invitation seems most appropriate, given that women and children are the primary subjects of the welfare state in general and child welfare in particular and yet their voices have not been heard. In this spirit, how might this case study inform child protection policy and practice?

**Interpreting Children's Interests, Needs, and Rights:
The Place of Women**

In embarking upon a feminist critique of the welfare state, Nancy Fraser (1989) suggests that we begin with an appreciation for the ways in which issues get framed. Typically, she notes, social welfare issues are framed as follows:

> Shall the state undertake to satisfy the social needs of a given constituency, and if so, to what degree? Now this way of framing issues permits only a relatively small number of answers, and it tends to cast debates in quantitative terms. More importantly, it takes for granted the definition of needs in question, as if that were self-evident and beyond dispute. (p. 145)

Talk of need coexists, 'albeit often uneasily,' with talk of rights and interests (Fraser, 1990, p. 200). The satisfaction of needs, suggests Fraser, always entails interpretation, which can be disparate, controversial, and problematic, not to mention 'politically contested' (p. 202). To engage in the politics of needs interpretation is not without obstacles for feminist analysts. 'At the heart of such politics lie questions about what various groups of women really need and whose interpretations of women's needs should be authoritative' (Fraser, 1989, p. 145). In response to such challenging questions, Fraser offers the following insights. She reminds feminists that 'authoritative views purporting to be neutral and disinterested actually express the partial and interested perspectives of dominant social groups' (Fraser, 1990, p. 219). While it might be argued that all interpretations stem from specific, interested locations in society, we can ascertain who is advantaged and disadvantaged by a particular interpretation of need and whether or not societal patterns of dominance and subordination are challenged or accommodated (Fraser, 1990).

With this discussion in mind, the official, authoritative, and neutral view of children's needs following an experience of sexual abuse is, first and foremost, the need and right to protection as ensconced in legislation. Alongside protection are the principles of support for families in caring for children and the provision of help with as little intrusion and as much continuity as possible.

The overarching conclusion reached in this exploration of contemporary practice is that the protection mandate is shifted from state to mother through her transformation to mother protector. In essence, this process represents an interpretation of what children need as well as what women are constructed to be. As seen in Chapter 5, certain features of the problem of child sexual abuse are accentuated over others, resulting in a shift in focus from the offender's actions to women's deficiency as wives and mothers. The implication of women was found to be necessary to rewrite the problem from 'sexual abuse' to 'failure to protect.' As such, women were positioned as defective mothers, who 'needed' to improve their inadequacies and transgressions.

While this is not a particularly complimentary light in which to view protection practices, it nonetheless gives rise to a view of those practices as interpretations of children's and women's needs. As an interpretation, room for manoeuvre is found.

It seems imperative to name and acknowledge mother protector. From being the 'cornerstone' in the pathological incest family (Lustig, Spellman, Dresser, & Murray, 1966) to being the 'cornerstone of effective intervention' (James, n.d.), mothers have been central to our understanding of the problem of child sexual abuse and its resolution. As documented here, protection emerged as a feature of women's unpaid servicing and patching labour, labour which I have called 'mother protection.' Simultaneously, the labour of mother protection, with all its costs and consequences, was largely concealed. To name mother as protector is by no means a neutral act. Naming women as mother protectors renders visible a central tenet of intervention that necessarily casts a different light on women's relation to the state.

To identify mother as protector is to confront the positioning of women as 'mothers.' In this case study, the needs and rights of children eclipsed those of their mothers. The women's needs and rights were ignored, cast as irrelevant in relation to the child's need for (mother) protection. In explicitly designating mother as protector, my intent is not to deny her many dimensions as a woman, but rather to recognize that she is expected and compelled to undergo a transformation, experiencing costs and consequences that extend far beyond the protection mandate and its execution. In other words, to view mother as protector is to necessitate an exploration of her needs, her wants, and her rights as a woman who actually 'chooses' how to engage herself – to what extent and by which rules – in the protection process. If child welfare analysts and practitioners continue to hold that the well-being and protection of children are contingent upon mother's well-being, then we cannot continue to disregard the many dimensions of women's lives, including mothering.

Placing 'Mother Protector' Front and Centre

The identification of mother as protector offers an opportunity to view women's relation to the state differently. For one, she can be seen as a state resource. She can be identified as a central feature of intervention. In both instances, I accept that children need protection and that using mother as protector may well be preferable to apprehending the child. I also accept that the transformation process is intrusive, unsettling, and costly, and thus I ask how mothers can be helped to protect in ways that are less costly to her and her children.

What would happen if mother protectors were thought of as a state resource, much akin to foster parents? As a state resource, she would be eligible for financial remuneration, emotional support, and respite service. Though it could be argued that payment for her labour places her at risk for increased scrutiny by the state, Miller (1991) notes that value is often associated with remuneration. The question of how much to pay for women's work (caring, servicing, patching, and protecting) is by no means a small matter nor one that is confined to mother protecting.

Another way of repositioning the concept of mother protector in relation to the state is to recognize her centrality in intervention. Her effectiveness can be maximized when her needs are taken into consideration. Here, the intent is to dispel the assumption that women's caring responsibilities are individual, private matters, detached from their social and economic context (Parton & Parton, 1988/89).

Throughout these accounts, mothers were expected to protect and assumed to be able to protect their children from sexual abuse. How can this protection be enhanced? To answer this question is to challenge how the welfare state operates as a juridical-administrative-therapeutic (JAT) state apparatus (see Chapter 2) (Fraser, 1989). As a JAT, state practices rewrite needs and impose meaning. As has been the case in this book, children's need for protection was interpreted to mean that children need mothers to protect. Most of what followed was the pursuit of this need through the transformation of women into mother protectors. As a JAT, there is little room for mother protectors to participate in the definition of need. This process was found to be counterproductive and rife with tensions between workers and mothers, ranging from the construction of the problem, to impressions of contributing factors, to desired outcomes and their effects. Given that the understanding of a problem is intimately connected with the institution charged with its resolution, accepting mothers' construction of the problem and its resolution is almost unimaginable. Their conceptions of the problem would, after all, entail removal of women as central to the problem, redesign of the child welfare response that no longer requires mother/wife blame, and attention to prevailing power relations. However, to continue to dismiss or challenge tensions in the name of protection is to risk alienating mother as protector. Where, then, is there room for manoeuvre?

For starters, the focus should be shifted back to the offender, who, of all people, definitely knows of the abuse, certainly fails to protect his child's well-being, and almost always denies his behaviour. Mothers should be commended for making efforts to handle the problem. The gender-specific features of the problem and its resolution should be recorded in case files, court orders and agreements, conference proceedings, and so forth. And the gendered composition of protection as women's work should be documented. Both workers and mothers know that it is mother who is expected (and vows) to be there to watch and supervise, forecast and identify warning signs, and report them. Nothing prevents practitioners from accurately portraying protection, with all its costs and consequences for women, throughout official documentation.

From the assessment to the investigation and its aftermath, women described experiences that were predominantly unpleasant and unnerving. They were blamed for failing to protect, pressured to embrace the protection priority, denied support and aid, and refused a voice in the direction of the protective effort, from the first hours of the investigation and lasting through their experiences with the child welfare agency. From the cases described in this book, the major part of intervention consisted of transforming women into mother protectors, denying their several dimensions, coercing them to 'choose' to protect, and offering little else. Not surprisingly, mother protectors were left with the impression that the state worked against them.

To turn this outcome around, intervention might proceed in a more forthright manner. Practitioners might detail the dearth of options available to the mother, the sacrifices, adjustments, and consequences that she can expect, and the degree of control she will have. Though this candour sounds idealistic, it seems even more unrealistic to intervene on the assumption that the transformation of women into mother protectors is a natural, painless, and problem-free labour of love.

Intervention might also be tailored to increase control and lower demand on women as they shift into mother protector gear. As long as women serve as the primary protectors of children, questions around allocation of resources to this task must consider their needs. This is no minor recommendation. It flies in the face of one of the 'key characteristics or skills which professionals are deemed to possess': the right to define need (Dale & Foster, 1986, p. 104). It also contradicts the notion of mother protector as a cheap (unpaid), ever-flexible, and available 'service worker' who transforms the state mandate into actual protection.

Room for manoeuvre may be found by listening and responding to women's articulation of the material needs they require in their protective efforts. Most of the resources required would not emanate from the child welfare agency and thus would not affect its budget. For those resources that have budgetary implications, such as transportation services, I am reminded of the mothers' descriptions of agency-based services that were required but not particularly wanted nor deemed useful (e.g., therapeutic sessions that focused on marital affairs or communication defects). If state services really want to support children in families, then administrators need to replace rhetoric with hard cash.

While developing a flexible service system could prove to be a daunting task, Marilyn Callahan reminds us that

> all talk of empowerment fades ... if a service system is unable to listen to what clients say they need, cannot design flexible services to meet those needs, and refuses to allow clients to select services as they wish, particularly clients who by virtue of age, sex, class, and race are profoundly disadvantaged. (1993b, p. 197)

Of course, listening to women express their needs and fulfilling those needs are not the same thing. Procuring scarce resources is beyond the control of individual social workers. However this feature of the working environment need not be concealed. Practitioners can and should record with precision the conditions within which they function to aid in the protection of children from mistreatment. Should more 'intrusive' protective measures be required, the obstacles to protection ought to be examined. Whether women express fear of or need or love for the offender or concerns about loss of home or income, social workers must accept, document, and respond to what women want, need, and feel.

Beyond 'Mother' as the 'Only' Protector: Father's Obligations Considered

Through this book I have suggested that, rather than constructing women as one-dimensional 'mother protectors,' we should view women as a central feature of contemporary intervention strategies. This emphasis on mother is not intended to propose that only she can function as protector. The roles and responsibilities of fathers must be factored into the protection equation as well.

Given that the majority of sexual offences against children and youths are perpetrated by males, one might wonder how fathers or father-figures could be considered protectors of children. While it has been suggested that males of all ages predominate as child sexual abusers, survey studies provide an analysis of offenders that differs from the types of abusers that come to child welfare attention. For example, approximately 60 per cent of abusers that come to the attention of a CAS are relatives; the remaining 40 per cent are unrelated or extrafamilial. Of 'related' offenders, biological, step-, and foster fathers comprise about 35 per cent of total offenders. In the context of the total list of offenders (familial and nonfamilial), father-figures represented 21 per cent of total offenders (IPCA, n.d.). As noted earlier, surveys reveal that related offenders comprise about 30 per cent of the total population of offenders, and that father-figures account for about 7 per cent of all identified offenders. Methodological and contextual issues aside,[3] fathers and father-figures account for about one-quarter of reported cases and less than one-tenth of those noted by adult survivors. This means that fathers can be expected, if not obligated, to engage in the protection process in 75 per cent of those incidents reported, investigated, assessed, and treated by a child welfare agency.

To help mother to protect in ways that are less costly to her, I suggest that nonoffending fathers be considered as co-protectors. The overwhelming tendency for male offenders and nonoffenders alike to consistently fade from the fore reinforces the notion that mothers are the best and the only protectors. While protection by the child's parent(s) is preferable to protection by the state, it does not logically follow that mother is the only protector available in most cases. Thus, assessments of prior knowledge of abuse and responses to abuse, as well as casework objectives, must take into consideration the nonoffending mother and, whenever applicable, the nonoffending father/father-figure too. This means that the nonoffending father/father-figure would be asked to support and believe his child and be informed of the dynamics and signs of abuse. His involvement in aiding his child to address the sexual abuse could prove beneficial for all involved.

That fathers/father-figures in no way comprise the 'majority' of child sexual offenders should be startling, given that men have rarely been constructed as 'nonoffenders.' Women, in contrast, are almost always constructed as 'Mother.' Not just a double standard, this conception of men as either perpetrators or distinterested bystanders in the protection of the child effectively ensures that they will continue to be excused from the care, concern, and responsibility for their children.

To include men in the care and protection of children is neither a straightforward matter nor one that engenders consensus among feminists. As Eisenstein (1981, p. 187) pointed out, when we ask men to 'help' rear and protect children, we must understand that we are 'speaking of a fundamental reorganization of society':

> The entire social organization of the way people live their lives, as well as think about them, is involved. The organization of wage labour, the relationship between home and work, the conception of public life, and the definition of masculine and feminine have to be completely rethought and restructured. (p. 187)

To abstain from thinking of fathers as 'nonoffending' parents supports dominant conceptions of the problem. The configuration of 'father–daughter incest' has, almost unfailingly, shaped understandings of child sexual abuse in scholarly and professional discourse as well as everyday practice, regardless of the divergent forms of abuse. Conceptual frameworks for understanding the dynamics of child sexual abuse need to be adjusted. The extent to which abuses perpetrated by relatives differ from those committed by nonrelatives with respect to dynamics and effects must be tackled in order to rethink child protection policy and practice. By challenging the traditional image of child sexual abuse as a problem of dysfunctional 'family' dynamics, implicating all members and particularly mother, a different concept of women as mothers can be constructed.

The final point to be raised regarding fathers' involvement concerns how women can better manage following a separation from the abuser. In many cases, the removal of a male partner might also mean the loss of his wage and her withdrawal from the labour force. As I have suggested, mother protectors' intimate and labour-related relationships are regarded as flexible, negotiable, even severable. To borrow Laura Balbo's words, 'let us be sure that we fully understand what this implies, in the context where the majority of adult women are both housewives and workers in the labour force' (1987, p. 51). Of course, in response to the sexual abuse of a child, the demands and expectations placed upon women are overwhelming, and whether by choice or necessity or fear, some women forsake their place in the public labour force. For those men who have offended, we might ask for maintenance or financial support.

Revisiting Child Welfare Discourse and Practice

A key issue that emerges in child welfare discourse is the place of the state in the private lives of families. Child welfare analysts have pondered the definitions of mistreatment, the situations that justify state intervention, and the principles upon which such interventions should proceed. A perusal of child welfare discourse reveals repeated references to state intrusion, concern with the benefit-to-harm ratio of interventions, and the relative merits of interventionist and family-autonomy approaches to protection.

When we talk of intrusion and coercion, disruption and restriction, benefits and risks, and the interventionist or noninterventionist state, we must ask whose perspectives we have drawn our conclusions from. These debates seem to have been generated without concern for the primary caretakers of children: women. To recognize that women, not the state, are the expected and assumed protectors of children is to call for an evaluation of the relationship between the state and family from the perspective of mothers. In this study, interventions were experienced as intrusive and often coercive for mother protectors. Protection was rife with pressure, force, and threats, and women were burdened with obligations and expectations, as was seen during the investigation phase of intervention.

During the investigation, the worker must assess, almost immediately, the degree of risk to the child in her or his home. This assessment thus focuses on the capacity of mother to protect the child from further sexual abuse. At a time when a mother is most vulnerable, least informed, and frequently ill equipped, she is appraised for her protective responses and priorities. While workers are pressured to make an evaluation in the best interests of the child, it seems to me that children's interests are not best served if the interests of the primary carer are not also fully appraised. As explicated throughout this book, the shift in the protection mandate from state to mother tends to occur almost immediately; workers push past multidimensional woman to get at mother protector. This pattern is not unusual. Child welfare analysts have well-documented protection services that place great emphasis on investigating complaints while providing little in the way of follow-up services and supports. However, while success may be inferred once compliance from the mother has been secured, the longer-term effect is far from successful, with anger and alienation between women and their social workers being a common result.

We are thus compelled to investigate what measures might aid in thwarting the estrangement of mother protectors from child protection workers. To do so requires us to step back and consider the context within which child welfare workers operate. By now, it is clear that the best practice of intervening through the mother as protector ought to be subject to critical analysis. In exploring how protection comes about, I do not want to understate the real dangers facing some children and their need for protection. Social workers do need ways to identify avenues of protection. As argued here, 'mother protector' as a central feature of intervention promotes the rapid scrutiny of mothers in such a way so as to conceal the ideological and material contexts in which the mothering of children takes place.

As I have argued elsewhere (Krane & Davies, 2000), social workers, in their everyday child protection practice, confront mothers struggling to care for their children, often under extremely trying conditions. Some workers attempt to understand and address mothers' complex lives and concerns. They may be well aware of the constraints mothers face and may even struggle with the pursuit of (mother) protection. However, child protection workers are held to account for the well-being and security of children. Nowhere is this more striking than in the recent case of a protection worker who was charged (alongside the mother) with criminal negligence causing the death of a baby. This is a stark reminder of workers' vulnerability in their efforts to ensure the protection and well-being of children.[4] Social workers in child protection must make judgments as to what constitutes appropriate protection and safety, but the statutory context of their practice necessitates an emphasis on children's needs and interests. Despite an appreciation of a given mother's situation, workers must appraise how a woman's behaviour affects her children and their safety (Featherstone, 1997a).

From the frontline perspective, this is no easy task. While workers might make every effort to refrain from mother blame, at the same time they cannot exonerate 'women from any responsibility at all, as this would diminish women's sense of effectiveness and agency altogether' (Burck & Speed, 1995, p. 3, cited in Featherstone, 1997b, p. 178). In the arena of child protection, further attention to what constitutes appropriate protection seems wanting, as does consideration of 'whether any standards of evaluation are needed and, if so, what these might be' (Featherstone 1997a, p. 8). To evade these dilemmas, Featherstone points out, is to leave 'social workers unsupported in the face of ... maternal neglect and abuse' (1997a, p. 8).

As Burck and Speed (1995) suggested, we need to find ways to simultaneously 'hold macro understandings about cultural tendencies to blame mothers alongside micro understandings about the complexities and variations in women's and children's own experiences' (cited in Featherstone 1997b, p. 178). How might this occur in practice? We might imagine creating practice environments that allow the opportunity to explore and reflect upon subjective and material contexts of maternal care and protection. In this vein, Parton advocates a rehabilitation of the concept of uncertainty in practice contexts:

> The rehabilitation of the idea of uncertainty, and the permission to talk about an indeterminacy which is not amenable to or reducible to authoritative definition or measurement, is an important step ... for recognizing the contemporary complexities of practice. Rather than seeing a commitment to uncertainty as undermining and lying at the margins of practice ... [Parton] would suggest it lies at the heart, and, that its recognition provides an opportunity for valuing practice, practitioners, and the people with whom they work. Notions of ambiguity, complexity and uncertainty are at the core of social work and should be built upon and not defined out. A commitment to uncertainty opens up creativity and novel ways of thinking. (Parton, 1998, p. 23)

To build upon this recommendation, the integration of a 'mothering narrative' might prove fruitful (Krane & Davies, 2000). Such a narrative could provide women with the space to tell their own stories as mothers, to give voice to their actual daily physical and emotional caregiving labour and the context within which their mothering occurs. Such a narrative might enable women to reflect on their subjective experiences of mothering, including its stresses, emotional intensity, challenges, and pleasures. The mothering narrative could make visible the complex and often contradictory nature of mothers' feelings in relation to the sexual abuse of their children and its disclosure. It could allow their interpretations of events to become a meaningful component in both assessment and the development of 'relationship-based' practice (Howe, 1998). For social workers, the narrative might engender a deeper appreciation of the conditions faced by women and their children and allow a more accurate evaluation of their situation.

In addition to the mother narrative, social workers might be encouraged to critically question their assumptions of (mother) protection and how these ideals are derived from their own social locations and maternal experiences. Space in worker supervision could be created where practitioners might explore these themes and the 'complexity of the relationships they encounter' (Featherstone, 1997b, p. 168) and freely express the sometimes intense emotions produced by their contact with mothers and children. Such a climate of reflection might promote an emphasis on support for both mothers and social workers, not to mention for the children.

These suggestions may not be so easily accomplished within a statutory framework for practice that is all too often 'defensive and adversarial' in nature (Featherstone, 1997b, p. 174). Differing opinions about what is needed in a given case do arise between social workers and their clients, as do disagreements over children's safety and protection. In this arena, child protection workers occupy positions of power and authority in relation to their clients. Indeed, the mere presence of the child protection worker is an ever-present reminder to the mother of the threat of losing her children.

Feminist social work theorists have wrestled with the issue of power relations between workers and clients. Some critics have challenged simplistic understandings of power as exercised only one way, that is, from professionals to clients (Ferguson, 1997; Gordon, 1988; Healy, 1998). Others have taken issue with uncritical prescriptions for relationships between workers and clients marked by rational ideals of mutuality and shared power (Healy, 1998). Family relationships, feminists have argued, are also active arenas of power relations. Healy states that we need to acknowledge the productive and necessary use of statutory power for the redistribution of power within families, for example, between children and parents, men and women. She recommends that child protection workers make judgments and be prepared to exercise authority to protect children where they see it is necessary. They must also be willing to acknowledge their observations and the sense they make of them. The problem is not in judgment itself, but in the lack of reflexivity in the way judgments have been developed and applied. Professional judgments should be transparent and open to critical reflection and challenge (Healy, 2000). This process could be enhanced by a more in-depth understanding of maternal subjectivities, an acknowledgment of the physical and emotional demands of mother protection and the conditions in which women struggle to support their children and secure their protection.

Closing Thoughts

By the end of my investigations, the agency that formed the basis of this study was in the process of considering ways to better engage women at the onset of the protection process. One suggestion was to ask 'successful' mother protectors to help other mothers by sharing their experiences of involvement with the agency. This endeavour may provide a kind of support that an already overburdened worker, even with the best of intentions, could not possibly offer. It might also reinforce the mother protector mandate with a disregard, albeit less forceful, for the many dimensions of women's lives, and the costs and consequences of protection. Further research into this matter would be valuable.

As I conclude this book, I admit that I have refrained from suggesting what women 'should' do with respect to accepting, challenging, or refuting the protection mandate with all its costs and consequences. I have not advocated separation from their partners nor have I identified ways to encourage her to protect her child. I am, however, committed to pursuing paths to protecting children that are less costly for women as mother protectors, more compatible with their needs and goals, and of course helpful to children. As seen in this study, women differed in the extent to which they supported their male partners, believed in their children's allegations, and were willing to embrace the protection priority. Regardless of these variations, the women spoke of a future when their families would be reunited. Yet, regardless of their efforts as mother protectors, they expressed caution about declaring that it was 'safe enough' to allow their families, which may include children and offenders, to reunite. This scepticism is both telling and distressing. It asks us to question practices that respond to atrocities against children by featuring women's inadequacies as part of the problem and its resolution. It suggests unrelenting expectations and evaluations of women, and it warns us that as long as protection is realized through mothers in the private sphere, neither the state nor men will have to carry the costs or share in the protection of children.

Notes

1 Introduction

1 This story received worldwide attention. Excerpts reported here were obtained from the following newspaper articles: 'Family ties: Judge orders teen-age daughter chained to her mother for a month,' *The Sun Sentinel*, 15 December 1995: 3A, and 'Tethered teen's mom hospitalized: Woman treated for anxiety drug overdose,' *The Sun Sentinel*, 11 January 1996: 9A.
2 This phrase is borrowed from the title of the groundbreaking work of Canadian feminist scholar Betty Carter (1990).
3 Jaclyn Miller (1991) refers to the 'missing persons' phenomenon in child welfare.
4 Discussions with each worker revealed few choices in case selection. BW identified four possible cases. In two, the allegations were unfounded and the files were closed at Intake. In another case, the mother refused to participate as she was moving to another city. She also identified AM, who took part in the study.

CW had no current cases. As she was the investigating worker on the IM case, which was discussed with IM's family service worker, it was reviewed with CW for the 'intake' perspective.

GW ran a support program for victims and did not conduct investigations. No cases were available from her. She was interviewed for her insights gleaned from her years of involvement with women in the mothers' support group.

DW identified three cases. One closed case was used for the pretest. The two remaining cases (IM and EM) participated and were also discussed with their respective intake workers (CW and AW). Both of these cases were near closure.

FW had four cases. The HM case provided a most recent disclosure. It was investigated by FW and represented the longest case on her workload. FM was her second most recent case. Both HM and FM agreed to take part. In another case, the mother and children moved out of the county. In the fourth case, the mother refused to participate.

EW was the only worker with a pool of cases from which to sample. Of her eight cases, four were inappropriate: one moved; in another, both parents were deaf and mute, and funds were unavailable for an interpreter for research purposes; DM, whose common-law partner's brother sexually assaulted their children, chose not to participate, though her case was discussed with the worker; in another case, EW 'suspected' intrafamilial sexual abuse but no disclosure had yet been made. Four cases were left to consider: CM refused to participate; BM, the worker's most recent case, agreed to participate; JM, the second most recent case, also agreed to participate. The final case identified was GM. In this case, GM was the adoptive mother of her husband's four grandchildren, who had been sexually and physically abused prior to relocating with the Ms. GM was selected to participate because, as the data collection phase commenced, it was obvious that few cases were available for inclusion in the study.

5 Of the eight women eliminated, one participated in the pretest. In two cases, the allegations were unfounded. Three women moved, one case needed an interpreter, and one case involved suspected but unsupported evidence of intrafamilial child sexual abuse.

2 Women and the Welfare State

1 This is not to deny historical variations in what constitutes the public and the private or to reinforce the gendered division, given that 'the split does not always equal a male/female distinction' (Dahlerup, 1987, p. 105).
2 The ideology of domesticity, which emerged by the early nineteenth century, established women as responsible for 'the moral and everyday affairs of the home' (Andersen, 1988, p. 150); women's experiences were limited to the 'private world of the family' (p. 150). Though large numbers of working-class women performed wage labour, the 'definition of womanhood as idealized femininity stemmed from the bourgeois origins of the cult of domesticity' (pp. 150–1).
3 Findlay (1987), Pupo (1988), Schneider (1990), and Walker (1990) examine the ways in which feminist appeals to the state are acknowledged, absorbed, and transformed. These writers variously address how state responses to women's issues appear liberating but fail to inspire substantial changes in

women's everyday lives or in relations of power between women and men.
4 A similar analysis was undertaken by Barbara Nelson (1990, p. 124), who views the U.S. welfare state as 'fundamentally divided into two channels': one designed for predominantly white male workers and the other for predominantly white female mothers.
5 For women raising children without a male breadwinner, a striking contradiction appears. Women are supposed to, but cannot, be 'normative mothers' because they are not offered daycare, job training, or a family wage but rather are stigmatized, humiliated, and harassed (Fraser, 1989, p. 153).

3 Family Ties: Child Welfare and the Protection of Children from Sexual Abuse

1 Headline and story details are cited from the Ottawa *Citizen*, 16 August 1996, p. C1.
2 Child sexual abuse is not only a child welfare matter. Federal initiatives during the 1980s clearly established sexual abuses of children as a criminal matter. In fact substantial changes were made to the criminal justice system as a medium for protection (see Badgley, 1984; Stewart, 1987; Wells, 1990). As well the 1980s saw a proliferation of treatment and support programs for victims, family members, and offenders (Rogers, 1988). Though child sexual abuse is complex and involves a nexus of social institutions, the everyday activities of protection remain under the purview of the child welfare arm of the state.
3 More detailed descriptions of the investigative and clinical components of the interview with the child victim are available elsewhere (Cage, 1988; Dawson, 1982; Sgroi, Porter, & Blick, 1985; Spencer & Nicholson, 1988).
4 Whether or not criminal charges are laid or a finding of guilt results from criminal proceedings, one cannot imply that a child is not in need of protection. As noted in the protocol, the police/CAS team may have reasonable grounds to suspect that abuse occurred but are unable to attain a conviction in criminal court due to lack of corroborating evidence or inadmissibility of the child's testimony (MTSCCA, 1986).
5 In his examination of the relationship between poverty and risk of violence towards children, Gelles (1992) determined that while violence towards children is found across social classes, severe violence is more likely to occur in economically impoverished families. He further reported that conditions of poverty have a greater impact on women's risk of child abuse in general, and on single mothers' propensity to engage in child abuse in particular.

While these findings are understandable given cultural norms that bestow child care responsibilities upon women with minimal material resources and structural and institutional supports for meeting such demands, it is economic deprivation that explains such abuse (Gelles, 1992).

4 Understanding Child Sexual Abuse: Highlighting the Inadequacies of Women

1 Headlines and story details regarding the case of Sarah Dutil are cited from the Montreal *Gazette*, 22, 25, 27, and 29 January 1994.
2 The 'manual' refers to Ontario's *Child Sexual Abuse*, Part I: *Investigation and Assessment*, and Part II: *Intervention with Children and Their Families* (IPCA, n.d.) in circulation in the late 1980s. Commentary on the 'latest version' refers to the training manual entitled *Investigating Sexual Offences against Children*, which was published jointly in 1999 by the Ontario Association of Children's Aid Societies and the Ontario Police College.

9 Protection as Gendered and En/Gendering: Implications for Theory, Practice, and Research

1 Dahlerup (1987) argues that the state is not the only site of women's oppression: 'The oppression of women does not derive from a single set of social relations but from a complex system of interrelated structures and relations' (p. 102). In my study, the focus has been on one particular, albeit central, segment of the state that ensures or provides protection to children in response to sexual abuse.
2 This is not to suggest that workers set out to erode women's control. In fact, workers often wished for better conditions for mothers and children, as seen in Chapter 8.
3 Discrepancies between national or state-wide survey results and provincial child welfare findings should be expected. While such surveys describe the nature and extent of child sexual abuse based on retrospective accounts of adult 'survivors,' child protection statistics document those incidents reported to the agency.
4 This example was derived from a memo of 14 August 1997, issued by the executive director of a Catholic Children's Aid Society. It was circulated to local Children's Aid Society directors across the province of Ontario.

References

Adamson, N., Briskin, L., & McPhail, M. (1988). *Feminist organizing for change: The contemporary women's movement in Canada*. Toronto: Oxford University Press.

Alter, C. (1985). Decision-making factors in cases of child neglect. *Child Welfare*, 64(2), 99–111.

Andersen, M. (1988). *Thinking about women: Sociological perspectives on sex and gender* (2nd ed.). New York: Macmillan.

Armitage, A. (1993). The policy and legislative context. In B. Wharf (Ed.), *Rethinking child welfare in Canada* (pp. 37–63). Toronto: McClelland & Stewart.

Armstrong, L. (1995). *Of 'sluts' and 'bastards': A feminist decodes the child welfare debate*. Monroe, ME: Common Courage Press.

Armstrong, P., & Armstrong, H. (1990). *Theorizing women's work*. Toronto: Garamond Press.

Badgley, R. (1984). *Report of the committee on sexual offences against children and youths. Sexual offences against children in Canada: Summary*. Ottawa: Canadian Government Publishing Centre, Supply and Services Canada.

Bagley, C. (1985). Child sexual abuse: A child welfare perspective. In K.L. Levitt & B. Wharf. (Eds.), *The challenge of child welfare* (pp. 66–92). Vancouver: University of British Columbia Press.

Baker, M. (1996). Families. Changing trends in Canada. (3rd ed.). Toronto: McGraw-Hill Ryerson.

Bala, N. (1991). An introduction to child protection problems. In N. Bala, J.P. Hornick, & R. Vogl (Eds.), *Canadian child welfare law* (pp. 1–16). Toronto: Thompson Educational Publishing.

Balbo, L. (1987). Crazy quilts: Rethinking the welfare state debate from a woman's point of view. In Anne Showstack Sassoon (Ed.), *Women and the state: The shifting boundaries of public and private* (pp. 45–71). London: Hutchinson.

Barnhorst, D., & Walter, B. (1991). Child protection legislation in Canada. In N. Bala, J.P. Hornick, & R. Vogl (Eds.), *Canadian child welfare law* (pp. 17–32). Toronto: Thompson Educational Publishing.

Belenky, M., Clinchy, B., Goldberger, N., & Tarule, J. (1986). *Women's ways of knowing: The development of self, voice, and mind*. New York: Basic Books.

Birns, B., & Meyer, S. (1993). Mother's role in incest: Dysfunctional women or dysfunctional theories? *Journal of Child Sexual Abuse*, 2(3), 127–35.

Bogdan, R., & Biklen, S. (1982). *Qualitative research for education*. Toronto: Allyn and Bacon.

Borchorst, A., & Siim, B. (1987). Women and the advanced welfare state – A new kind of patriarchal power? In Anne Showstack Sassoon (Ed.), *Women and the state: The shifting boundaries of public and private* (pp. 128–57). London: Hutchinson.

Boushel, M. (1994). The protective environment of children: Towards a framework for anti-oppressive, cross-cultural and cross-national understanding. *British Journal of Social Work*, 24, 173–90.

Braverman, L. (1991). Beyond the myth of motherhood. In M. McGoldrick, C. Anderson, & F. Walsh (Eds.), *Women in families. A framework for family therapy* (pp. 227–43). New York: W.W. Norton.

Cage, R. (1988). Criminal investigation of sexual abuse cases. In S.M. Sgroi, *Vulnerable populations: Vol. I. Evaluation and treatment of sexually abused children and adult survivors* (pp. 187–227). Toronto: Lexington Books, D.C. Heath and Company.

Callahan, M. (1985). Public apathy and government parsimony: A review of child welfare in Canada. In K.L. Levitt & B. Wharf (Eds.), *The challenge of child welfare* (pp. 1–27). Vancouver: University of British Columbia Press.

Callahan, M. (1993a). The administrative and practice context: Perspectives from the front-line. In Brian Wharf (Ed.), *Rethinking child welfare in Canada* (pp. 64–97). Toronto: McClelland & Stewart.

Callahan, M. (1993b). Feminist approaches: Women recreate child welfare. In Brian Wharf (Ed.), *Rethinking child welfare in Canada* (pp. 172–209). Toronto: McClelland & Stewart.

Callahan, M., & Attridge, C. (1990). *Women in women's work: Social workers talk about their work in child welfare*. University of Victoria, November 1990. A study funded by The Social Science and Humanities Research Council. Research monograph #3.

Cammaert, L.A. (1988). Nonoffending mothers: A new conceptualization. In L.E.A. Walker (Ed.), *Handbook on sexual abuse children* (pp. 309–25). New York: Springer Publishing.

Canadian Centre for Justice Statistics (CCJS). (1998). Statistics Canada.

Uniform Crime Reporting Survey. Retrieved 26 January 2002, from http://www.statcan.ca/english/sdds/3302.htm.
Caplan, P. (1989). *Don't blame mother: Mending the mother–daughter relationship.* Toronto: Harper & Row.
Carter, B. (1990). *But you should have known: Child sexual abuse and the non-offending mother.* Unpublished doctoral dissertation, University of Toronto, Toronto.
Carter, B. (1993). Child sexual abuse: Impact on mothers. *Affilia, 8*(1), 72–90.
Carter, B. (1999). *Who's to blame? Child sexual abuse and non-offending mothers.* Toronto: University of Toronto Press.
Conte, J.R. (1985). Clinical dimensions of adult sexual abuse of children. *Behavioral Sciences and the Law, 3*(4), 341–54.
Contratto, S. (1986). Child abuse and the politics of care. *Journal of Education, 168*(3), 70–9.
Dadds, M., Smith, M., Webber, Y., & Robinson, A. (1991). An exploration of family and individual profiles following father–daughter incest. *Child Abuse & Neglect, 15*, 575–86.
Dahlerup, D. (1987). Confusing concepts – confusing reality: A theoretical discussion of the patriarchal state. In Anne Showstack Sassoon (Ed.), *Women and the state: The shifting boundaries of public and private* (pp. 93–127). London: Hutchinson.
Dale, J., & Foster, P. (1986). *Feminists and state welfare.* Boston: Routledge & Kegan Paul.
David, M. (1991). Putting on an act for children? In M. Maclean & D. Groves (Eds.), *Women's issues in social policy* (pp. 95–116). New York: Routledge.
Davies, L. (1990). A critical reappraisal of control and autonomy in state social work. *Canadian Review of Social Policy, 25*, 47–55.
Dawson, R. (1982). *Sexual abuse training program.* Toronto: Ministry of Community and Social Services.
Dawson, R. (1984). Therapeutic intervention with sexually abused children. *Journal of Child Care, 1*(6), 29–35.
Deblinger, E., Hathaway, C., Lippmann, J., & Steer, R. (1993). Psychosocial characteristics and correlates of symptom distress in nonoffending mothers of sexually abused children. *Journal of Interpersonal Violence, 8*(2), 155–68.
Dietz, C., & Craft, J. (1980). Family dynamics of incest: A new perspective. *Social Casework, 61*(10), 602–9.
Djao, A.W. (1983). *Inequality and social policy: The sociology of welfare.* Toronto: John Wiley & Sons.
Dooley, D. (1984). *Social research methods.* Toronto: Prentice-Hall Canada.
Eichler, M. (1988). *Nonsexist research methods: A practical guide.* Boston: Allen & Unwin.

Eisenstein, Z. (1981). *The radical future of liberal feminism*. New York: Longman.

Elbow, M., & Mayfield, J. (1991). Mothers of incest victims: Villians, victims, or protectors? *Families in Society: The Journal of Contemporary Humans Services*, 72(2), 78–86.

Esparza, D. (1993). Maternal support and stress response in sexually abused girls ages 6–12. *Issues in Mental Health Nursing*, 14(1), 85–107.

Everson, M., Hunter, W., Runyon, D., Edelson, G., & Coulter, M. (1989). Maternal support following disclosure of incest. *American Journal of Orthopsychiatry*, 59(2), 197–207.

Faller, K. (1988a). Decision-making in cases of intrafamilial child sexual abuse. *American Journal of Orthopsychiatry*, 58(1), 121–8.

Faller, K. (1988b). The myth of the 'collusive mother.' *Journal of Interpersonal Violence*, 3(2), 190–6.

Featherstone, B. (1997a). Introduction: Crisis in the western family. In W. Hollway and B. Featherstone (Eds.), *Mothering and ambivalence* (pp. 1–16). New York: Routledge.

Featherstone, B. (1997b). 'I wouldn't do your job!' Women, social work and child abuse. In W. Hollway and B. Featherstone (Eds.), *Mothering and ambivalence* (pp. 167–92). New York: Routledge.

Ferguson, H. (1997). Protecting children in new times: Child protection and the risk society. *Child and Family Social Work*, 2, 221–35.

Findlay, S. (1987). Facing the state: The politics of the women's movement reconsidered. In Heather Jon Maroney & Meg Luxton (Eds.), *Feminism and political economy: Women's work, women's struggles* (pp. 31–50). Toronto: Methuen.

Finkelhor, D. (1979). *Sexually victimized children*. New York: The Free Press.

Finkelhor, D. (1984). *Child sexual abuse: New theory and research*. New York: The Free Press.

Fraser, N. (1989). *Unruly practices: Power, discourse, and gender in contemporary social theory*. Minneapolis: University of Minnesota Press.

Fraser, N. (1990). Struggle over needs: Outline of a socialist-feminist critical theory of late capitalist political culture. In Linda Gordon (Ed.), *Women, the state, and welfare* (pp. 199–225). Madison: The University of Wisconsin Press.

Furniss, T. (1984). Organizing a therapeutic approach to intra-familial child sexual abuse. *Journal of Adolescence*, 7(4), 309–17.

Garbarino, J. (1993). Is good science bad sexual politics? Commentary on 'Mother's role in incest: Dysfunctional women or dysfuntional theories?' *Journal of Child Sexual Abuse*, 2(3), 13–140.

Gelles, R. (1992). Poverty and violence towards children. *American Behavioral Scientist*, 35(3), 258–74.

Giarretto, H. (1982). A comprehensive child sexual abuse treatment program. *Child Abuse and Neglect, 6*(3), 263–78.

Glaser, B., & Strauss, A.L. (1967). *The discovery of grounded theory: Strategies for qualitative research.* New York: Aldine Atherton.

Glaser, D., & Frosh, S. (1993). *Child sexual abuse* (2nd ed.). Toronto: University of Toronto Press.

Glenn, E. (1994). Social constructions of mothering: A thematic overview. In E.N. Glenn, G. Chang, & L.R. Forcey (Eds.), *Mothering: Ideology, experience, and agency* (pp. 1–29). New York: Routledge.

Gordon, L. (1988) *Heroes of their own lives.* New York: Viking.

Gordon, L. (1990). Family violence, feminism, and social control. In Linda Gordon (Ed.), *Women, the state, and welfare* (pp. 178–98). Madison: The University of Wisconsin Press.

Groth, A.N. (1985). The incest offender. In S. Sgroi (Ed.), *Handbook of clinical intervention in child sexual abuse* (pp. 215–39). Toronto: D.C. Heath.

Harris, J., & Melichercik, J. (1986). Age and stage-related programs. In Joanne C. Turner & Francis J. Turner (Eds.), *Canadian Social Welfare* (2nd ed., pp. 159–81). Don Mills: Collier Macmillan Canada.

Heald, S. (1990). 'Making democracy practicable': Voluntarism and job creation. In R. Ng, G. Walker, & J. Muller (Eds.), *Community organization and the Canadian state* (pp.147–64). Toronto: Garamond Press.

Healy, K. (1998). Participation and child protection: The importance of context. *British Journal of Social Work, 28,* 897–914.

Healy, K. (2000). *Social work practices: Contemporary perspectives on change.* London: Sage.

Hooper, C. (1992). *Mothers surviving child sexual abuse.* New York: Tavistock/Routledge.

Hoorwitz, A.H. (1983). Guidelines for treating father–daughter incest. *Social Casework, 64*(9), 515–24.

Horejsi, C., Bertsche, J., Francetich, S., Collins, B., & Francetich, R. (1987). Protocols in child welfare: An example. *Child Welfare, 66*(5), 423–31.

Howe, D. (1998). Relationship-based thinking and practice in social work. *Journal of Social Work Practice, 12*(1), 45–56.

Hunter, W., Coulter, M., Runyan, D., & Everson, M. (1990). Determinants of placement for sexually abused children. *Child Abuse & Neglect, 14*(3), 407–17.

Hutchison, E. (1992). Child welfare as a woman's issue. *Families in Society: The Journal of Contemporary Human Services, 73*(2), 67–78.

Hutchison, E. (1993). Mandatory reporting laws: Child protective case finding gone awry? *Social Work, 38*(1), 56–63.

Hutchison, E., Dattalo, P., & Rodwell, M. (1994). Reorganizing child protective

services: Protecting children and providing family support. *Children and Youth Services Review, 16*(5/6), 319–38.
Institute for the Prevention of Child Abuse (IPCA). (n.d.). *Child sexual abuse. Part I: Investigation and assessment. Part II: Intervention with children and their families.* Resource manual. Toronto, Ontario.
Jack, G. (1997). Discourses of child protection and child welfare. *British Journal of Social Work, 27,* 659–78.
Jackson, S. (1995). Looking after children better: An interactive model for research and practice. In J. Hudson & B. Galaway (Eds.), *Child welfare in Canada: Research and policy implications* (pp. 324–36). Toronto: Thompson Educational Publishing.
James. (n.d.). Mothers of incest victims. In IPCA, *Child sexual abuse. Part II: Intervention with children and their families* (pp. 25–31). Resource manual. Toronto, Ontario.
Johnson, J. (1992). *Mothers of incest survivors: Another side of the story.* Bloomington: Indiana University Press.
Kalichman, S., Craig, M., & Follingstad, D. (1990). Professionals' adherence to mandatory child abuse reporting laws: Effects of responsibility attribution, confidence ratings, and situational factors. *Child Abuse & Neglect, 14*(1), 69–77.
Kamerman, S., & Kahn, A. (1990). Social services for children, youth, and families in the United States. *Children and Youth Services Review, 12*(2), 1–179.
Keller, R., Cicchinelli, L., & Gardner, D. (1989). Characteristics of child sexual abuse treatment programs. *Child Abuse & Neglect, 13*(3), 361–8.
Kelley, S. (1990). Responsibility and management strategies in child sexual abuse: A comparison of child protective workers, nurses, and police officers. *Child Welfare, 69*(1), 43–51.
Krane, J. (1989). *Patriarchal biases in the conceptualization of child sexual abuse.* Toronto: Faculty of Social Work, University of Toronto, Working Papers on Social Welfare in Canada.
Krane, J. (1994). *The transformation of women into mother protectors: An examination of child protection practices in cases of child sexual abuse.* Unpublished doctoral dissertation, University of Toronto, Toronto.
Krane, J., & Davies, L. (2000). Mothering and child protection practice: Rethinking risk assessment. *Child and Family Social Work, 5*(1), 35–45.
Land, H. (1991). Time to care. In Mavis Maclean & Dulcie Groves (Eds.), *Women's issues in social policy* (pp. 7–19). New York: Routledge.
Lang, R.A., Langevin, R., Van Santen, V., Billinsley, D., & Wright, P. (1990). Martial relations in incest offenders. *Journal of Sex & Martial Therapy, 16*(4), 214–29.

Levine, H. (1985). The power politics of motherhood. In Joan Turner & Lois Emery (Eds.), *Perspectives on women in the 1980s* (pp. 28–40). Winnipeg: The University of Manitoba Press.

Levitt, K.L. (1985). Preface. In K.L. Levitt & B. Wharf (Eds.), *The challenge of child welfare* (pp. x–xiii). Vancouver: University of British Columbia Press.

Lindsey, D. (1994). *The welfare of children.* New York: Oxford University Press.

Lofland, J., & Lofland, L. (1984). *Analyzing social settings: A guide to qualitative observation and analysis.* Belmont: Wadsworth.

Lustig, N., Spellman, J., Dresser, S., & Murray, T. (1966). Incest. *Archives of General Psychiatry, 14,* 31–40.

Macintyre, E. (1993). The historical context of child welfare in Canada. In Brian Wharf (Ed.), *Rethinking child welfare in Canada* (pp. 13–36). Toronto: McClelland & Stewart.

MacKinnon, C.A. (1987). *Feminism unmodified: Discourses on life and law.* Cambridge: Harvard University Press.

MacLeod, M., & Saraga, E. (1988). Challenging the orthodoxy: Towards a feminist theory and practice. *Feminist Review, 28,* 16–55.

Mandell, N. (1988). The child question: Links between women and children in the family. In Nancy Mandell & Ann Duffy (Eds.), *Reconstructing the Canadian family: Feminist perspectives* (pp. 49–81). Toronto: Butterworths.

Maroney, H. (1985). Embracing motherhood: New feminist theory. *Canadian Journal of Political and Social Theory, 9*(1/2), 40–64.

McDonough, H., & Love, A. (1987). The challenge of sexual abuse: Protection and therapy in a child welfare setting. *Child Welfare, 66*(3), 225–35.

Melichercik, J. (1978). Child welfare in Ontario. In Shankar Yelaja (Ed.), *Canadian Social Policy* (pp. 187–206). Waterloo: Wilfrid Laurier University Press.

Melichercik, J. (1987). Child welfare policy. In Shankar Yelaja (Ed.), *Canadian Social Policy* (Rev. ed., pp. 195–223). Waterloo: Wilfrid Laurier Press.

Metropolitan Toronto Special Committee on Child Abuse (MTSCCA). (1986, June). *Child sexual abuse protocol: Guidelines and procedures for a coordinated response to child sexual abuse in Metropolitan Toronto* (2nd. ed.). Toronto: Metropolitan Toronto Special Committee on Child Abuse.

Miller, J. (1991). Child welfare and the role of women: A feminist perspective. *American Journal of Orthopsychiatry, 61*(4), 592–8.

Muram, D., Rosenthal, T.L., & Beck, K.W. (1994). Personality profiles of mothers sexual abuse victims and their daughters. *Child Abuse & Neglect, 18*(5), 419–23.

Myer, M.H. (1985). A new look at mothers of incest victims. *Journal of Social Work and Human Sexuality, 3*(2/3), 47–58.

Nelson, B. (1990). The origins of the two-channel welfare state: Workmen's compensation and mother's aid. In Linda Gordon (Ed.), *Women, the state, and welfare* (pp. 123–51). Madison: The University of Wisconsin Press.

Ng, R., Walker, G., & Muller, J. (1990). Problematizing community organization and the state. In R. Ng, G. Walker, & J. Muller (Eds.), *Community organization and the Canadian state* (pp. 13–28). Toronto: Garamond Press.

Ontario. (1984). *Bill 77: An act respecting the protection and well-being of children and their families*. Toronto: Queen's Printer for Ontario.

Ontario Association of Children's Aid Societies (OACAS). (1991). *Fact sheets: Extracted from OACAS Services Survey for the year 1991*. Toronto: Ontario Association of Children's Aid Societies.

Ontario Association of Children's Aid Societies. (1999). Trainers' notes and lesson plans for ISOAC (Investigating Sexual Offences against Children). Toronto: Ontario Association of Children's Aid Societies.

Ontario Ministry of Community and Social Services (MCSS). (1986). *Standards and guidelines for management of child abuse cases*. Toronto: Ontario Ministry of Community and Social Services.

Ontario Ministry of Community and Social Services (MCSS) (1999). *Handout. CFSA amendments*. Toronto: Ontario Ministry of Community and Social Services

Parton, C., & Parton, N. (1988/89). Women, the family and child protection. *Critical Social Policy, 24*, 38–49.

Parton, N. (1992). The contemporary politics of child protection. *Journal of Social Welfare and Family Law, 2*, 100–13.

Parton, N. (1998). Risk, advanced liberalism and child welfare: The need to rediscover uncertainty and ambiguity. *British Journal of Social Work, 28*, 5–27.

Pascall, G. (1986). *Social policy: A feminist analysis*. New York: Tavistock Publications.

Pellegrin, A., & Wagner, W. (1990). Child sexual abuse: Factors affecting victims' removal from home. *Child Abuse and Neglect, 14*(1), 53–60.

Pelton, L. (1990, Fall). Resolving the crisis in child welfare: Simply expanding the present system is not enough. *Public Welfare*, 19–25.

Pezdek, K. (1994). Avoiding false claims of child sexual abuse: Empty promises. *Family Relations, 43*, 258–60.

Piven, F. (1990). Ideology and the state: Women, power, and the welfare state. In Linda Gordon (Ed.), *Women, the state, and welfare* (pp. 250–64). Madison: The University of Wisconsin Press.

Prevent Child Abuse America (2000). *Child Sexual Abuse, 19*. Chicago, IL.

Pupo, N. (1988). Preserving patriarchy: Women, the family and the state. In Nancy Mandell & Ann Duffy (Eds.), *Reconstructing the Canadian family: Feminist perspectives* (pp. 207–37). Toronto: Butterworths.

Reinharz, Shulamit. (1992). *Feminist methods in social research*. New York: Oxford Uiversity Press.

Rist, K. (1979). Incest: Theoretical and clinical views. *American Journal of Orthopsychiatry, 49*(4), 680–91.

Rivers, B. (1993). From baby snatcher to family builder: Paradigm shifts in child welfare. In Leslie Bella (Proceedings Editor and Conference Co-Chair), *Rethinking social welfare: People, policy and practice*. Proceedings of Sixth Biennial Social Welfare Policy Conference, St John's, Newfoundland, June 27–30, 1993.

Rosenberg, H. (1988). Motherwork, stress, and depression: The costs of privatized social reproduction. In Bonnie Fox (Ed.), *Family bonds and gender divisions: Readings in the sociology of the family* (pp. 379–99). Toronto: Canadian Scholars Press.

Ruffolo, M. C., Sugamele, M., & Taylor-Brown, S. (1994). Scapegoating of mothers: A study of mother-blaming in case studies included in core foundation social work practice textbooks. *Journal of Teaching in Social Work, 10*(1/2), 117–27.

Russell, D.E.H. (1986). *The secret trauma: Incest in the lives of girls and women*. New York: Basic Books.

Sapiro, V. (1990). The gender basis of American social policy. In Linda Gordon (Ed.), *Women, the state, and welfare* (pp. 36–54). Madison: The University of Wisconsin Press.

Sassoon, A. (1987a). Introduction: The personal and the intellectual, fragments and order, international trends and national specificities. In Anne Showstack Sassoon (Ed.), *Women and the state: The shifting boundaries of public and private* (pp. 15–42). London: Hutchinson.

Sassoon, A. (1987b). Women's new social role: Contradictions of the welfare state. In Anne Showstack Sassoon (Ed.), *Women and the state: The shifting boundaries of public and private* (pp. 158–88). London: Hutchinson.

Saunders, B.E., Lipovsky, J.A., & Hanson, R.F. (1995). Couple and familial characteristics of father–child incest families. *Journal of Family Social Work, 1*(2), 5–25.

Schneider, E. (1990). The dialectic of rights and politics: Perspectives from the women's movement. In Linda Gordon (Ed.), *Women, the state, and welfare* (pp. 226–49). Madison: The University of Wisconsin Press.

Sedlak, A., & Broadhurst, D. (1996). *Executive summary of the third national incidence study of child abuse and neglect*. Westat, Inc.

Sgroi, S., & Dana, N. (1985). Individual and group treatment of mothers of incest victims. In S.M. Sgroi (Ed.), *Handbook of clinical intervention in child sexual abuse* (pp. 191–214). Toronto: Lexington Books, D.C. Heath and Company.

Sgroi, S., Blick, L., & Porter, F. (1985). A conceptual framework for child sexual abuse. In Suzanne Sgroi (Ed.), *Handbook of clinical intervention in child sexual abuse* (pp. 9–37). Toronto: D.C. Heath.

Sgroi, S.M., Porter, F., & Blick, L. (1985). Validation of child sexual abuse. In S.M. Sgroi (Ed.), *Handbook of clinical intervention in child sexual abuse* (pp. 39–79). Toronto: Lexington Books, D.C. Heath.

Smith, B., & Smith, T. (1990). For love and money: Women as foster mothers. *Affilia, 5*(1), 66–80.

Smith, D.W. & Saunders, B.E. (1995). Personality characteristics of father/perpetrators and nonoffending mothers in incest families: Individual and dyadic analyses. *Child Abuse & Neglect, 19*(5), 607–19.

Spencer, C., & Nicholson, M. (1988). Incest investigation and treatment planning by child protective services. In L.E.A. Walker (Ed.), *Handbook on sexual abuse of children* (pp. 152–74). New York: Springer Publishing.

Statistics Canada. (1996). Census families in private households by family structure, presence of children and labour force activity of husband/male common-law partner, showing labour force activity of wife/female common-law partner or lone parent, for Canada, 1996 census (20% sample data). Retrieved 18 November 2002, from http://www.statcan.ca/english/census96/june9/f3can.htm.

Stewart, C. (1987). *Understand the new law on child sexual abuse. Bill C-15: Implications and issues* (A discussion paper). Toronto: The Institute for the Prevention of Child Abuse.

Summit, R. (1983). The child sexual abuse accommodation syndrome. *Child Abuse and Neglect, 7*(2), 177–93.

Summit, R. (n.d.). Role of the mother. In IPCA, *Child sexual abuse. Part II. Intervention with children and their families*. Resource manual. Toronto, Ontario.

Swift, K. J. (1995). *Manufacturing 'bad mothers': A critical perspective on child neglect*. Toronto: University of Toronto Press.

Trocmé, N. (1991). Child welfare services. In R. Barnhorst & L.C. Johnson (Eds.), *The state of the child in Ontario* (pp. 63–91). Toronto: Oxford University Press.

Trocmé, N., McPhee, D., & Tam, K.K. (1995). Child abuse and neglect in Ontario: Incidence and characteristics. *Child Welfare, 74*(3), 563–86.

Truesdell, D., McNeil, J., & Deschner, J. (1986). Incidence of wife abuse in incestuous families. *Social Work, 31*(2), 138–40.

Valentine, M. (1994). The social worker as 'bad object.' *British Journal of Social Work, 24*, 71–86.

Voight, L. (1986). Welfare women. In Helen Marchant & Betsy Wearing (Eds.), *Gender reclaimed: Women in social work* (pp. 80–92). Sydney: Hale & Iremonger.

Waerness, K. (1984). Caring as women's work in the welfare state. In Harriet Holter (Ed.), *Patriarchy in a welfare society* (pp. 67–87). Oslo: Universitetsforlaget.

Walker, G. (1990). *Family violence and the women's movement: The conceptual politics of struggle.* Toronto: University of Toronto Press.

Waterhouse, L., & Carnie, J. (1992). Assessing child protection risk. *British Journal of Social Work, 22,* 47–60.

Wells, M. (1990). *Canada's law on child sexual abuse: A handbook.* Ottawa: Department of Justice Canada/Minister of Supply and Services Canada.

Wells, S. (1994). Child protective services: Research for the future. *Child Welfare, 73*(5), 431–47.

Wharf, B. (1985). Preventive approaches to child welfare. In K. Levitt & B. Wharf (Eds.), *The challenge of child welfare* (pp. 200–17). Vancouver: University of British Columbia Press.

Wharf, B. (1995). Organizing and delivering child welfare services: The contributions of research. In J. Hudson & B. Galaway (Eds.), *Child welfare in Canada: Research and policy implications* (pp. 2–12). Toronto: Thompson Educational Publishing.

Wyatt, G., & Mickey, M.R. (1987). Ameliorating the effects of child sexual abuse: An exploratory study of support by parents and others. *Journal of Interpersonal Violence, 2*(4), 403–14.

Yin, R. (1984). *Case study research: Design and methods.* Beverly Hills, CA: Sage.

Zuelzer, M.B., & Reposa, R.E. (1983). Mothers in incestuous families. *International Journal of Family Therapy, 5*(2), 98–110.

Index

Adamson, N., Briskin, L., & McPhail, M., 17, 24, 25, 28
Alter, C., 46
Andersen, M., 26, 30, 31, 198
Armitage, A., 20, 55
Armstrong, L., 56
Armstrong, P., and Armstrong, H., 17, 28

Badgley, R., 46, 60, 61, 199
Bagley, C., 52
Baker, M., 21–2
Bala, N., 40, 41, 45, 55
Balbo, L., 25, 27, 31, 32, 179, 191
Barnhorst, D., & Walker, B., 43, 44
Belenky, M., Clinchy, B., Goldberger, N., & Tarule, J., 14
Birns, B., & Meyer, S., 74
Bogdan, R., & Biklen, S., 15
Borchorst, A., & Siim, B., 29, 30
Boushel, M., 54, 62
Braverman, L., 26

Cage, R., 47, 49, 199
Callahan, M., 7, 12, 27, 39, 55, 189
Callahan, M., & Attridge, C., 56, 57, 155

Cammaert, L.A., 52
Canadian Centre for Justice Statistics (CCJS), 60, 61, 62
Caplan, P., 69
Carter, B., 6, 7, 13, 53, 62, 79, 80, 197
case study method, 9–10, 13–15
  generalizability of findings in, 15
  identifying mothers for participation, 13–14, 197–8n. 4, 198n. 5
child protection
  boundaries of, 19,
  defined 5, 19, 176
  historical role of state in, 39–41
  inattention to mothers' experience of, 6, 192
  as neutral and gender-free, 6, 37, 130–3
  preference of family care, 6, 19, 43, 54
child protection workers
  and ambivalence, 194
  assert their authority and expertise, 109–10, 123–4, 154
  beliefs in offenders' abilities to change, 162–5
  and critical reflections on judgments, 195

child sexual abuse (cont.)
  daunting nature of protecting children at risk, 56
  experiences of the work, 57, 155–6
  frustrations with women who failed to protect, 160–1, 166–7
  tensions in securing the protection of children, 49, 157–60
  understanding of relations between mothers and offenders, 152–3, 161–2
  urgency of securing protection, 106–7, 192–3
child sexual abuse
  characterization of mothers in training manuals, 66–9, 74
  child protectionists' understandings of, 62–4
  as criminal offence, 199n. 2
  debates about court involvement in cases of, 50–1
  disclosure as critical, 48
  disclosure to peers, 62
  dominant discourse on, 6, 65–82
    critique of, 78–9
  as form of male prerogative, 101
  as function of dysfunctional family dynamics, 65–75, 83–8, 97–101
  implication of mothers, 6, 53
  intrafamilial vs. extrafamilial, 47, 61–2
  preoccupation with incest, 6
  prevalence of, 60–1, 64
  redefined as maternal failure, 7
  women activists' understandings of, 64–5
child sexual abuse investigation
  assessment of nonoffending parent in, 49, 51–2
  discrepancies between workers' and mothers' experiences of, 113–15
  disregarding women's multiple dimensions in, 115–26
  investigative protocol in, 45–54
  maternal support as predictor of child's protection, 52–4, 105–9
  principle of 'least intrusion' in, 49, 129, 175, 176, 181
  securing immediate protection of children in, 49
child sexual abusers
  absolution from blame, 67, 71, 74, 82, 88
  as characterized in training manuals, 66–7, 75–9
  as fading from view in the problem of child sexual abuse, 95, 99
  as fixated or regressed, 75–7
  needs for power and control, 85–6,
  profile of, 61–2, 189–90
child welfare system
  current criticisms of, 55–6
  emphasis on 'failed families,' 54
  and heavy investigative focus in contemporary practice, 54–5
  profile of, 19, 39
  residual approach to, 20
Conte, J.R., 78
Contratto, S., 24, 26

Dadds, M., Smith, M., Webber, Y., & Robinson, A., 72
Dahlerup, D., 198, 200
Dale, J., & Foster, P., 32, 33, 37, 182, 183, 188
David, M., 20, 55, 176
Davies, L., 44
Dawson, R., 48, 50, 51, 52, 62, 66, 67, 199

Deblinger, E., Hathaway, C., Lippmann, J., & Steer, R., 53, 68, 73
Dietz, C., & Craft, J., 68, 82
Djao, A.W., 20
Dooley, D., 15

Eichler, M., 23
Eisenstein, Z., 191
Elbow, M., & Myfield, J., 72
Esparza, D., 53
Everson, M., Hunter, W., Runyon, D., Edelson, G., & Coulter, M., 49, 53

Faller, K., 49, 51, 80
Featherstone, B., 193, 194, 195
Ferguson, H., 195
Findlay, S., 198
Finkelhor, D., 61, 62, 64, 65, 75, 77
Finkelhor's four preconditions model, 77–8
Fraser, N., 24, 32, 34, 35, 36, 179, 180, 184, 185, 187, 199

Garbarino, J., 74
Gelles, R., 55, 199, 200
Giarretto, H., 51
Glaser, B., & Strauss, A.L., 15
Glaser, D., & Frosh, S., 38, 65, 69, 75, 78
Glenn, E., 26
Gordon, L., 25–9, 185
Groth, A.N., 75, 76, 77

Harris, J., & Melichercik, J., 40
Heald, S., 18
Healy, K., 195
Hooper, C., 7, 62, 64, 79, 80
Hoorwitz, A.H., 51, 53
Horejsi, C., Bertsche, J., Francetich, S., Collins, B., & Francetich, R., 45, 49, 51
Howe, D., 194
Hunter, W., Coulter, M., Runyan, D., & Everson, M., 52
Hutchison, E., 5, 26, 55
Hutchison, E., Dattalo, P., & Rodwell, M., 55

Institute for the Prevention of Child Abuse (IPCA), 68, 75, 79, 180, 200

Jack, G., 43, 49
Jackson, S., 43
James, 68, 69, 186
Johnson, J., 7, 12, 79, 80, 81
Juridical-administrative-therapeutic (JAT) state apparatus, 34–5, 36, 56

Kalichman, S., Craig, M., & Follingstad, D., 82
Kammerman, S., & Kahn, A., 55
Keller, R., Cicchinelli, L., & Gardner, D., 51
Kelley, S., 81
Krane, J., 6, 10, 53, 80
Krane, J., & Davies, L., 193, 194

Land, H., 12
Lang, R.A., Langevin, R., Van Santen, V., Billinsley, D., & Wright, P., 72
Levitt, K.L., 39, 46, 55
Lofland, J., & Lofland, L., 15
Lustig, N., Spellman, J., Dresser, S., & Murray, T., 65, 66, 185

MacKinnon, C.A., 65
MacLeod, M., & Saraga, E., 65, 69
Mandell, N., 24

Maroney, H., 26
maternal expectations
  cultural constructions of, 25
  glorification and idealization of, 25
  for keeping children safe, 60, 87, 110–15
  for meeting partners' needs, 85,
  to protect children, 103–4, 107–9, 126–8, 166–7
  for recognizing warning signs of child sexual abuse, 89–101
  western conceptions of, 4
maternal inadequacies, 87
  emphasized over offender's inadequacies, 123
  as feature of redefining the problem of child sexual abuse, 102
  in need of repair through casework practices, 145–6, 146–7
  as paramount in supervision orders, 134–43
  in relation to their intimate relations, 149–52
  in relation to private efforts to protect, 92–6
  workers' discomfort with a focus on, 102–4
maternal responsibilities
  to choose to protect, 123–6
  following disclosure of child sexual abuse, 53
  to learn to protect, 87–8, 143–5
  protection shifted from public to private sphere, 4, 176–7
McDonough, H., & Love, A., 53
Melichercik, J., 39, 40
Metropolitan Toronto Special Committee on Child Abuse (MTSCCA), 46, 47, 48, 49, 50, 199
Miller, J., 187, 197

'Mom finds child in dumpster' story, 58–9
  mother blame and, 60,
mother blame
  as central to protection, 104
  as central to understanding dynamics of child sexual abuse, 66–75
  as central to understanding feminist critiques, 79–81
  as experienced during investigations, 96–101
  as pervasive feature of child protection discourse and practice, 7–8
  in professional practice, 81–2
  reproduced in child welfare practice, 8
  in setting up abuse, 88–9
  in social work education, 81
mother protectors
  alienated from social workers, 170–3
  as central feature of child protection intervention, 87–88, 134–43, 186–9
  choice vs. obligation, 126–8, 130–4, 143
  counterproductive effects of, 7, 168–70, 175
  dearth of support for, 9, 116–22, 167–8
  as instance of social relations, 177–84
  involvement in access and visitation, 147–9
  as negotiated in investigations, 123–6
  obligatory and invisible nature of, 7, 57, 166–7, 174

overview of processes that transform women into, 7, 9, 105, 157, 176–7
positive experience, 173–4
rendered visible, 185–6
and roles of nonoffending fathers, 189–91
using a mothering narrative to understand, 194–5
Muram, D., Rosenthal, T.L., & Beck, K.W., 72
Myer, M.H., 53, 80

Nelson, B., 199
Ng, R., Walker, G., & Muller, J., 15, 17, 18

Ontario Association of Children's Aid Societies, 45, 62
Ontario child welfare legislation, 41–5
  definition of child in need of protection, 43–4
    as crucial provision in the legislation, 44
    worker discretion in assessing, 44–5
  functions of child welfare agencies, 42–3, 45–54
  principles of Child and Family Services Act, 41–2, 192
Ontario Ministry of Community and Social Services (MCSS), 45, 51

participants' accounts
  in context of 'best practice,' 9–10
  interview sample, 6, 10–12, 13
  interview themes, 6–7, 14
  vs. official discourse, 7, 15–16
Parton, C., & Parton, N., 55, 187

Parton, N., 54, 55, 194
Pascall, G., 24, 28, 29, 30, 31, 32, 181, 182
Pellegrin, A., & Wagner, W., 49
Pelton, L., 56
Pezdek, K., 48
Piven, F., 29
Prevent Child Abuse America, 60, 61
Pupo, N., 23, 30, 198

Reinharz, Shulamit, 10
reproduction of gender relations, 4
  everyday practices and, 9, 18
  unwittingly by social workers, 8
Rist, K., 66
Rivers, B., 43
Rosenberg, H., 26, 180
Ruffolo, M., C., Sugamele, M., & Taylor-Brown, S., 81
Russell, D.E.H., 14, 61, 62

Sapiro, V., 29, 31, 183
Sassoon, A., 4, 23, 30, 31, 32, 179, 181, 182
Saunders, B.E., Lipovsky, J.A., & Hanson, R.F., 73
Schneider, E., 198
Sedlak, A., & Broadhurst, D., 61
Sgroi, S., & Dana, N., 52, 71
Sgroi, S.M., Porter, Frances, & Blick, Linda, 62
Smith, D.W., & Saunders, B.E., 27, 72, 73
Spencer, C., & Nicholson, M., 50, 53, 199
Statistics Canada, 21–2
Stewart, C., 199
Summit, R., 62
Supervision Orders 134–43
Swift, K.J., 7, 27, 36

'Tethered teen' story, 3–4, 5
Trocmé, N., 55
Trocmé, N., McPhee, D., & Tam, K.K., 41
Truesdell, D., McNeil, J., & Deschner, J., 68

Valentine, M., 56, 57
Voight, L., 12
Voluntary Agreements, 49–51
  different from supervision and wardship orders 129–30
  example of, 91
  and maternal expectations to protect, 130–4

Waerness, K., 32
Walker, G., 18, 198
Waterhouse, L., & Carnie, J., 52
welfare state
  and bifurcation of public/private spheres, 20, 21–3
  feminist critique of, 30–3, 177–9
  historical variations, 198n. 1
  definition of, 17–18
  predominance of women as clients and workers in, 12, 26, 27, 33
welfare state as gendered and en/gendering, 7, 33–7, 177–9, 187–8
  child sexual abuse as example of, 36–7, 187–9
  needs as interpretations, 35–7, 179–80, 184–5
  politicized and open to dispute, 36
  neglect as example of, 36
  two-tiered system as way of understanding, 33–4
Wells, M., 46, 199
Wells, S., 43, 55
Wharf, B., 20, 39
'Woman sues mother' story, 38
women and the welfare state
  contradictory effects of, 28–30, 180–4
  dearth of attention in child welfare, 5
  debates about social control, 28–30, 180–4
  feminist analysis of, 4, 23, 198n. 3
  'missing persons' in child welfare, 8
  mother protectors as state service, 179–80
  relations between, 8, 24–7
  women as employed providers, 27
  women as patchworkers, 26
  women as recipients or consumers, 26
  women as unpaid caregivers and motherworkers, 24–6, 30–3
Wyatt, G., & Mickey, M.R., 53

Yin, R., 10

Zuelzer, M.B., & Reposa, R.E., 70, 71